For the Healing of the Nations
Baptist Peacemakers

For the Healing of the Nations
Baptist Peacemakers

Paul R. Dekar

Smyth & Helwys Publishing, Inc.
Macon, GA

ISBN 1-880837-16-1

For the Healing of the Nations: Baptist Peacemakers
by Paul R. Dekar

Copyright © 1993
Smyth & Helwys Publishing, Inc.

All rights reserved.
Printed in the United States of America.

The paper used in this publication meets the minimum requirements of
American Standard for Information Sciences—Permanence of Paper
for Printed Library Materials, ANSI Z39.48–1984.

Library of Congress Cataloging-in-Publication Data

Dekar, Paul R. 1944–
    For the healing of the nations : Baptist peacemakers / Paul R. Dekar.
      xxiv+287pp.   6x9" (15x23 cm.)
    ISBN 1-880837-16-1 9alk. paper)
    1. Baptists—Biography. 2. Peace movements—Biography.
    3. Peace—Religious aspects—Biography. I. Title.
BX6493.D45   1993
261.8'73'00922—dc20
[B]   93-14910
                                                                                   CIP

Contents

Preface by Nancy Sehested vii

Foreword by Martin E. Marty xi

Introduction xvii

1. Identifying the Legacy 1

Section One. Voices Against War: Negative Peace   17

2. Early Non-Resistants 19

3. British Baptists in Nineteenth-Century Peace Societies 33

4. American Baptists in Nineteenth-Century Peace Societies 47

5. John Clifford (1836–1923) 61

6. James Henry Rushbrooke (1870–1947) 75

7. Douglas Clyde Macintosh (1877–1948) 87

Section Two. Voices Against War: Positive Peace   101

8. Champions of Liberty 103

9. Freedom at Midnight 117

10. Following the North Star 131

11. The Missionary as Peacemaker 143

12. Voices from the Developing World 155

13. Howard Thurman (1900–1981) 169

Section Three. Prophetic Voices 181

14. Martyrs 183

15. Walter Rauchenbusch (1861–1918) 197

16. Muriel Lester (1883–1968) 211

17. Martin Luther King, Jr. (1929–1968) 227

18. British Conscientious Objectors 241

19. The Baptist Peace Fellowship of North America 255

Conclusions 271

Index 279

Preface

Where have all the heroes gone? In our age of instant media magnification of the human frailties of public people, it has been difficult to find heroes anymore. Heroes just disappoint us in time. So who needs them, anyway?

Well, I do. I especially need to hear of heroes in the faith, for it is with human story that I can most vividly see God's story incarnated among us. As a Baptist, I have longed to know stories of Baptist heroes who have incarnated the gospel call to peacemaking.

In recent years, Baptists in my part of the world have been more identified with brawls and battles than with peacemaking. Some of us have been embarrassed by our Baptist family name. We have felt isolated and alone in our commitment to answer God's call to work for peace and justice. We have felt alienated from some of our Baptist family who insist on narrowly defining salvation in only personal terms. We have wondered if there was anyone else like us. We have wondered if there were Baptist heroes of peacemaking to follow.

The answer is a resounding "Yes." Yes, there are other Baptist peacemakers all over the globe. Yes, there are Baptist heroes who have boldly and courageously championed Christ's call to reconciliation.

For some of us, the "yes" came in the summer of 1986. About 130 Baptists from across the United States and Canada gathered in Green Lake, Wisconsin, for the first annual conference of the Baptist Peace Fellowship of North America. Excellent preaching, teaching, and music-making stirred us as a community of Baptists to renewed hope and vision as Christ's emissaries of peace and justice.

One of the most lasting memories of the week came from a professor from McMaster Divinity School, Paul Dekar. At each of the morning and evening sessions, Paul presented brief narratives in answer to the question: "Who Are Our Baptist 'Saints'?" Paul vividly painted oral portraits of mostly unnoticed Baptist peacemakers of the last 200 years.

We were captivated and inspired to hear the stories of our long lost relatives. We found ourselves greatly encouraged by the witness of so many Baptist men and women who have gone before us. Some of us even began to feel proud to be identified as a Baptist. We had found some heroes.

The stories of their witness to God's reign of peace and justice were empowering for us. The cloud of witnesses surrounding us included Baptist names. We were not alone.

Over the years of the BPFNA summer gatherings, Paul Dekar's stories of our Baptist saints have remained a highlight. We have stepped beside a slave named Samuel Sharpe as he led a nonviolent slave uprising in Jamaica. It cost him his life. We stepped around the Lord's Table with missionary Isabel Crawford and the Kiowa Indians of Oklahoma. She encouraged them to fight for their rights, seeing the root cause of injustice as the theft of their land. We listened to turn-of-the-century British preacher John Clifford denounce militarism and materialism while advocating for relief for the poor.

We shook with the enduring prophetic words of Walter Rauschenbusch who spoke the language of the biblical prophets. He called for a radical discipleship to Christ's law of love. Rauschenbusch gave new meaning to evangelism, insisting that the gospel is a social gospel that engages in healing in the world. We moved among the poor with pacifist Muriel Lester in her life as minister, prophet, pastor, and healer in England. Lester called on women to take the lead in ending wars. She demonstrated an empowerment model of leadership in her lifelong commitment to marginalized people.

This book is Paul's expansion of our Baptist family album of peacemakers. He has offered us numerous snapshots to view that include the unknown—like pioneer pastor Jennie Johnson—to the well-known—like Martin Luther King, Jr. We see a rich and wide diversity of Baptists from all over the world. We glimpse the multiple expressions of peacemaking: from preaching to teaching to writing to organizing.

The differences among this group of Baptist peacemakers are vast. Yet some common denominators do seem to exist. One is a continued commitment to the biblical word about justice and mercy. Another is the longing to do all they could to alleviate human suffering.

These peacemakers caught God's vision of a new heaven and a new earth. They clearly incarnated their faith, expressing their conviction that matters of freedom and liberation for the human community were matters of faith. Like the roll call of the faithful witnesses in Hebrews, these Baptist peacemakers endured resistance to their message through affliction and hardships and sometimes even death. As Hebrews recounts, "the world was not worthy" of them (Heb 11:38). The world was not ready for them, any more than it was ready for the witness of Jesus Christ. "They did not receive what was promised" (Heb 11:38), but they got a good, long glimpse at the promise in their step into God's transforming work in the world.

As a strong and courageous Baptist peacemaker himself, Paul Dekar has a keen and sensitive eye to the joys and struggles of announcing God's reign. He has provided us with the gift of a heritage in this collection of stories. We had no idea that we were surrounded by so great a cloud of Baptist peacemaking witnesses. With renewed encouragement and hope from their lives, we can "run with perseverance the race that is set before us, looking to Jesus the pioneer and perfecter of our faith" (Heb 12:1-2). God is still active, creating heroes of the faith for the healing of the nations. Thanks be to God.

Nancy Hastings Sehested
Pastor, Prescott Memorial Baptist Church
Memphis, Tennessee

Foreword

Baptist Peacemakers: the title sounds like an oxymoron. The two words together, given the experience of recent decades in several parts of the Baptist world, form a contradiction in terms. Paul Dekar is aware of that as he sets out to trace the ancestry of the small but significant movements or the often lonely individuals who *do* represent peacemaking. He is interested only in those to whom being Baptist is not an accidental or casual feature of life. These are not "Peacemakers who happened to have been or to be Baptist." They are people who take their Christian life, received and appreciated through Baptist heritages and forms, and try to contribute to a world of peace. Their existence may always have irritated the majority of Baptist believers, just as, nowadays, their story must surprise bystanders. Those of us who hope for wide use of this book might even hope that it should sell for its "surprise factor."

Baptist Peacemakers: the wags will say again, as wags in two other denominations do when they are being playful and, at the same time, serious, that this sounds like *Active Episcopalians* or *United Methodists*. The in-house critical loyalists in those denominations are bemoaning the apathy of so many fellow Episcopalians, the disunities of a group whose very name suggests peace and harmony in their house. *Baptist Peacemakers* could belong in the similar linguistic sphere: the in-house critical loyalists bemoan the violent, pro-gun, pro-big-defense, pro-aggression, and sometimes pro-war stance of many Baptist institutions, movements, and individuals.

Before addressing the ways in which it is clear that Professor Dekar is not trying to be waggish or oxymoronic, we should spend a moment mentioning why Baptists and what they represent and hope for are important. The non-Baptist author of this Foreword brings credentials for that. Some years ago I wrote an article on and have on occasion tried to patent the term "Baptistification." Observing global Christian trends, I argued that at least the near future of Christianity will have a large Baptist component. That future includes a growing Roman Catholicism, an uncertain Orthodoxy, a booming part-Baptist, part-anti-Baptist Pentecostalism and Charismatism, a languid "old established Protestantism" [Anglican, Lutheran, Reformed, Methodist, etc.], and, a major player, Baptistdom.

Why? Not all Baptists in all nations are in burgeoning groups. Great Britain, Canada, the Western European continent, the northern United States—heartlands of the Baptist world most frequently visited by Dekar—are not seeing the Baptist growth so much as the South of the United States and much of what used to be called the Third World. "Baptistification" meant the appeal in the modern world of movements that are aggressively missionary and conversionistic; the attraction of movements that call for adult conversion, including expression of will and choice, of personal commitment and the movement of individuals through "an ordeal of passage" to adult mature appropriation of faith; the lure of Christianity that relies on local autonomy, individualism, and personal freedom, and more. On the soil where that form of Baptist expression reigns, are there *Baptist Peacemakers*?

Perhaps I write too much out of the context of the northern United States, where citizens look at the largest Protestant body in their nation, the Southern Baptist Convention, taken over—most observers put it that way—by a fundamentalistic leadership that is increasingly assertive in political life. This Foreword reflects the perceptions of someone who has read the newspapers for the past twenty years and seen Baptists as part of the New Christian Right. That has meant not only oppositional stances on "social issues"—abortion, homosexuality, prayer in public schools, anti-pornography, and the like (positions on which many non-Baptists and non-Christian Rightists might often also agree). It has meant support for the biggest arms build-ups, the largest appropriations for defense, the most rigorous support of nationalist and military verbal (and other) muscle-flexing, the most criticism of movements for disarmament and peace talks. Baptist Billy Graham risked and received more criticism from Baptists to his right—are they now a majority?—for his support of nuclear disarmament as for anything he has done.

On the morning in which I complete this Foreword, the newspaper—in this case, the *New York Times* (June 7, A7) reports on the Christian Right takeover of Republican political organizations in Virginia, South Carolina, and more. B. Drummond Ayres, Jr., writes that "in both Virginia and South Carolina, . . . [these movements have been energized by] an evangelical fervor to restrict abortion, limit homosexual rights, *defeat gun-control measures* and control what children learn in school." Anyone who consults the religious atlases of those states learns that the overwhelming majority of Protestants there are Baptist and whoever interviews delegates to conventions of these movements learns that they are overwhelmingly Baptist in their affiliation.

Why "defeat gun-control measures?" Why buy into the language and support of that which poises nations for war and even neighbor against neighbor? Is such support integral to the Baptist vision of life?

Not at all, Paul Dekar says, offering not banners or slogans but quiet and consistent testimony. The peacemaking voice, from that of conciliation all across the spectrum to consistent pacifism, has never been in the majority in mainstream Baptist groups; only Quakers, Brethren, a few other Anabaptist groups, have kept the peacemaking vision consistently and centrally. But it has not been absent, muffled, or silent. Dekar obviously believes that the act of telling or reading the story of Baptist Peacemakers can stir the hearts of those not yet convinced to entertain the peacemaking vision. He clearly suggests that to adopt that vision and to work toward its realizations is not a betrayal of Baptist principle but is a consistent attempt to understand and act upon Baptist understandings of gospel, of scripture, of devotion to God in Christ, and of the expression of Baptist soul liberty. In fact, the only little lapses from the pure-historian stance throughout this book are closing lines in numbers of chapter Conclusions. The good professor turns pastor and preacher at such times with injunctions: "Let us then . . ." or exhortations or expressions of wishes and dreams.

The book has something of a *tour de force* character. As Dekar visits the many original outbursts of modern Baptist thought and life, he finds that pioneers were often peacemakers and regarded their approach to be the only way one could live out the gospel as Jesus taught it, evangelists portrayed, and heroes and heroines of faith [and this book, happily, includes the heroines] have pursued it. I said this is a *tour de force* because the force of one's preconceptions is to think of Baptists as being preoccupied with other things than peacemaking, as being minor contributors to the pro-peace endeavor in Christianity. Instead, Dekar, without straining, finds many of the best-known Baptists belonging to this camp. Without wanting to sound provincial, let me revisit his United States pages one more time: Roger Williams, Walter Rauschenbusch, and Martin Luther King, Jr., are three of the best-known and most widely influential Christians in a half millennium of North American life. They are all, in their various ways—Williams was essentially a "seeker" —Baptists. And they belong in anyone's annals of peacemaking.

The book will present less familiar names from Great Britain, Canada, the United States, and the old "missionary fronts" as well. This is not just a new version of familiar stories but the presentation of stories that few knew until now. The cast of characters in this book, then, is not just a "bunch of radicals," a mix of mavericks, an aegis of eccentrics, and connection of uninfluential misfits. Instead the people who people these pages are strong Christian believers, Baptist to the core, whose stories when well-told, as they are here, judge the complacent—which means most of us—and should inspire anyone who is ready to reexplore conscience and commitment. One may read this and go other ways than the ways of the peacemakers, but not without having seen at least the examples of the heroic, the glimpses of the saintly, and the dedication of those who would follow gospel before they follow opinion polls or the signals of the culture around them.

Martin E. Marty
The University of Chicago

To Nancy, Nathaniel, Matthew.
Love is the secret.

Introduction

This book has arisen from commitments I have made as a Christian, a pacifist, a husband, a father, and a scholar. As a child, I was introduced to the gospel of Jesus Christ. Gradually, I discerned a call from God to make peace with myself, God, and all God's creation. This call led in the direction of Christian pacifism. More than a theological or political stance, pacifism became for me a comprehensive way to live out the Christian life.

Several influences have directed me along my journey to God and into active peacemaking. Studying the Bible and Christian history have been central. My confession, "Jesus is my savior," has found resonance in the language of Ephesians 2:14: Jesus Christ is our peace. Through his death and resurrection, Jesus has effected reconciliation between God and myself and with the whole of humanity. There is no enmity with God or with others. Participating in the divine nature, I am restored to the fullness of God's image and likeness (2 Pet 1:4). This new status before God and the whole of creation is not my doing. It is God's gift. My re-creation is God's handiwork, and it is still taking place. As shoes for the journey, I am to put on whatever makes me ready to proclaim the gospel of peace (Eph 6:15). I am to find a community of commitment, joining others whose calling is rooted in a deep faith in Jesus Christ, who is our peace, in whom everything holds together, and through whom we are empowered to a ministry of healing among the nations.

Biblical teaching about human liberation, peace, and reconciliation encouraged me to take part in small ways in two powerful currents of the 1960s: the civil rights movement and the movement against military engagement by the United States in Southeast Asia. Community organization work, marches, and civil disobedience sharpened my commitment to pacifism. So did participation in a development project organized by Crossroads Africa. Working in Chad during the summer of 1965, I met poor people suffering from the scourges of malnutrition, poverty, racism, religious intolerance, underdevelopment, and war. I came to understand the need to change unjust social structures into ones that utilize the resources of the created order and of human ingenuity and wisdom for the benefit of all.

Around 1967, three events strengthened my commitment to active peacemaking: I met Nancy Rose; I joined the Fellowship of Reconciliation (FOR); and I became a conscientious objector. Ordinary milestones in the normal flow of life, these three events were interwoven and informed each other. Nancy's formative years shaped her own quest for non-violent means of social change and human betterment. Two separate pilgrimages came together. By marrying, we covenanted to grapple with the exigencies of peacemaking in family life. As a conscientious objector, I was permitted by my draft board to do service overseas. As a result, Nancy and I spent nearly three years in Cameroon, where we confronted issues such as war, degradation of the environment, poverty, and violation of human rights. We dreamed that the polluted, ravaged creation might become a new creation of peace, joy, righteousness, and wholeness. As parents, later, we wanted to bequeath to our sons Nathaniel and Matthew a different, better world than we inherited from our parents' generation.

Through the FOR, a network of women and men who recognize the essential unity of humanity and have joined together to explore the power of love and truth for resolving human conflict, we came to appreciate a simple phrase that summarized the direction our lives were taking. In the words of Second World War French resistance leader Maurice Schwartz, "There is no way to peace. Peace is the way."[1]

A few years after our return to North America, we settled in Hamilton, Ontario, Canada, where we have identified with small groups and quiet circles that foster idealism and transformative processes. Through organizations such as Amnesty International and the Hamilton Disarmament Coalition, we work for social change. Through MacNeill Baptist Church, we seek to assist battered women and children, refugees, or students from developing nations. Through colleagues, professional contacts, and students, my career as a teacher in a Baptist theological college and a secular university links us with a global network of concerned individuals resisting war and working towards a just and lasting peace in several areas of conflict. Through a network of Baptist peacemakers from countries such as Canada, El Salvador, India, Burma (now Myanmar),

---

[1]The quotation is often attributed to A. J. Muste. He indicated its origins in A. J. Muste, "Peace Is the Way. A Christmas Meditation," *Fellowship* 42 (December 1976): 3-5.

Nicaragua, Puerto Rico, South Africa, Sri Lanka, and the United States, we have sought to share in the healing of the nations.

To identify Baptists as peacemakers may be a surprise. The Baptist denomination is not a so-called historic peace church. While the first Christians as well as Brethren, Mennonites, members of the Society of Friends and Christians from virtually every branch of the Church have been peacemakers, rarely does one think of Baptists in this light. Yet peace is an emphasis in Baptist life that has flowed at varying times as an underground stream or as a mighty current.

As successors of the sixteenth-century continental Anabaptists and seventeenth-century British Baptists, Baptist peacemakers share a legacy that has inspired Baptists from all walks of life and in every part of the world to work against war and the demonic fallout that wars always bring. Some have done so by opposing specific wars. Others have done so as champions of a broad conception of peace. Some have defended religious freedom. Others have promoted justice by joining struggles for the abolition of slavery, against colonialism, for women's rights or for human rights. Many have clothed the naked, fed the hungry, comforted the sorrowful, sheltered the destitute, served those that meant them harm, and bound up the victims of wars.

For sixty years, Baptist peace groups have existed as leaven within Baptist bodies and as channels for Baptist peacemaking. In the United Kingdom, the Baptist Pacifist Fellowship (BPF) began in 1929 when a pastor, William Henry Haden (1875–1952), took the initiative to circulate a letter among 2000 Baptists inquiring about organizing a peace group. He received sufficient encouragement from among 400 respondents that, in 1932, the BPF was organized. American and Southern Baptist pacifist groups also took shape during the dark days before the Second World War.

Baptist pacifist organizations served important war-time functions. Subsequently, they went into decline, prompting several times pundits prematurely to pronounce them dead. They are not. Within the Baptist Union of Great Britain, the BPF claims nearly a thousand members. It holds conferences, publishes a newsletter, and witnesses against war and militarism. In the United States, peacemaking groups within the American and Southern Baptist conventions took the initiative to form, in 1984, the Baptist Peace Fellowship of North America (BPFNA). By 1992, it embraced Baptists from eleven denominations, over thirty regional organizations, and peacemaker groups in local congregations. Through its publications, including *The Baptist Peacemaker* and newsletters, the BPFNA reaches nearly 30,000 readers. Glen Stassen's book, *Journey into Peacemaking*, published by the Southern Baptist Brotherhood Commission in 1983, sold over 5,000 copies and went into its second edition.

North American Baptist peacemakers form part of a wider network. In August 1988 a historic gathering in Sjövik, Sweden, brought together 200 Baptists from thirty countries. Under the theme "seek peace and pursue it" (Ps 34:14), participants explored the Baptist peacemaking heritage and practical strategies for implementing peace and justice ministries. The final communiqué envisioned development of new peacemaking initiatives among Baptists around the world.

The second international Baptist peace conference took place in Nicaragua in July 1992. Jointly sponsored by the Baptist Peace Fellowship and the Baptist Convention of Nicaragua, the conference brought together over 200 registrants from thirty-five countries under the theme "Thy Kingdom Come." The objectives were: (1) to explore parts of our Baptist heritage that relate to the biblical promise of God's coming reign of justice and peace, (2) to examine from a biblical point of view the history of colonization in light of the 1992 quincentenary of the arrival of Columbus in the Americas, and (3) to strengthen commitment on the part of Baptists to address issues of justice and peace by sharing experiences of biblical witness in many parts of the world.

Keynote speaker Gustavo Parajon, medical doctor, pastor of the First Baptist Church, Managua (whose choir led in music), and president of CEPAD [Nicaraguan Evangelical Committee for Aid and Development] began with readings from Isaiah 58 and Matthew 25. Parajon surveyed the history of his country from colonization to the present. He described the existing situation as one of crisis resulting from natural disasters, twelve years of war, and the general disparity in wealth between industrialized and poorer nations. Parajon deplored the fact that "800 million people in the North control the lives of four billion people in the South." He urged governments and international financial institutions to lift the burden of poverty by canceling usurious debts.

Several persons whose cultures are indigenous to the Americas gave leadership. Reaves Nahwooks (Kiowa), Clydia Nahwooksy (Cherokee), and Ava Doty (Comanche) offered prayers each morning. Olivia Juarez Dominguez (Nahualt), professor at a Baptist seminary in Mexico, stressed contributions of indigenous peoples to the growth of advanced, culturally sophisticated civilizations. Citing the relationship between military coercion and religious conversion, she spoke of new possibilities:

> Our roots are deep. They have broken our branches, but our sprouts are growing and will flower. Now we join together just as many suffering peoples are clamoring for the Kingdom. We ask, above all, for respect for the humblest, who are suffering from war, hunger, and injustice.

Luis N. Rivera-Pagan, professor at the University of Puerto Rico, spoke on "the tragic convergence of conquest and Christianization."

Several speakers provided first-hand reports of conflict and peacemaking. Miguel Thomas Castro, onetime prisoner of conscience and former pastor of Hispanic work at Wentworth Baptist Church, Hamilton, Ontario, Canada, returned four years ago to El Salvador. He reported the suffering and martyrdom of Baptists during years of civil war. He was one of a delegation from Emmanuel Baptist Church, San Salvador. Forged in suffering, the Emmanuel Baptist wagers of peace shared a faith that allows no room for despair. Castro urged: "Do not forget us. Tell our stories. Be present with us in your prayer. Be present with us here as witnesses to our reality. Be companions on our road."

Recalling the slaughter of forty-two sleeping people in Boipatong, South Africa, Diba Madolo, General Secretary of the Baptist Convention of South Africa, indicated his fear that when liberation finally comes to that battered country, there will be no one to enjoy it. Madolo stressed that peace is not a passive activity. Echoing the theme from a different context, Jualynne Dodson, an African American sociologist and ecumenical liaison for the Progressive National Baptist Convention, stressed the connection between personal prejudice and institutionalized racism, between overt and covert racism. She warned that the sin of racism is fuel that explodes into the open conflict. She concluded, "If you are serious about peace, you work for justice."

Despite the desperation that grips many throughout the world, we live as people captive to a vision of God's coming realm. With the power of the Holy Spirit, let us find ways to act on the basis of practical suggestions provided in the closing conference statement: to study the Bible for the witness of peace and justice, to be doers of the Word and not hearers only, to amplify the voices of peace workers, to encourage ambassadors of reconciliation, to focus resources and efforts on the exploding crisis of racial/ethnic conflict, and to reclaim our responsibility as stewards of "the earth and all that dwells therein" (Ps 24:1).

In some sense, I have written this book to meet a need deep within myself to chart my pilgrimage, to identify myriad influences that have shaped it, and to understand it as it unfolds. I am writing amidst dark days of dashed hopes and war. I envision Baptist peacemakers hastening along the road of human interdependence, a wide boulevard of people finding one another's hands for the long journey ahead. I offer this book to those walking with me: Baptist peacemakers who need to discover the tradition in which they move and other Christians who need models and exemplars of the peaceable realm Jesus proclaimed and brought into being. If readers gain a sense of meaning, direction, and encouragement from the book, it will have served a purpose. As well, I offer this book as the fruit of research. Scholars have not given adequate attention to this neglected dimension of Baptist historiography.[2]

A comment on language is in order. When quoting authors who use male language to express inclusive ideas, I leave the text unchanged. Otherwise, following guidelines in *Woman, Language, and the Church* (London: Association for Inclusive Language, 1988), I endeavor to use inclusive language throughout the book.

Acknowledgements

A year's research leave from McMaster Divinity College in 1990–1991 made possible completing this book. The Arts Research Board of McMaster University provided grants in 1988 and 1989 that enabled me to meet key figures and visit archives. I am indebted to Judith Colwell, Canadian Baptist Archives, Hamilton, Ontario, Canada; Sue Mills, Librarian-Archivist, Regent's Park College, Oxford, Great Britain; and, in the United States, Richard Deats of the Fellowship of Reconciliation,

---

[2]The only Baptists with entries in Harold Josephson, ed., *Biographical Dictionary of Modern Peace Leaders* (Westport: Greenwood Press, 1985) are Harry Emerson Fosdick (1878–1969), Henry Holcombe (1762–1824), Martin Luther King, Jr. (1929–1968), Muriel Lester (1884–1968, whose Baptist roots are not noted), and Francis Wayland (1796–1865).

Nyack, New York, Wilma Mosholder, Swarthmore College Peace Collection, Swarthmore, Pennsylvania, and Jim Lynch and Lois Hayes, American Baptist-Samuel Colgate Library, Rochester, New York. I have also consulted holdings in the American Baptist Archives Center, Valley Forge, Pennsylvania; British Library, London; Bristol Baptist College; Dr. Williams's Library, London; Fellowship of Reconciliation, London, Ireland, and Holland; Friends Library, London; the London Peace Society; the Martin Luther King, Jr. Center for Nonviolent Social Change, Atlanta, Georgia; and the Special Collections Library, Yale Divinity School, New Haven.

As part of the process of research, one collects many IOUs. Many have read draft material. I have benefitted from conversation and hospitality from many individuals, including Gay Albaugh, Paul Barlow, Alan and Margaret Betteridge, Cawley Bolt, William H. Brackney, John Briggs, Dan and Sharon Buttry, Martin Ceadel, Keith Clifford, Ann Connor and A. B. Short of the Community of Hospitality in Atlanta, Georgia, Paul Fiddes, Ruth Fraser, Shirley Gordon, Mary Haddow, Norman and Pat Kember, Debbie Kirk, Graeme MacQueen, Donald and Dorothy Nicholl, LeeAnn Purchase, Marc and Linda Rafael, David Sharma, Reid and Jennelle Trulson, and Jill Wallis. Any deficiencies in this book are not their responsibility.

A special word of acknowledgement is in order. In September 1984, George Williamson, pastor of First Baptist Church, Granville, Ohio, called. "Will you come to Granville for a meeting of a newly formed Baptist peace network? Our structure is intentionally wide open, and we are eager to explore contacts with Canadian brothers and sisters." For several reasons, I was reluctant to go. Nevertheless, I went and was seized by a vision of a community of Baptist peacemakers seeking to witness to the gospel of peace. Though we had no idea how the proposed budget was to be met, we named Ken Sehested, executive director of the fledgling Baptist Peace Fellowship of North America.

About a year and several meetings later, Ken called. He was dreaming an event to be billed part conference, part revival. Ken asked me to share some brief stories of Baptist "saints." Again, for a number of reasons, I was reluctant to go. Again, I went. The gathering at Green Lake, Wisconsin, June 30–July 5, 1986 was a transformation moment. The Holy Spirit created an environment in which many of us experienced God's reign as real. The conjoining of spiritual renewal with an emphasis on work for peace with justice led many of us to affirm God's call to peacemaking as our fundamental vocation. We discovered that there is something special about being both Baptist and peacemakers.

Subsequently, through many friendship tours, gatherings, board meetings, and informal "networking," members of the BPFNA have found practical ways for involving our congregations and denominational structures in specific forms of reconciling ministry. Along the way, we have struggled to become a genuinely multi-racial, international community of peacemakers bearing witness to the oneness we experience in Christ. We have taken risks. George, Ken, and many others, including Karen Chaponis, Kyle Childress, Anne Whirley, Kim Whitehead, Paula Womac, and co-Canadian board members Neil and Bonnie Hunter and John and Carol Sabean have inspired, prodded, and patiently bolstered me. One result is that a community of conviction has directly shaped this book. Understanding that the foundation of peace is justice, that the force of peace is love, we have found in our tradition seeds of God's peaceful realm from which will spring the tree of life and bring healing among the nations. Thanks to you all.

Courtesy of Publications

I acknowledge with thanks use of material which has appeared in the following journals and books: *American Baptist Quarterly*; *Atlantic Baptist*; *Baptist Quarterly*; *Link and Visitor*; *McMaster Journal of Theology*; H. Wayne Pipkin, ed., *Seek Peace and Pursue It* (Memphis: BPFNA and Ruschlikon: Institute for Baptist and Anabaptist Studies, 1989); Jarold K. Zeman, ed., *Costly Vision. The Baptist Pilgrimage in Canada* (Burlington: Welch, 1988).

Apart from passages in quotations from the work of other authors, references from the Bible are from the *New Revised Standard Version* (Oxford: Oxford University Press, 1989).

Chapter One

Identifying the Legacy

Aims

This book has two aims. The first is to recover the legacy of Baptist peacemakers. The second is to explore the faith that has led Baptist peacemakers to follow Jesus' pathways of peace. The title, "For the Healing of the Nations: Baptist Peacemakers," expresses the interdependence of these two objectives.

The title draws upon John's vision in Revelation 21-22 of a new heaven and new earth. The seer is shown the river of life, sparkling like crystal, flowing from the throne of God and of the Lamb down the middle of a city street. On either side of the river stands the tree of life: "the leaves of the tree are for the healing of the nations" (Rev 22:2).

For centuries this image of the healing of the nations has inspired Christians, including Baptists. As an example, from 1957–1960 during the height of the Cold War, Edwin Theodore Dahlberg (1893–1986), Baptist pastor and a founder of the Baptist Pacifist Fellowship, served as head of the National Council of Churches in the United States of America. In an address delivered 6 December 1957, he scrutinized in the light of the gospel of Jesus Christ the theory of "massive retaliation . . . bomb for bomb, rocket for rocket, sputnik for sputnik." Dahlberg explained,

> When Jesus was reviled he reviled not again. His four point program in relation to his enemies, according to the Sermon on the Mount, was to love, to bless, to do good and to pray. The task of the Christian church, if we would be faithful to the express command of our Lord, must be one of massive reconciliation on a world scale.

Dahlberg challenged his audience by condemning doleful expenditures by governments for social needs in contrast with military spending. He urged Christians to follow the model of churches in St. Louis, Missouri (where he was a pastor) to achieve reconciliation in race, religion, economics, and other areas of life.

Dahlberg believed that we must draw upon the deep resources of faith if we are going to have massive reconciliation. In one letter he spelled out the scope of the challenge for Christians: "We have an opportunity to lead a war stricken world to a higher level of patriotism and understanding among all nations." In another talk, he returned to the theme of massive reconciliation. He concluded, "Massive reconciliation may seem like an impossible task. But man [sic] has been given the intelligence, the imagination, and the power to effect it. Will he have the faith?"[1]

Edwin Dahlberg's challenge has not lost its urgency. For an entire generation, two of the most compelling symbols of the deep estrangements and human wounds in need of healing have been the Berlin Wall and the imprisonment of Nelson Mandela in South Africa. Suddenly, on 9 November 1989, nonviolent struggle brought down the Berlin Wall, ended the Cold War, and fueled dreams for a peace dividend. Three months later, on 11 February 1990, Nelson Mandela walked out of jail. This culminated another long, generally nonviolent struggle for social change. Dreams soared. A new world was dawning. Soon all peoples of the world would walk in the ways of freedom, justice, and peace.

Euphoria over these developments has disappeared. War has devastated the Persian Gulf region. In Burma (Myanmar), Central America, Ethiopia, and elsewhere, wars continue unabated. Conflicts in Israel, Lebanon, and Northern Ireland are no closer to resolution. Collapse of the Union of Soviet Socialist Republics has heightened concern about nuclear weapons. In Africa, thousands die of starvation. Environmental degradation encroaches everywhere. We have, in short, crossed some rivers along the long journey to a world of security, cooperation, and peace.

---

[1]" 'The Task Before Us,' Text of Address by Rev. Dr. Edwin T. Dahlberg, 6 December 1957," Swarthmore College Peace Collection (hereafter, SCPC); memo regarding the Dahlberg Peace Award, 15 June 1973, Office on Peace Concerns, Board of National Ministries, American Baptist Churches; "Massive Reconciliation," *Baptist Peace News*, August 1979.

A comment on language is required. When quoting directly authors who use male language to express inclusive ideas, I leave the text unchanged. Otherwise, following guidelines in *Woman, Language, and the Church* (London: Association for Inclusive Language,1988), I endeavour to use inclusive language throughout the book.

Mountains remain to be climbed. John's vision of the old order passing away and of a new heaven and a new earth has not yet become reality.

People and social structures have never corresponded with God's purposes as the Bible reveals them. Insofar as these can be summarized, the life and teaching of Jesus have to do with restoring in us the fullness of God's image and likeness marred by sin and renewed through union with Jesus (2 Pet 1:1-11), proclaiming God's realm, and reordering earthly priorities.

Jesus brought about a new reality. He also left tasks undone and dreams unfulfilled. Drawing on a body of Jewish apocalyptic expectation about the impending end of history, a time when the world as it was known would disappear and God would usher in a new age of peace and righteousness, early Christians expected Jesus to return soon. When this did not happen, they adjusted to living in the here-and-now. How should they go about this? They experienced a tension between what they affirmed as accomplished fact and what they expected to occur soon.

Christians have never fully resolved this tension. At times, expectations about the imminent second coming of Jesus have soared, only to be dashed. More generally, Christians have come to terms with living out Jesus' teachings and building up God's earthly realm in ordinary ways, ever hopeful about the future.

This book is about a few Christians who offer guidance to those seeking a safer and saner world. They have not ushered in God's realm. This is something for God to accomplish. They have lived as though God's realm is a reality unfolding. God has worked through them (among others) to reshape the world around them. Baptist peacemakers are signs of God's activity in the world. Through their espousal of differing approaches to peace and through the variety of initiatives they have undertaken, they provide us "resources for a journey of hope."[2]

Baptist peacemakers are not saints, if by the word "saint" we mean perfection. They are ordinary women and men with weaknesses and limitations common to all people. As companions for our own journeys, Baptist peacemakers may make contemporary readers uncomfortable. Historians have found vivid labels for them. For example, recent books identify radical Baptists as "a turbulent, seditious, and factious people,"

---

[2]James Hinton, *Protests and Visions. Peace Politics in Twentieth-Century Britain* (London: Hutchinson Radius, 1989) vii.

"trouble makers," or "troublesome people."[3] Stories about these Baptists put us in touch with human suffering and summon us to do something about the pain of the world. Baptist peacemakers raise our sights. They inspire us with their dreams. By leaving tasks undone, they do not make things particularly easy for us. Memory of them may help to revitalize the peacemaking traditions of Christianity. Their stories may motivate us to seek the healing of the nations.

The Baptist Peace Legacy

In modern religious historiography, the place of Baptists is secure among the radicals of the seventeenth-century Puritan revolution, the eighteenth-century evangelical awakening, the nineteenth-century nonconformist conscience, and the free-church tradition of the twentieth century. Historians disagree about the source of Baptist radicalism. Some have identified a "trail of blood" running from the martyrdoms of the first Christian centuries, through the Montanists, Donatists, and various sectarian groups persecuted during the Middle Ages to the martyrs of the sixteenth-century Protestant reformation, including the Anabaptists. Others have noted continuity in British radicalism from Wyclif through the Separatists to the Baptist denomination that, along with the Congregationalists, Friends, and Presbyterians, emerged out of the religious ferment of seventeenth-century Britain. Both perspectives provide clues concerning Baptist origins and attitudes towards peace.

What was the relationship between the early British Baptists and the continental Anabaptists of the sixteenth century? The extent of indebtedness to Anabaptism is very controversial. A survey of early Baptist confessions of faith and treatises reveals some influence, in particular, regarding oaths, "the sword," and civil government. We can identify Baptist concern for these issues as early as 1610. In that year, the first modern people called Baptist (they did not use this name themselves) signed a confession of faith. John Smyth (d. 1612) and forty-one others

---

[3]Christopher Hill, *A Turbulent, Seditious, and Factious People. John Bunyan and his Church* (Oxford: Clarendon Press, 1988); A. J. P. Taylor, *The Trouble Makers. Dissent over Foreign Policy 1792–1939* (London: Hamish Hamilton, 1957); Caroline Moorehead, *Troublesome People. The Warriors of Pacifism* (London: Hamish Hamilton, 1986).

indicated their accord with a position Anabaptists called non-resistance. It is plausible to suppose that they might have come to this stance by virtue of their devotion to the Bible, but contacts with Anabaptists among Dutch settlers in Britain and while exiled in Holland also swayed them.

The majority of Baptists probably owed more to the teachings of the sixteenth-century reformer John Calvin than other spiritual forbearers. Thomas Helwys (d. 1616), leader of the faction that returned to Britain, explicitly rejected Smyth's views on taking oaths and bearing arms. Historian Walter H. Burgess summarized: "A few were ready to accept the Mennonite belief on these two points, but the majority held that the taking of an oath and bearing arms were legitimate in some circumstances, though not in a spiritual cause."[4]

In their views on the atonement and church organization, Helwys and his followers adopted many of the views of the Dutch theologian Jacob Arminius, who taught that the death of Christ is valid more generally. This became the doctrinal basis of the General Baptists. Other Baptists followed the views of seventeenth-century British Calvinists who believed that Christ died not for all but only for a particular few, the elect. This became the doctrinal basis of the Particular Baptists. A third group, the Seventh-day Baptists, were Calvinist in most areas but emphasized observance of the seventh day.

All Baptists agreed on the question of religious liberty. A treatise by Leonard Busher (b. ca. 1571), *Religion's Peace: A Plea for Liberty of Conscience* (1614), exemplified the stance of Baptists. Writing while he was in exile in Holland, Busher compared religious persecution and forced worship to rape. Citing Isaiah's vision of the peaceable realm, he concluded, "Little David overcame great Goliath, yet not brought up in war. Unlearned Peter confuted the learned priests, yet by calling a fisherman. Attend and help and you shall see the wonderful work of God."[5] Busher did not believe that Christians should renounce the sword.

---

[4]Walter H. Burgess, *John Smyth the Se-Baptist, Thomas Helwys and the First Baptist Church in England with Fresh Light upon the Pilgrim Fathers' Church* (London: James Clarke & Co, 1911) 333. Subsequent research has not altered the conclusion.

[5]Leonard Busher, *Religion's Peace: A Plea for Liberty of Conscience* (1614), in Edward Bean Underhill, *Tracts on Liberty of Conscience and Persecution 1614–1661* (London: J. Haddon, 1846) 80-81; Leon McBeth, *The Baptist Heritage. Four Centuries of Baptist Witness* (Nashville: Broadman Press, 1987) 104; Richard L. Greaves and Robert

He defended use by civil authorities of force to establish religious liberty and defend justice. This commitment to justice and religious liberty shaped a Baptist alternative to non-resistance. In a recent article, Timothy George argued,

> Basic to the Baptist defense of "the sword" was the belief that not only social tranquility but also religious toleration required some measure of magisterial coercion. Helwys upbraids the Dutch Mennonites for considering the office of the magistrate "a vile thing" while at the same time basking in the liberty and peace which the magistrate by use of the sword had won for them. As we shall see, the Baptists strongly objected to any form of established religion but they saw no reason why "religious peace" should not be defended by the sword and civil power. The coercive power of the magistrate also extended to the execution of moral and judicial law of the Old Testament, though not to its ecclesiastical laws which had been abrogated by Christ. Hence, the Baptists did not hesitate to call for strict enforcement of capital punishment against crimes such as adultery. [6]

Between 1640 and 1660, some Baptists supported taking up arms. Baptists numbered among the most prominent figures in the New Model Army and, by 1653, reached the zenith of their military and political influence. Then, as disillusionment with the Protectorate grew, a diverse group of radicals known as the Fifth Monarchists claimed the right, even the duty, to take up arms to overthrow the existing regime and to establish the millennium. While some leading Fifth Monarchists were Baptist, Baptists generally distanced themselves from the apocalyptic tenets of the movement. By 1660, when the monarchy was restored, Baptists had reclaimed Smyth's vocabulary of non-resistance.

In 1660 and at the end of the century, most Baptists welcomed the end of the turmoil. Suffering and persecution did not give way to full toleration, however. Baptists had to strengthen commitments characteristic of their radical origins by defending freedom of conscience and separation of church and state. While concern for mission focused on the salvation of individuals, peacemaking had found a place within Baptist life through non-resistance and work for justice.

Zaller, eds., *Biographical Dictionary of British Radicals in the Seventeenth Century* (Brighton: Harvester Press, 1982).

[6]Timothy George, "Between Pacifism and Coercion: The English Baptist Doctrine of Religious Toleration," *Mennonite Quarterly Review* 58 (1984): 38-39.

Since the seventeenth century, Baptists have opposed war and the demonic fallout that wars always bring. Prominent Baptists have numbered among the ranks of modern peace crusaders. Though many names are lost to the historian, Baptists have joined myriad campaigns for peace, protested every war right up to the recent war in the Persian Gulf region, extended wartime relief, promoted reconciliation, and sought to eliminate the causes of war.

Baptists did not become one of the so-called "historic peace churches," a category generally reserved for Anabaptist groups such as the Mennonites and Hutterites, the Society of Friends (or Quakers), and the Church of the Brethren. Unlike Anabaptists, whose position against use of the sword has been constant since the Schleitheim Confession of 1527, or Quakers, who renounced bearing arms in a statement of 1660, Baptists have no similar document that defines a coherent or unifying Baptist peace testimony. There has never been a consistent Baptist position on peace. Individuals and voluntarism preclude Baptist agreement to a common stance on non-resistance, ways to achieve justice, *or any other issue*. Baptists have diverse views on virtually every question. What unites them is their attempt to be faithful to biblical truth as they understand it. Irrespective of culture, circumstance, or hermeneutical principles, all frame thought and action by drawing on biblical teaching.

To arrive at a useful idea of the legacy of Baptist peacemakers, it is necessary to examine the witness of many figures from many times and places. Countless Baptists have been peacemakers. As an attempt to recover the Baptist peace heritage, this book identifies the life-giving forces that have guided and energized Baptist peacemakers. We probe the peace witness of Baptists by asking questions within four broad categories: conversion, scripture, action, and analysis.

(1) What conversion experiences led to peacemaking? How was the breakthrough experience interpreted?

(2) What passages of the Bible or beliefs are central to understanding peace? Have these convictions changed over the years? Who or what nourished these convictions?

(3) How have these convictions found expression in action? In taking action, has the individual Baptist peacemaker identified with Baptists?

(4) How are the causes of war and roads to peace understood? Has the individual's analysis changed over the years?

Definitions

Some discussion of the word "peace" is necessary. This is because the word is multi-dimensioned, emotive, capable of being misused, and problematic for scholars. Peace can refer to inner tranquility, social tranquility, or tranquil relations between political groups. Peace can also refer to war. Those who "fight for peace" or defend a particular conflict may do so because they believe a specific war to be a way to peace. In speaking of peace, one may have in mind relating to God, others, and the earth; ending conflict, or seeking to remove the sources of conflict; moving toward a better world, or building utopia. In each of these understandings of peace, peace is a complex reality. Peace is a valid end in itself. Peace also refers to the means by which one strives to realize the goal. This is the meaning of the slogan, "There is no way to peace. Peace is the way." While working for a dream that may not be realized in one's lifetime, one lives as though peace were an accomplished fact.

In this book, peacemaking denotes a process by which one endeavors to live at harmony with oneself, the created order, and the Creator God. The biblical phrase, "seek peace, and pursue it" (Ps 34:14), suggests two dimensions of peacemaking. The first is practical. Baptist peacemakers seek peace by using peaceful methods such as conciliation and arbitration to resolve conflicts and build more just and stable relationships. The second is visionary. Baptist peacemakers pursue a better world in which injustice, violence, and war no longer exist.

Baptists think of themselves as biblical people. This provides a clue to understanding the specific contribution of *Baptist* peacemakers. For most Baptist peacemakers, peace with God in Christ is at the heart of the Bible and the lifestyle it calls forth. Peace is an outlook on life deeply rooted in an understanding of the work of Jesus. A great company of heavenly voices announced his birth with promises of peace on earth (Luke 2:14). Through him we have peace with God (Rom 5:1). He blessed peacemakers (Matt 5:19) and warned disciples against hoarding material possessions and allowing themselves to be tempted by wealth and power (Matt 6:19-21). A later writer affirmed that true justice is the harvest reaped by peacemakers from seeds sown in a spirit of peace (Jas 3:18); wealth and power remained for him the source of conflict and quarrels (Jas 4:1-5). Jesus effected peace among Gentiles and Jews, thus making peace among all the nations, and so he came and proclaimed the Good News of the Gospel of Peace (Eph 2:11-22). Christians are to put on the sandals of peace (Eph 6:15).

Christians have not agreed on how to put these teachings into practice, or even that they should. Since the fourth century, most Christians have accepted war as a matter of tragic necessity. Only a minority of Christians has opposed participating in service requiring them to kill. The only consistent voice for peace has been that of the historic peace churches, and even that witness has not been uniform. Some members of those churches have accepted the authority of earthly powers to engage in war. In the past, the complicity of Christians in war-making and vacuous bleating by Christians about love or peace have discredited Christianity. Only recently has this changed as more and more Christians give moral leadership about issues of war and peace.

Quite apart from practical dimensions of making peace in personal, interpersonal, and wider relationships, peace is also a utopian ideal. Throughout Christian history, followers of Jesus have looked forward to an end of time when God will intervene to bring about true peace. The Baptist movement began amidst a period of enormous eschatological, or apocalyptic, expectation of the imminent arrival of such an age of peace. Especially during the past eighty years when humanity has devised technologies capable of destroying all life, this sort of language has informed the tradition. Thus, many Baptist peacemakers have drawn strength from the biblical image of a new world order (as one edition of the Jerusalem Bible puts it) when God promised that,

> As long as the earth endures,
> seedtime and harvest, cold and heat,
> summer and winter, day and night,
> shall not cease. (Gen 8:22)

Among the ranks of Baptist peacemakers, many are energized by the vision of the new world order in which swords will be hammered into plowshares and nations shall not lift sword against nation nor even study war (Isa 2:4); when the proud shall be scattered, the mighty pulled down, the lowly ones exalted, the hungry filled with good things and the rich sent away empty (Luke 1:51-53); when creation shall be set free from its bondage to decay (Rom 8:19-24); when death itself will be vanquished and every tear wiped away, for there shall be neither mourning nor crying nor pain anymore (Rev 21:4).

In developing a biblical ethic of peace, one should be careful not simply to turn to the Bible for a definition of peace.[7] Numerous biblical passages refer to peace, but the word means different things in different contexts. To say that the Hebrew word for peace suggests wholeness, balance, integrity, and harmony between people, the natural world, and the Creator, or that the Greek word for peace suggests friendship with God is not sufficient to understand specific excerpts or to relate ancient texts to modern times. Our world-views are different from those of biblical writers.

The *Oxford English Dictionary* devotes three pages to the word and its derivatives. Among various definitions is one which has wide acceptance: "freedom from, or cessation of, war or hostilities; that condition of a nation or community in which it is not at war with another." This has the merit of simplicity. A nation or community is at peace when it is not at war with another. But is the absence of armed conflict necessarily peace? A nation may in fact not be engaged directly in hostilities against any other nation. This is a desirable condition, but repressive means may be applied internally to suppress the rights of individuals, to block the self-determination of communities longing to be free, to foster activities short of war such as terrorism, or to conceal the intent to go to war with another state. Similarly, communities not at war with each other may co-exist with a high degree of enmity and aggressive behavior short of war. In these cases we may speak of peace as the absence of war, but we may legitimately question whether the measures taken to maintain "peace" are peaceful or engender future wars.

To illustrate the problem, histories of Europe often describe the period from 1815–1914 as a century of peace. The word "peace" here can only refer to a narrow definition of peace, for war was not absent as such between the end of the Napoleonic wars and the outbreak of the First World War. By some criteria, for example, conflict avoidance or the scale of deaths, the years were peaceful. There were, in the helpful terminology of pioneer peace researcher Lewis Fry Richardson (1881–1953), nearly a hundred "deadly" or "fatal quarrels." Some went

---

[7]T. Raymond Hobbs, *A Time for War. A Study of Warfare in the Old Testament* (Wilmington, Delaware: Michael Glazier, 1989).

before various courts of arbitration. Some involved great loss of human life. But none of the fatal quarrels, even the two most deadly, Crimea (1854–1856) and Anglo-Boer (1899–1902), disrupted the capacity of the European powers to balance contending interests. None threatened to destroy civilization. None was a "Great War."[8]

There is another outlook, according to which a second, complementary definition of peace is required. From the perspective of African and Asian peoples conquered and "pacified" by deadly means during the years from 1815–1914, this was a century of war. The magnitude of disaster was enormous. In the words of another definition in the *Oxford English Dictionary*, what was lacking was "a state or relation of peace, concord, and amity." From this definition, we note that peace is bound up with freedom, justice, respect for human rights, and other conditions. Peace is the absence not only of war, but also of all that contributes to war. In the words of John William Graham (1859–1932), in his classic study of the conscription controversy in the United Kingdom during World War I, "Peace is no mere negative of war, but a splendid positive ideal of the active life and co-operative endeavour of which war and all the things that make for war are the denial."[9]

Thus far, the word *pacifism* has not been used. Pacifism signifies many things to many people. It can mean conscientious objection, or refusal to bear arms and, in some cases, to pay for the preparation of war. It can refer to love of enemy. Some pacifists withdraw from society. Others engage in active politics. Some devote themselves to "life service for the enthronement of love in personal, social, commercial and national life."[10] Others pledge to resist war. Some equate pacifism with weakness or appeasement. Others identify pacifism with nonviolent struggle. Some regard pacifism as a faith. Others see it as ideology. Many pacifists eschew use of the word altogether. Others think they ought to.

A story told by a Canadian pacifist, Walter Klaassen, expresses some of the emotions pacifists elicit. As a student, he went before a committee

---

[8]Oliver M. Ashford, *Prophet or Professor? The Life and Work of Lewis Fry Richardson* (Bristol: Adam Hilger Ltd, 1985) 170-88; Hinton, 1.

[9]John W. Graham, *Conscription and Conscience. A History 1916–1919* (London: George Allen and Unwin, 1922) 38; Harold Josephson, ed., *Biographical Dictionary of Modern Peace Leaders* (Westport: Greenwood Press, 1985) 352-53.

[10]Statement of the British Fellowship of Reconciliation.

to assess his credentials for ministry in the Baptist denomination. Asked if he was a pacifist, Klaassen replied, "Yes." "I expect that you will not make a point of it" was the response.[11]

A cognate word is *pacificism*, which refers to the advocacy of peaceful processes such as arbitration and conciliation. Some use the words pacifism and pacificism interchangeably. Historian Alan John P. Taylor, however, distinguishes pacifism, the doctrine of non-resistance advocated by Smyth or Anabaptists, and pacificism, which typified nineteenth-century peace movements. In his studies of British pacifism, Martin Ceadel refines this terminology to differentiate those who oppose all war or participation in war (pacifists) and those who rule out aggressive wars and some defensive ones (pacificists).[12]

Etymologically, the words were not in use before this century and did not appear in the original 1905 *Oxford English Dictionary*. According to *The Shorter Oxford English Dictionary* of 1936, pacifism refers to the doctrine or belief that it is desirable and possible to settle international disputes peacefully. Pacifism can refer to a great variety of peace advocacy. In this book, following usage since the late 1930s, we refer to pacifism as principled opposition to all war.[13]

Scope

Some discussion of the scope of this book is necessary. This is because there is no consensus regarding criteria to define who is a Baptist. Also, limited space and lack of access to relevant sources have led to decisions as to who may be included in this book. I have followed these criteria.

---

[11]Interview, 1 November 1985. In studies as a candidate for ministry in the Baptist denomination, Dr. Klaassen discovered his Mennonite roots. He became a distinguished Anabaptist teacher and scholar. The questioner, George Peel Gilmour, was President of McMaster University.

[12]A. J. P. Taylor, 51, n. 5; Martin Ceadel, *Pacifism in Britain 1914–1945. The Defining of a Faith* (Oxford: Clarendon Press, 1980) and id., *Thinking about Peace and War* (Oxford: Oxford University Press, 1987).

[13]A. Ruth Fry, *Victories without Violence* (London: Peace Book Company, 1939; 1943 and 1950 editions expanded), uses pacifism as the word is now understood. John Howard Yoder, *Nevertheless. . . . The Varieties of Religious Pacifism* (Waterloo: Herald Press, 1972), explores twenty forms of Christian pacifism.

The first criterion concerns Baptist identity. We focus on women and men who called themselves Baptist at some point in their lives, accepted "believer's baptism," and were members of Baptist congregations for a discernible period of time. Historians regard them as part of "The International Baptist Family."[14] Anabaptists, German Brethren, and Quakers are largely absent from the pages of this book, despite their influence on Baptist life.

The second criterion concerns the character of Baptist peacemaking. We focus on women and men of concrete action. This is not a book about theory or arm-chair theologians. Baptist peacemakers have experienced pain in their own lives. They have confronted real evil in a real world. Like Jesus, Baptist peacemakers have taken on the plight of slave and refugee, the imprisoned victim and battered child, and sought to restore them to the fullness of the divine image and likeness. Baptist peacemakers recall an insight from 2 Peter 1:4: in God's divine power, we participate in the divine nature.

The third criterion concerns movements for social change. There is a place for solitary witness and action. One should never disparage the contribution of an individual, especially a person motivated for peace activism by outraged conscience. Nonetheless, peace workers rarely function exclusively as solo artists. More commonly, they help mobilize large numbers of people over long periods of time to achieve their goal of meaningful change. For example, in this book we examine William Carey (1761–1834) as part of the modern missionary enterprise he helped to shape, William Knibb (1803–1845) within the context of the anti-slavery movement, Martin Luther King, Jr. (1929–1968) as part of civil rights and anti-war movements, and so on.

The names of many peace workers are lost to posterity. We forget them at our own loss. In this book, one regrets limited attention to Germans, Italians, Russians, Scandinavians, or Baptists from the dynamic churches of the developing nations. To redress imbalance at least in part, we have included two remarkable Christians from the subcontinent of India. Otherwise, we have excluded living figures.

---

[14]I have consulted William H. Brackney, ed. *Baptist Life and Thought: 1600–1980* (Valley Forge: Judson Press, 1983); id. *The Baptists* (New York: Greenwood Press, 1988); William L. Lumpkin, *Baptist Confessions of Faith* (Chicago: Judson Press, 1959); McBeth (n. 5); Robert G. Torbet, *A History of the Baptists* (Valley Forge: Judson Press, 1963).

Some figures warrant more attention than has been possible. For example, Frederick Brotherton Meyer (1847–1929) and Joseph James Doke (1861–1913) exercised an influence on Gandhi. While their story is recounted briefly in chapter five, readers are directed through the footnotes to other literature.[15] Where there are lacunae, an agenda exists for future researchers.

This book is organized into three broad sections, each with six chapters. To illuminate the breadth of Baptist peace work, we cast a wide net. Each chapter contains biographical vignettes. Each could be a book. Precedents for this approach abound in Baptist historiography.[16] While often the literature is hagiographical, this is not necessarily bad. We need heroes and exemplars of the peaceable realm Jesus came to establish.

The broad sections introduce three concepts: negative peace, understood here as opposition to war; positive peace, understood as effort to eliminate the causes of war; and prophecy, understood as critique of religion and wider society based on a biblical vision of a better world. The categories are not airtight. When military service is not at issue, a pacifist may focus energy on work for justice. One may oppose war but believe that some wars are justifiable. Prophets call people to repentance, conversion, and amendment of life. Some may confront war and militarism, others injustice.

Martin Luther King, Jr., a seminal figure discussed at length in chapter seventeen, introduced these categories into contemporary analysis of social change. King coined the phrases "negative peace" and "positive peace." As early as the mid-1950s, during the Montgomery campaign, King summarized:

---

[15]In this case, see James D. Hunt, *Gandhi and the Nonconformists: Encounters in South Africa* (New Delhi: Promila and Company, 1986).

[16]The first Baptist history, Thomas Crosby's *The History of the English Baptists*, 4 vols. (1738–1740) attempted to provide not only a narrative of Baptist beginnings and subsequent development, but also biographical sketches of specific Baptist leaders, to vindicate the notion of Baptists as true successors of the original apostles. Other examples of the genre include W.S. Stewart, *Early Baptist Missionaries and Pioneers* (Philadelphia: Judson Press, 1925); Austin Kennedy de Blois, *Fighters for Freedom* (Philadelphia: Judson Press, 1929); Gordon Jones, *Greatness Passing By* (Brantford: Baptist Federation of Canada, 1967); James E. Tull, *Shapers of Baptist Thought* (Valley Forge: Judson Press, 1972). A recent example of the genre in the historiography of peace is John Ferguson, *Give Peace a Chance* (East Wittering, West Sussex: Gooday, 1988).

> Peace is not merely absence of some negative force—war, tension, confusion—but it is the presence of some positive force—justice, goodwill and the power of the kingdom of God. . . . Peace is not merely the absence of (tension in race relations) but it is the presence of justice. . . . If the Negro accepts his place, accepts exploitation, accepts injustice, there will be peace. But it would be a peace boiled down to stagnant complacency, deadening passivity, and if peace means this, I don't want peace. If peace means accepting second-class citizenship, I don't want it. If peace means keeping my mouth shut in the midst of injustice and evil, I don't want it.

In his "Letter from a Birmingham Jail," King returned to the phrases to contrast negative peace, a way of subjugating others in the name of decorum, law, and order, while positive peace connotes a way of living justly, nonviolently, and with respect for the dignity of all.[17]

The source of King's phrases is uncertain.[18] Ultimately, King drew his categories, including prophecy, from the Bible. King understood prophecy to mean something other than prediction of events. Prophecy is visionary in the sense that many of the images prophets use to describe God's holy ways cannot be humanly realized and will come to fruition only at some ill-defined future time. More commonly in the Bible, prophecy refers to the activities of women and men called by God to remind the people of what God requires—faithful obedience—and of the covenants established to direct the people along God's holy ways. The biblical prophets awakened hopes that God would restore things to the way they should be. They denounced sin and all that prevents realization of God's purposes. They called people to conversion, to turn from their evil ways, and to follow in the ways of peace. Generally, those named prophets in this book exercised such functions.

---

[17]"When Peace Becomes Obnoxious," sermon preached on March 29, 1956, King Papers, Atlanta, Series 111. In *Stride Toward Freedom: The Montgomery Story* (San Francisco: Harper and Row, 1958) 40, King contrasted negative peace with true peace. King's "Letter from a Birmingham Jail" circulated as a pamphlet and in *Why We Can't Wait* (Toronto: New American Library, 1964).

[18]The two concepts have wide usage. Kenneth E. Boulding, *Stable Peace* (Austin: University of Texas, 1979) 5, sees positive peace as a skill in the management of conflict and the development of a larger order than that which involves warring parties. Ronald J. Glossop, *Confronting War. An Examination of Humanity's Most Pressing Problem*, 2d ed. (Jefferson and London: McFarland and Co., 1987) 1-12, uses negative peace to denote absence of war and positive peace to describe a situation in which individuals and groups are not exploited.

This book is historical. It has been written for Christians who need a living past. As part of a living tradition, historic Baptist peacemakers continue to inform contemporary peacemakers through their lives and witness. What is their legacy? At the heart of it are two potent Christian symbols, the cross and empty tomb. Martin Luther King, Jr. wrote amidst the Montgomery campaign, "The cross is the eternal expression of the length to which God will go in order to restore broken community. The resurrection is a symbol of God's triumph over all the forces that seek to block community."[19] He went on to urge that we make love a reality through creation of the beloved community. Empowered by the Spirit of Christ who overcame death on the cross, we too shall overcome all that engenders bitterness, hatred, and violence. As we seek a better world in this way, we will witness the healing of the nations.

---

[19] *Stride toward Freedom*, 71.

Section One

Voices Against War: Negative Peace

As indicated in chapter one the first section presents Baptist peacemakers who opposed preparation for war, and war itself. Six chapters identify aspects of Baptist non-resistance, pacifism, and conscientious objection. Ensuing chapters examine the witness of those who advanced peacemaking principally through the work for positive peace and prophetic vision.

Chapter two explores early Baptist thinking about the sword and non-resistance. Chapter three introduces British Baptists in nineteenth-century peace societies. Chapter four introduces North American Baptists in nineteenth-century peace societies. On both sides of the Atlantic, some campaigners were pacifists. Others opposed only specific wars. Some were internationalists. Others stressed anti-imperialism.

After these collective portraits, we examine the lives of three individuals who opposed war without necessarily adopting pacifism. Two British Baptists, John Clifford (1836–1923) and James Henry Rushbrooke (1870–1947), resisted the Anglo-Boer War and sought to break the drift towards the First World War. Ultimately, they supported Britain's involvement in the war. Similarly, the Canadian Baptist theologian Douglas Clyde MacIntosh (1877–1945) served in the First World War as a military chaplain. Later, he questioned his support for the war. A legal battle ensued when he sought United States citizenship. The case established the legal principle of selective conscientious objection in the United States. These figures provide a bridge between the peace campaigners of the early twentieth century and those who founded contemporary Baptist peace groups.

Chapter Two
Early Non-Resistants

Non-Resistants in Christian History

Pacifism manifested itself early in Christian history. The first Christians believed that military service and killing were contrary to Jesus' teaching. In the second and third centuries, prominent leaders such as Tertullian and Origen condemned war and military service. Gradually, the church accommodated itself to admitting soldiers into membership. By the fourth century, when Christianity became the official religion of empire, the church accepted the role of the state as protector of peace and defender of orthodoxy. Two western bishops, Ambrose and Augustine, formulated what became known as the just war theory. They held that a Christian could sanction a war fought under certain conditions for a just cause and in a just manner.

Pacifism did not disappear. During the early middle ages, it persisted among monastic movements.[1] Later, persecuted groups such as the Italian Waldensians and Czech Brethren adopted pacifism, as did several theologians, including John Wyclif (d. 1384) and Desiderius Erasmus (ca. 1467–1536). In early modern times, pacifism manifested renewed vigor among Anabaptists, the Society of Friends (Quakers), and the Church of the Brethren.

The first of the historic peace churches traced its roots to sixteenth-century Anabaptism. Initially attracted to Zwingli's reform at Zurich, Conrad Grebel, Michael Sattler, and other colleagues rejected the sword and restated Jesus' teaching about non-resistance. In a "programmatic letter" to Thomas Müntzer (1524), and in seven articles formulated during a gathering at Schleitheim (1527), they agreed that Christians should separate themselves from "unchristian, devilish weapons of force." They added,

---

[1] John T. McNeill, "Asceticism versus Militarism in the Middle Ages," *Church History* 5 (1936): 3-28.

the sword is ordained of God outside the perfection of Christ. It punishes and puts to death the wicked, and guards and protects the good. . . . The sword is ordained to be used by the worldly magistrates. In the perfection of Christ, however, only the ban is used.[2]

Finally, Christians should not hold office or swear an oath. Over the next fifty years, Grebel and 2,500 others died amidst severe persecution. Tolerated in Holland and eastern Europe, followers of Menno Simons, Jacob Hutter, and other Anabaptist leaders taught non-resistance.

A second peace church, the Society of Friends, began between 1640–1660 during the English civil war. Initially, many early Friends were not pacifist. Some joined the Levellers and Fifth Monarchists. These movements included advocates of force to unseat ungodly governments. As late as December 1659, Richard Hubberthorne, a Friend, rebuked Baptists for declaring against armed rebellion.

Margaret Fell, George Fox, and others checked this non-pacifist strand of Quakerism. In June 1660, Fell drafted a statement given to King Charles II. Fell, Fox, Hubberthorne, and ten others declared they could not engage in wars to defend realms of this world. Their weapons would be spiritual and not carnal. As the basis of the Quaker peace testimony, they stated, "We utterly deny all outward wars and strife, and fightings with outward weapons, for any end, or under any pretence whatsoever; this is our testimony to the whole world."[3]

The third peace church, the Church of the Brethren, took shape early in the eighteenth century. Influenced by Pietism and Anabaptism, Alexander Mack and some followers renounced military service. Persecuted, they found refuge in Pennsylvania. Despite kinship with German Baptists, they formed a distinct body emphasizing non-resistance and conscientious objection.[4]

---

[2] William L. Lumpkin, *Baptist Confessions of Faith* (Chicago: Judson, 1959), 26-28.

[3] Initially, Quakers were not pacifist. Peter Brock, *The Quaker Peace Testimony* (York: Sessions Book Trust, 1990); Douglas Gwyn, *Apocalypse of the Word. The Life and Message of George Fox (1624–1691)* (Richmond: Friends United Press, 1986) esp. 141; Christopher Hill, *The Experience of Defeat. Milton and Some Contemporaries* (London: Faber and Faber, 1984) 153-63. A modern Quaker statement is "The Gulf Crisis and the Quaker Peace Testimony," *The Friend*, 7 December 1990, 1577.

[4] Rufus D. Bowman, *The Church of the Brethren and War 1708–1941* (Elgin: Brethren Publishing House, 1944).

At the start of the seventeenth century, similar ideas about non-resistance and the military found expression among British Baptists. A group led by John Smyth, one of several exiled congregations that separated from the established church, questioned the validity of their baptism. Smyth baptized himself and his followers in late 1608 or early 1609. Soon, Smyth had doubts about this procedure and attempted to lead his congregation into the Mennonite church. For this purpose, in 1609, he drafted a confession of faith in twenty articles. He made no reference to distinctive Mennonite views on oath-taking or bearing arms. Despite Smyth's contacts with Mennonites, he was not yet one of them. Ten members of Smyth's congregation did not want to join the Mennonites and, in 1612, followed Thomas Helwys back to Britain to form the first Baptist congregation there.

Still in Holland, the exiled British community received encouragement from the Mennonites who asked the petitioners to explain their views more fully. In response, Smyth and forty-one others formulated a confession of faith closer doctrinally to Mennonite convictions than the 1609 draft. They agreed that Jesus called Christians to follow

> his unarmed and unweaponed life, and his cross-bearing footsteps . . . (upon the office of the worldly authority many other things depend, as wars . . . to hurt his enemies in body or good . . . which evilly or not at all will fit or consort with the Christ, and the crucified life of the Christians), so hold we that it beseemeth not Christians to administer these offices.[5]

Sometime before his death in August 1612, Smyth drafted a fuller statement.[6] Published after Smyth's death, the manuscript reflected the extent to which Smyth and his party accepted Anabaptist views regarding civil magistrates and the duties of followers of Christ. They held that as for magistrates, by virtue of office they are,

> not to meddle with religion, or matters of conscience, to force or compel men to this or that form of religion, or doctrine: but to leave Christian religion free, to every man's conscience, and to handle only civil transgressions.

---

[5]"A Short Confession of Faith," 1610, in Lumpkin, 112.

[6]"Propositions and Conclusions concerning True Christian Religion, containing a Confession of Faith of certain English people, living at Amsterdam," in Lumpkin, 140.

As for a disciple of Christ, they asserted,

> he must love his enemies and not kill them . . . suffer persecution and affliction with Christ, and be slandered, reviled, blasphemed, scourged, buffeted, spit upon, imprisoned and killed with Christ; and that by the authority of magistrates, which things he cannot possibly do, and retain the revenge of the sword.

Smyth's non-resistance was not an isolated phenomenon. From 1624–1630, five or six General Baptist congregations sought union with Mennonites. Although they differed on some matters, regarding war they stated, "Some of us are of the same with you."[7] In future decades, Baptists did not unite on this stance. While non-resistance became a persistent theme in Baptist life, Baptists developed no consistent alternative that would permit adherents to know if, when, or how they ought ever to go to war.[8]

Period of the English Civil War

The years 1640–1660 were revolutionary.[9] Thomas Edwards (1599–1647), a Presbyterian pamphleteer, charged that a great swarm of

---

[7]Robert G. Torbet, *A History of the Baptists* (Valley Forge: Judson Press, 1963) 44; Robert Barclay, *The Inner Life of the Religious Societies of the Commonwealth* (London: Hodder and Stoughton, 1879) 73.

[8]Baptist theologians rarely explore just war thought. Exceptions include Francis Wayland, *The Elements of Moral Science*, reprint ed. by Joseph L. Blau (Cambridge: Harvard University Press, 1963) and the contemporary thinker James Wm. McClendon, Jr., *Systematic Theology: Ethics* (Nashville: Abingdon, 1986).

[9]The secondary literature is voluminous. Aspects of Baptist origins are treated by Timothy George, "Between Pacifism and Coercion: The English Baptist Doctrine of Religious Toleration," *Mennonite Quarterly Review* 58 (1984): 30-49; Christopher Hill, *The World Turned Upside Down. Radical Ideas during the English Revolution* (London: Temple Smith, 1972); Glen Stassen, "Anabaptist Influence in the Origin of the Particular Baptists," *Mennonite Quarterly Review* 36 (1962): 322-48; and Heather M. Vose, "Attitudes toward War and Peace Reflected by Some Puritan-Separatist Spiritual Descendants—the Baptists," *Mennonite Quarterly Review* 64 (1990): 371-84. For the New Model Army, see Charles H. Firth, *Cromwell's Army* (2d ed, London, 1912) and Leo F. Solt, *Saints in Arms. Puritanism and Democracy in Cromwell's Army* (London: Oxford University Press, 1959).

"illiterate mechanick preachers, yea of Women and Boy Preachers!" threatened the deformation of true religion:

> Among all the confusion and disorder in church matters both of opinions and practices, and particularly of all sorts of mechanicks taking upon them to preach and baptize, as Smiths, Taylors, Shoomakers, Pedlars, Weavers, etc., there are also some women-Preachers in our times, who keepe constant lectures, preaching weekly to many men and women.[10]

Sharing Edwards' alarm, the poet John Taylor (1578–1653) railed against the "rattlesnakes . . . unlearned men" who were turning things upside down and tearing religion into pieces.[11]

Albeit in an extreme manner, Edwards and Taylor provided a window into the formative period of the Baptist movement. Along with other radical groups, the Baptists extended Protestant ideas to new conclusions. They sought a pure church of "visible saints." They had the audacity to baptize ("dip") each other in the frigid lakes and muddy rivers of Britain. Dripping with the waters of new life, they championed the gospel of Jesus Christ with power. They preached the gospel where it was not known. They distributed relief to the poor. They experienced the presence of Christ amongst them and expected fully that Christ would daily cause more truth to appear.[12]

During the English civil war, women and laity asserted themselves in new roles such as preaching and evangelism. Critic John Taylor lamented, "When women preach and cobblers pray, the fiends in hell make holiday."[13] Among Baptists, women and men assumed equality in terms of ministries of care, compassion, and outreach. One woman

---

[10] *Gangraena, or, A Catalogue and Discovery of Many of the Errours, Heresies, Blasphemies and Pernicious Practices of the Sectaries of This Time. . . .* (1646, in three parts, 2d ed., enlarged) Epistle Dedicatory, 8, 116.

[11] John Taylor, *A Swarm of Sectaries and Schismatiques: Wherein is discovered the strange preaching (or prating) of such as are by their Trades Coblers, Tinkers, Pedlers, Weavers, Sowgelders, and Chymney-Sweepers* (1641).

[12] London Confession, 1644, in Lumpkin, 155.

[13] *Lucifer's Lackey, or The Devil's New Creation* in Leon McBeth, *Women in Baptist Life* (Nashville: Broadman, 1979) 30.

preacher was Dorothy Hazzard (d. 1674).[14] She was the wife of Anthony Kelly, a Bristol shop keeper. After his death in 1631, Dorothy ran the shop. "Very famous for Piety and reformation," she made a point of rejecting state religion by opening her store on Christmas and protecting itinerant separatist preachers. She remarried a pastor, Matthew Hazzard. In the face of criticism her husband backed his wife's nonconformity.

Dorothy began to preach. Out of this ministry evolved the Broadmead Chapel. For nearly thirty years, Dorothy played a role as "godly minister." The Bristol congregation employed paid women deaconesses who considered themselves servants, modelled after the servant Jesus. As the occasion required, they spoke words of support and consolation. Keeping the commandment that Christians are to love God and others, they built up a spiritual faith in Jesus Christ. "There is not an office of Christ in his church, but it is dipped in the blood of our Lord Jesus."

The Bristol band elicited a peacemaking ministry based on courageous leadership, patient suffering, and non-resistance in the face of injustice. John Bunyan (1628–1688) provides striking evidence of this particular contribution of Baptist women during the seventeenth century. According to his autobiography, *Grace Abounding*, his first wife gave him books that greatly influenced him, while the testimony of "three or four poor women" whom Bunyan happened to overhear set in motion his conversion. Later, when he was in prison, Bunyan's second wife presented petitions on his behalf, and various women carried on the ministry of his Bedford congregation. While women were notoriously absent from the first part of his *Pilgrim's Progress*, they dominated the second part.[15] Bunyan had an innkeeper named Gaius observe:

> 'Twas a woman that washed his [Christ's] Feet with Tears, and a Woman that anointed his Body to the Burial. They were Woman that wept when he was

---

[14]Roger Hayden, ed., *The Records of a Church of Christ in Bristol 1640 to 1687*, Bristol Record Society's Publication 27 (Bristol: Bristol Record Society, 1974) 12-18, 85-91, 154; McBeth, *Women*, 27-37; Claire Cross, "'He-Goats before the Flocks': A Note on the Part Played by Women in the Founding of Some Civil War Churches," in G. J. Cuming and Derek Baker, eds. *Popular Belief and Practice*, (Cambridge: Cambridge University Press, 1972) 195-202; Richard L. Greaves, "The Role of Women in Early English Nonconformity," *Church History* 52 (1983): 299-311.

[15]John Bunyan, *The Pilgrim's Progress from this World to That which is to Come*, ed. James Blanton Wharey, rev. Roger Sharrock (Oxford: Clarendon Press, 1960) 261.

going to the Cross; and Women that followed him from the Cross, and that sat by his Sepulchre when he was buried. They were Women that was first with him at his Resurrection morn, and Women that brought Tidings first to his Disciples that he was risen from the Dead. Women therefore are highly favoured, and shew by these things that they are sharers with us in the Grace of Life.

Dorothy Hazzard, John Bunyan, and most Baptists were not pacifists. Like other Baptists during the 1640s, they supported Cromwell's New Model Army and considered his cause as just with regard to liberty of conscience. To usher in a new age in politics and religion many wanted to bring down the old regime. Among the first to call for execution of a corrupt king were Baptist Levellers John Lilburne (1614–1657) and Richard Overton (fl. 1642–1663). "Hath not Charles Stewart committed treason against King Charles? Sure I am he hath done it against the kingdom of England."[16]

Not all Baptists shared their conviction. In tracts written in 1649, Particular Baptist Elizabeth Poole coupled support for the transfer of power to Parliament with a plea for clemency for King Charles I. When he died, she expressed sorrow. Surprised by her espousal of clemency, supporters repudiated her witness.

Amidst revolutionary events Baptists enjoyed unprecedented freedom and success in attracting members. By July 1653 they reached the zenith of political and military power. But regicide failed to usher in Christ's millennial reign. Liberation threatened to give way to anarchy. The apocalyptic mood fueled wars and rumours of war:

War and its miseries have overspread all lands. States have been shaken and subverted. Love, meekness, gentleness, mercy, the truest badges of Christianity, have been damned and banished; and, in their room, cruelty, hardheartedness, respect of persons, prisons, tortures, etc., things that our blessed Lord and Master and his apostles never proved, unless upon their own afflicted bodies, have had great sway for many hundred years. Hence is it that instead of peace, we have frequently had the sword; instead of sweet tranquility, love, and

---

[16]*Regal Tyranny Discovered*, at least in part the work of Lilburne and Overton, in H. N. Brailsford, *The Levellers and the English Revolution*, ed. Christopher Hill (London: Cresset Press, 1961) 117.

affection, hatred, contention, disaffection, and the bitter fruits thereof, have reigned.[17]

Some Baptists moved in the direction of non-resistance or pacifism. Some joined the Quakers. Others became convinced that it was best to live peaceably under the government. As Cromwell moved backwards towards arbitrary power and Fifth Monarchists urged the saints to take up arms to bring about God's rule, many disillusioned Baptists recovered earlier convictions about non-resistance and religious liberty.

In 1654 General Baptists urged members "patiently to suffer, or humbly to entreat favour."[18] In a study of Baptist political activities during the Civil Wars, Louise Fargo Brown found, "there were among them some who adhered to the belief of their brethren on the Continent that Christians should not meddle with the sword." She cited General Baptists who, meeting at the Speldhurst church, decided it was exceedingly dangerous and entirely unlawful for officers to serve as soldiers:

> In answer to the enquiries about fighting we say that in some cases it may be lawful, but as the affairs of the nation now stand and is likely to continue till the appearing of the Lord Jesus, we account it exceedingly dangerous, and for officers of churches to enlist themselves either as private soldiers or commissioned officers—that is altogether unlawful.[19]

Restoration of the monarchy approached. Critics accused Baptists of several offences: opposition to magistracy; desire to destroy the public ministry of the nation; adopting the irregular practices of Quakers;

---

[17]H. B. (probably the Presbyterian Henry Burton, 1578–1648) 1646, introductory letter to an edition of Leonard Busher's *Religion's Peace*.

[18]"THE HUMBLE REPRESENTATION AND VINDICATION of many of the Messengers, Elders, and Brethren, belonging to several of the BAPTIZED CHURCHES IN THIS NATION, of and concerning Their Opinions and Resolutions touching the CIVIL GOVERNMENT of these Nations, and of their Department under the same," London, 1654, in W. T. Whitley, ed., *Minutes of the General Assembly of the General Baptist Churches in England, with Kindred Records*, Vol I: 1654–1728 (London: Kingsgate, 1909) 3.

[19]Louise Fargo Brown, *The Political Activities of the Baptists and Fifth Monarchy Men in England During the Interregnum* (London: Oxford University Press, 1912) 9. Minute book, British Library, Additional Manuscript 36709, fol. 131v.

endeavoring "a toleration of all miscarriages in things ecclesiastical and civil under [pretense of] Liberty of Conscience"; and desiring to "murder and destroy those that differ from us in matter of religion."[20] How did Baptists respond to their opponents?

The Freewill Baptists of London stated,

> We are to be subject to it [the Magistrates' sword] and not to resist it. . . . But the sword of slaughter without examination or due consideration, is many times put in execution to the slaying and destroying of friends as well as enemies . . . for our acting in this sword, we can find no warrant from Scriptures in the least.

They added, "we further declare we are to be a peaceable people"[21] In March 1660, a general assembly of General Baptists met in London and agreed to twenty-five articles of "A Brief Confession or Declaration of Faith." The twenty-fourth article appealed for absolute liberty of conscience, while the concluding article repudiated the charges against them with these words:

> Moreover we do utterly, and from our very hearts, in the Lords fear, declare against all those wicked, and divillish reports, and reproaches, falsly cast upon us, as though some of us (in & about the City of London) had lately GOTTEN KNIVES, HOOKED KNIVES, & the like, & great store of Arms besides what was given forth by order of Parliament, intending to cut the throats of such as were contrary minded to us in matters of Religion, and that many such KNIVES and Armes, for the carrying on some secret design, hath been found in some of our houses by search; we say, from truth of heart, in the Lords fear, that we do utterly abhor, and abominate the thoughts thereof, and much more the actions.[22]

---

[20](Henry Adis), *A Declaration of a Small Society of Baptized Believers, undergoing the name of Free-Willers, about the City of London*, broadside, 12 December 1659. Association records of Particular Baptists reveals scant evidence of radical politics. At the time Quakers and Baptists shared common language about "waiting on the Lord for further light" or "the Spirit being poured forth." B. R. White, ed., *Association Records of the Particular Baptists of England, Wales and Ireland to 1660* (London: Baptist Historical Society, 1971–1977). Quakers did recruit successfully from General Baptists. William J. Collins, "The General Baptists and the Friends," *Transactions of the Baptist Historical Society* 5 (1917): 65-73, 143.

[21]Adis, *A Declaration of a Small Society of Baptized Believers*.

[22]Broadside. Also Lumpkin, 234; Whitley, 20-21.

Despite protestations of their pacific intentions, the Baptists did not escape renewed persecution. When Charles the Second took his throne, four found themselves writing from prison,

> We do, without any deceit, promise to live peaceably under thy government, and in case any thing should be by thee commanded in spiritual matters, wherein we cannot obey, we shall not then take up any carnal or temporal weapon against thee or thy authority, but patiently suffer such punishment as shall be inflicted on us for our consciences.[23]

John Bunyan expressed his understanding that warfare enjoined of Christians was spiritual, not temporal. In *The Holy War* (1682) he wrote, "Remember therefore, O my Mansoul, that thou art beloved of me; as I have therefore taught thee to watch, to fight, to pray, and to make war against my foes, so now I command thee to believe that my love is constant to thee . . . hold fast till I come."

To summarize, in seventy years Baptists traveled from non-resistance to holy war back to non-resistance. While Baptists continued to share the radical hopes of many, after 1660 there is little evidence of support for violence to establish God's reign.[24] British Baptists tended towards political quiescence.[25]

Colonial North America

Baptist non-resistants numbered among those who made their way from Britain to North America. According to historian Peter Brock, the first known conscientious objector in British North America was Richard Bickley, who possibly came to pacifist views through contact with British

---

[23]"The Humble Petition and Representation of the Sufferings of several Peaceable, and Innocent Subjects, called by the Name of Anabaptists" (London, 1660), in Edward Bean Underhill, *Tracts on Liberty of Conscience and Persecution 1614–1661* (London: J. Haddon, 1846) 307. William Jeffery, John Reve, George Hammon, James Blackmore wrote this entreaty in prison.

[24]Along with other radicals, Bunyan's response to defeat is explored by Christopher Hill, *A Turbulent, Seditious, and Factious People. John Bunyan and His Church 1628–1688* (Oxford: Clarendon Press, 1988).

[25]D. W. Bebbington, "Baptist M.P.s in the Seventeenth and Eighteenth Centuries," *Baptist Quarterly* 28 (1980): 245-62.

Baptists. On 7 May 1627, a court at James City, Virginia, arraigned Bickley for refusing to follow the orders of Ensign John Uty. Charged with "denying to take arms and discharge his public duty," Bickley received a sentence requiring that he be "laid neck and heels 12 hours" in the stocks and to pay a fine of 100 pounds of tobacco at harvest time.[26]

Catherine Scott, Anne Hutchison's sister, was one of the earliest settlers in Rhode Island. Credited with leading Roger Williams to become a Baptist in 1639, she may have been a preacher holding Anabaptist views on non-resistance and the sword.[27] In November 1654, members of the Baptist congregation in Providence, including pastor Thomas Olney, William Harris, John Field, and Williams' brother Robert circulated a paper stating that, "It was blood-guiltiness, and against the rule of the gospel, to execute judgement upon transgressors, against the private or public weal." Roger Williams, who was president of the colony and accepted the principle of a limited right to bear arms, rejected their appeal for conscientious objection and prompted a furious debate. Several Baptists, including Catherine Scott, joined the Quakers.[28]

In the 1670s, a wealthy, educated, New London, Connecticut farmer and tradesman John Rogers (1648–1721) founded a Baptist group known as the Rogerenes. The Rogerenes adopted a ministry of healing for the sick, sabbatarianism, and non-resistance. Their non-resistance derived from the belief that Christians are citizens of a spiritual realm. Prohibited from taking part in the violence of this world, the Rogerenes rejected military service, payment of money in lieu of service, tithes, and slavery. For another century, Rogerenes maintained this stance. In 1810 Alexander Rogers circulated a petition that persecution arising from his pacifism was undermining his ability to support a family, while other Rogerenes were conscientious objectors during the Civil War.[29]

---

[26]Peter Brock, *Pacifism in the United States from the Colonial Era to the First World War* (Princeton: Princeton University Press, 1968) 159n.

[27]H. Leon McBeth, *The Baptist Heritage. Four Centuries of Baptist Witness* (Nashville: Broadman, 1987) 131. Chapter 7 explores the position of Williams in greater depth.

[28]Samuel Hugh Brockunier, *The Irrepressible Democrat. Roger Williams* (New York: Ronald Press, 1940) 225-26.

[29]William H. Brackney, *The Baptists* (New York: Greenwood Press, 1988) 253-54; Brock, *Pacifism in the United States*, 44-45; Edward Needles Wright, *Conscientious Objectors in the Civil War* (Philadelphia: University of Pennsylvania Press, 1931). McBeth, *Baptist Heritage*, 123, refers to them as a "Baptist mutation"; *Seventh Day*

Other colonial non-resistants included followers of George Keith (c. 1638–1716), who in 1692 broke away from the Quakers and adopted believer's baptism. Keith ultimately joined the Episcopalians, but two followers, Thomas Budd and John Budd, "solemnly declared against all use of the carnal Sword, or of any carnal Weapon to hurt the Body of any man, or take away the Life of any man or men in any case, whether offensive or defensive." They were among the first to protest against slavery.[30]

During the United States' war for independence, Baptists overwhelmingly supported the cause. There were, however, such exceptions as the black loyalist Baptists who fled to freedom in Canada or the West Indies. They did not necessarily reject war but recognized that injustice laid the seeds of future wars.

Among white colonial Baptists who gave witness to non-resistance, Elder Eseck Carr of Easton, Massachusetts, refused to go when drafted into the Army. Arguing that ministers should not be soldiers, Carr persuaded the town that his religious principles forbade him to fight. He was not alone. Noah Worcester, a Congregationalist and leader in the Peace Society, recalled a Baptist preacher who imbibed Quaker views of war. Ezra Stiles, another Congregationalist, wrote of two Baptist ministers, Elder John Maxson of the Seventh Day Baptist Church and Elder Erasmus Kelly of the First Baptist Church in Newport, Rhode Island, who on 11 July 1776 refused to sign a loyalty oath, pleading objection to war. Stiles wrote,

> Mr. Kelly took the Affirmation & dishonored himself by declaring against "the Unlawfulness of taking up Arms" in all cases—tho he said if any (war) was lawful, the present American War was so; and that he could pray for success to the Americans. He is the first Baptist in N. England that ever declared ag't the Unlawfulness of Arms—perhaps is the only Man in the World, that can pray for Success to Arms, while he believes their Unlawfulness.[31]

Baptists in Europe and America (Plainfield: Seventh Day Baptist General Conference, 1910) 136-37, refers to them as "Rogerene Quakers."

[30]Reid S. Trulson, "Baptist Pacifism: A Heritage of Nonviolence," *American Baptist Quarterly* 10 (1991): 199-217; Brock, *Pacifism in the United States*, 92-95; on Keith, see the entry by Rufus Jones in the *Dictionary of American Biography.*

[31]William G. McLoughlin, *New England Dissent 1630–1833. The Baptists and the Separation of Church and State* (Cambridge: Harvard University Press, 1971) v. 1, 581.

While most free colonial Baptists supported the revolution, Baptists also defended the rights of those who could not in good conscience perform military duty. The Warren Baptist Association of Rhode Island passed a resolution supporting anyone "who conscientiously scruples the lawfulness of it, if he will pay such equivalent." Association meeting minutes for 9-10 September 1777 reveals something of their thinking:

> Our Lord says, My kingdom is not of this world; if my kingdom were of this world, then would my servants fight. . . . From whence we observe, That fighting with the sword, or a defensive war, is allowed of in worldly states; but that the Saviour's kingdom receives neither its rise nor support from thence.[32]

From British forebears, Colonial North American Baptists inherited divisions between Arminian (General), Calvinist (Particular, or Regular), and Seventh Day Baptists. The First Great Awakening (ca. 1726–ca. 1760) saw the rise of the "Separate" or "New Light" Baptists who left established Congregational churches over issues of congregational autonomy, regenerate church membership, believer's baptism, and separation of church and state. New Light itinerant evangelists were especially effective in the south. Shubal Stearns (1706–1771), converted to New Light views when George Whitfield preached in Connecticut in 1745, was among their leaders. He established churches in Virginia and the Carolinas, among which the Sandy Creek, North Carolina, church became the largest Baptist congregation in the world. During a dispute with the government in 1771, Stearns and the church resolved to excommunicate any member who might take up arms against the government.[33] Stearns influenced other New Lighters to adopt non-resistance. As well, Freewill (General) Baptists manifested non-resistant views. Those

---

McLoughlin mentions non-resistant views of Peleg Burroughs. Ruth Wilder Sherman, ed., *Peleg Burroughs's Journal 1778–1798* (Warwick: Rhode Island Genealogical Society, 1981). Also, William L. Chaffin, *History of the Town of Easton, Massachusetts* (Cambridge: J. Wilson and Son, 1886) 185-87, and Henry Ware, Jr., *Memoirs of the Reverend Noah Worcester* (Boston J. Munroe, 1844) 61. I owe these references to Reid Trulson.

[32]R. E. E. Harkness, "Baptists and War," *Chronicle* 2 (1939): 150; K. Armstrong and Marjorie Moore Armstrong, *The Indomitable Baptists* (New York: Doubleday, 1967) 93.

[33]Brackney, 265-66; William L. Lumpkin, *Baptist Foundations in the South* (Nashville: Broadman, 1961), 72-86; McBeth, *Baptist Heritage*, 227-29. G. W. Paschal, "Shubal Stearns," *Review and Expositor* 36 (1939): 117.

influenced by Benjamin Randall (1749–1808), another Whitfield convert, affirmed that true Christians cannot bear weapons.[34]

Conclusion

This survey reveals that non-resistance was not an isolated phenomenon among early Baptists. Further research may uncover other evidence of support for the principles of non-resistance and conscientious objection. Until the founding of the peace societies at the end of the Napoleonic wars and the War of 1812, Baptist non-resistance was a persistent position among Baptists, notably General and Freewill Baptists. While Baptists did not join the ranks of the peace churches, many established a peace witness as a central part of the Baptist heritage.

---

[34]McBeth, *Baptist Heritage*, 712-14; Stephen A. Marini, *Radical Sects of Revolutionary New England* (Cambridge: Harvard University Press, 1982) 117.

Chapter Three
British Baptists in Nineteenth-Century Peace Societies

Amidst the tumultuous events of the seventeenth century, the Baptist bodies of Great Britain and British North America arose as part of the Protestant Reformation. During the eighteenth century, Baptists in Britain struggled for recognition and toleration, but their dynamism in politics and religion gave way to political quietism, ecclesiastical disunity, and spiritual aridity. Activism did not disappear altogether. Baptists shared in the broad movements of evangelical renewal and revivalism of the day. Some expressed concern to spread the gospel. Some joined various voluntary societies. Some proclaimed God's coming reign.

By the end of the century, British Baptists were coming out of the doldrums. Formation of the New Connexion of General Baptists in 1770, the Baptist Missionary Society in 1792, and the Baptist Union in 1813 signaled renewal. Caleb Evans (1737–1791), pastor of Broadmead Baptist Church, maintained a dual emphasis on salvation and humanitarian good works. Preaching before Bristol Education Society on 16 August 1775, Evans stated,

> When we pray for the advancement of this kingdom, if we are not willing to do all we can to advance it, our prayers cannot be genuine, they are hypocritical. . . . When we pray that the kingdom of God may come, we are supposed to express a willingness to do whatever God may enable us to do, as workers together with him.[1]

---

[1]*The Kingdom of God* in K. R. Manley, "The Making of an Evangelical Baptist Leader: John Rippon's Early Years, 1751–1773," *Baptist Quarterly* 26 (1976): 267. See D. W. Bebbington, *Evangelicalism in Modern Britain: A History from the 1730s to the 1980s* (Boston: Unwin Hyman, 1989); Raymond Brown, *The English Baptists of the Eighteenth Century* (London: Baptist Historical Society, 1986); H. Leon McBeth, *The*

Baptist leadership in effecting significant social change in education, slavery, and temperance has long been recognized. Baptist involvement in peace societies has been less documented. This chapter and the next introduce the story.

Nineteenth-Century Peace Crusade

Peace movements are collective efforts of private citizens to abolish war through such means as conferences, education, political mobilization, or civil disobedience. Organization of modern peace movements may be traced to the early nineteenth century. During the era of the Napoleonic wars, many in the western world expressed weariness with war by holding days of prayer, fasting, and repentance or by searching for alternatives to international conflict.

The nineteenth-century peace crusade was a trans-Atlantic phenomenon.[2] The first organized peace society began in New York in 1815, followed by societies in Massachusetts and Ohio. In 1816, the Society for the Promotion of Permanent and Universal Peace, or Peace Society, began in London with chapters scattered throughout Britain. Peace advocates established peace societies in Paris (1821) and Geneva (1830), but for three decades, most activity took place in Britain and North America.

The peace societies drew from two traditions: Christian nonresistance and the Enlightenment. Christian pacifists rejected war as incompatible with the life and teachings of Jesus Christ, while Enlightenment philosophers formulated projects for "perpetual peace."

Baptist Heritage. Four Centuries of Baptist Witness (Nashville: Broadman Press, 1987).

[2]For the title of this section, see Merle Eugene Curti, *The American Peace Crusade 1815–1860* (New York: Octagon Books, Inc., 1965; orig 1928). Standard sources include Peter Brock, *Pacifism in Europe to 1914* (Princeton: Princeton University Press, 1972) and *Pacifism in the United States from the Colonial Era to the First World War* (Princeton: Princeton University Press, 1968); Sandi E. Cooper, "Peace Movements of the Nineteenth Century," *World Encyclopedia of Peace* 2:230; W. H. van der Linden, *The International Peace Movement 1815–1874* (Amsterdam: Tilleul Publications, 1987). Chapter Three concentrates on peace activity in England. Chapter Four concentrates on peace activity in the United States. Further research is needed regarding peace groups in Ireland, Scotland, Wales, and Canada.

Generally liberal in their economic and political outlooks, peace advocates looked to the creation of a world order free from the tumult of war. To this end, they promoted several principles including arbitration, treaties, the establishment of an international tribunal or congress, codification of international law, and disarmament.

In Britain, Quakers took the lead in founding the Peace Society, but it drew members from virtually every denomination, including Congregationalists, Unitarians, and other non-conformist bodies. Baptists contributed substantially. At public meetings and through pamphlets, periodicals, and sermons they commented regularly about the need for peace and causes of war. Two prominent Baptists exemplified the general yearning for the abolition of war and establishment of a lasting peace.[3]

At the turn of the century Robert Hall (1764–1831), destined to be remembered as the greatest British Baptist preacher of the century before Charles Haddon Spurgeon (1834-1892), was serving as pastor in Cambridge. In a sermon preached on 1 June 1802, Hall expressed hope that "along with peace, the spirit of peace will return. How can we better imitate our heavenly Father, than, when he is pleased to compose the animosities of nations, to open our hearts to every milder influence?" He went on to indicate that, in addition to "burying in oblivion all national antipathies," the most important benefits from the return of peace would be enhanced security, progress of religion, reduction of poverty and prices for necessities of life, and honouring God and Christ. He concluded,

> You will then be convinced it is better to be endeared to the cottage than admired in the palace; when to have wiped away the tears of the afflicted and inherited the prayers of the widow and the fatherless, shall be found a richer patrimony than the favour of princes.[4]

Another Baptist peace advocate, the Reverend Benjamin Godwin (1785–1871), served in the navy during the Napoleonic wars. Converted

---

[3]Other examples of treatises by Baptists against war include John Evans, *The Golden Centenary; or, One Hundred Testimonies in Behalf of Candour, Peace, and Unanimity* (London: Baldwin, Cradock, and Joy, 1822); T. P. [Thomas Parsons, d. 1813] *Christianity, a System of Peace* . . . (Bath: R. Cruttwell, 1804).

[4]Robert Hall, "Reflections on War," *The Works of Robert Hall, A.M.*, ed. Olinthus Gregory (1831) 1:105–106, 121.

at sea, he became a pastor and theological tutor. In 1822, during an address before the Buckinghamshire Association of Baptist Churches, Godwin lamented that, during the greater part of his lifetime, nearly the whole civilized world had been in a state of warfare. He warned against the danger of glorifying war instead of the Prince of Peace. He urged Christian parents, guardians, teachers, or ministers to "use our utmost endeavours to give prevalence to sentiments and feelings of a pacific nature, and to instil into the minds of our youthful charge, especially, a horror of war, and a detestation of those depraved principles which lead to it."[5]

Though Hall and Godwin were not pacifists, both worked for positive peace. For example, Hall helped organize at Cambridge a benevolent society for the relief of the sick, and at Leicester an aged poor and framework knitters' friendly relief society. Godwin joined anti-slavery, Bible, education, and mission societies. In addition to championing social Christianity, they joined a growing number of Baptists in the trans-Atlantic peace crusade. Outstanding Baptist leaders included Benjamin Evans (1803–1871), Joseph Foulks Winks (1792–1866), James Hargreaves (1768–1845), Alfred Illingworth (1827–1907), Arthur O'Neill (1819–1896), and William Stokes (1803–1881). They anticipated involvement by Baptists in peace movements of this century.

British Baptists in the Peace Society

In Britain during the first phase of the peace movement, from 1816 until the outbreak of the Crimean War in 1854, many Baptists active in the Peace Society are known chiefly because of the indefatigable labours of George Pilkington (1785–1858). After studies at Trinity College, Dublin, Pilkington attained the rank of captain in the Corps of Royal Engineers. In 1814, he resigned his commission and worked as a civil engineer in colonial posts: two and a half years in Sierra Leone, seven in Brazil, and three in Trinidad. In 1821, conversion to Christianity convinced him that, "the military profession in which I had been engaged was perfectly unlawful to the disciple of Christ, and that all war, whether offensive or

---

[5]*Herald of Peace* 1, n.s. (1822): 52-53 following an extract from Robert Hall's sermon on war. For Godwin's obituary, see *Baptist Handbook* (1872) 220-25.

defensive was altogether anti-Christian."⁶ In 1831, Pilkington settled with his family in Bideford, Devonshire. He identified with dissenting churches and lectured on behalf of the Anti-Slavery Society. In 1834, Pilkington took up the cause of peace as an itinerant minister. He collected some two hundred testimonies by pastors, showing the unlawfulness to Christians of all war. Congregationalists, or Independents, contributed the most statements, eighty-six, followed by fifty Baptists who consistently stressed their desire, on behalf of the Prince of Peace, to promote Christian ideals of benevolence and goodwill to all.⁷ Biographical data are available for all but a handful of these Baptists. Several functioned as presidents and secretaries of the various chapters of the Peace Society. Others contributed in general ways to the growing campaign to reduce arms and find new methods to resolve international disputes.

Prominent among those whose peace testimony Pilkington recorded was James Hargreaves. From age three, Hargreaves was raised by a paternal uncle who compelled him to work in a public-house. While Hargreaves received no formal religious education, he began to read the Bible and to preach. He adopted Baptist convictions and was called to a succession of pastorates at Bolton (1794), Ogden (1798), Little Wild Street (1822) in London where he acknowledged the influence of John Howard, the prison reformer who was a "hearer" though not a member of the congregation, and Waltham Abbey (1829). An absolute pacifist, Hargreaves joined the Peace Society in 1818. A member for twenty-seven years, he served as its secretary for twenty years, during which period he spoke frequently on peace subjects.⁸

In several published sermons, Hargreaves described war as contrary to the mind of Christ and the spirit of Christianity, a religion of peace, love, and goodwill. In a sermon preached on 22 February 1818 he stated

---

⁶George Pilkington, *The Doctrine of Particular Providence; or the Divine Guardianship over the Most Minute Concerns of Man, Illustrated and Defended in Biographical Reminiscences* (London: Effingham Wilson, 1836) 68.

⁷*Testimonies of Ministers, of Various Denominations, Showing the Unlawfulness to Christians of All Wars, Offensive or Defensive* (London: G. Eccles, 1837).

⁸For details, *Herald of Peace* 4, n.s. (October 1845): 364; *Dictionary of National Biography*; Philip J. Saffery, "Memoir of the Late Rev. James Hargreaves," *Baptist Magazine* (1847): 196-201, 273-77.

that war is "a heathenish and savage custom of the most malignant, most desolating and most horrible character; the greatest curse and resulting from the grossest delusions, that ever affected a guilty world!" Quoting profusely biblical passages and the writings of Tertullian, Origen, and other Christian writers, he went on to focus on Isaiah 2:2-4 with its vision of Messianic times realized in Christ Jesus. Hargreaves wanted to show that peace is attainable. He dealt point by point with various objections. With reference to just war thinking, he condemned the tendency for both sides in a conflict to claim justice. He urged Christians to adopt alternatives to war by using weapons of peacemakers such as love, truth, and the disciplines of the Christian life. As for the Peace Society, its work was to draw in ministers of the gospel, to educate through holding meetings and printing tracts, and generally to promote the cause of humanity. He ended by asking, since peace is always the professed object, why not seek peace by peaceful means?[9]

In other sermons, Hargreaves concentrated on the evils of war but offered few specific alternatives. He used language common to the period, though, at times, he could be quite original. For example, he believed that Christian females had a special role, dissuading men from entering military service and banishing the nurture of war and that a connection exists between peace and social justice. As a Baptist, he argued that a connection exists between justification and holiness and that liberty of conscience should inspire Christians to live out the peaceful tenets of the gospel. Unlike some peace leaders, he did not emphasize secular arguments favouring peace.[10]

Another Baptist, William Stokes, succeeded Hargreaves as secretary of the Peace Society. Originally from Essex, Stokes served at Burton-on-Trent from 1833–1835 through the Baptist Home Missionary Society. Subsequently, he pastored Strict Baptist congregations at Bethel, West Bromwich (1838–1843, 1854–1855) and Newhall Street, Birmingham

---

[9]James Hargreaves, *Universal and Permanent Peace a Desirable Object* (London: Button and Son, 1818) preface.

[10]James Hargreaves, *The Connexion between Free Justification and Holiness of Heart and Life* (Rochdale: Joseph Littlewood, 1820); *Hints on the Nature of a Christian Church and on the Principles of Dissent* (London: W. Jones, 1823); sermons published in the Peace Society's *Annual Report* for 1833, 32-35; *Baptist Reporter and Missionary Intelligencer* 2, n.s. (1845): 343-46.

(1843–1846). After 1846, he combined church and literary work with involvement in the Peace Society.[11]

For the Peace Society, Stokes undertook research, wrote poetry, and traveled widely, giving up to two hundred speeches and sermons a year. He helped organize a series of international peace congresses that met between 1843 and 1853. As Great Britain embarked on its Crimean adventure, this phase of the peace crusade collapsed in the face of frenzied support for colonialism, nationalism, and imperialism. An absolute pacifist, Stokes denounced the Crimean War through a barrage of anti-war activity. While this did not and could not have prevented war in 1854, Stokes drew valuable conclusions about what might have been done with the money spent by Britain in Crimea and about the need for new international structures. After the war, he helped the peace movement to recover from its mid-century loss of momentum and to shape its post-war agenda around issues such as controlling the production and trade of deadly armaments and proposing mechanisms for the pacific resolution of disputes. Through prodigious efforts, Stokes sharpened the analysis of war by peace advocates. He formulated ideas for alternatives to military spending and anticipated by a century research regarding the relationship between military and social spending undertaken by the World Priorities Institute in Washington, D.C., and the International Peace Research Institute in Stockholm, Sweden.

A third British Baptist secretary of the Peace Society was Arthur O'Neill. After beginning medical studies in Glasgow, O'Neill turned to theology and philosophy. He adopted Chartist principles and established in Birmingham a Chartist Congregation. In 1842, during a speech to striking coal miners held at the Cradley Heath Baptist Church, O'Neill was arrested and convicted to a year's imprisonment for seditious language. From the start of his ministry, O'Neill represented a radical tradition of religious dissent. With these words he justified his time in jail and encouraged his followers:

---

[11]*Herald of Peace* 4, n.s. (October 1845): 363 announced the death of Hargreaves and appointment of Stokes. For details, Geoffrey R. Breed, *The Baptist Evangelical Society. An Early Victorian Episode* (Dunstable: Fauconberg Press, 1988); Frederic Boase, *Modern English Biography*, vol. 6, L-Z Supplement (Truro: Netherton and Worth, 1921).

> I believe in the mysterious ways of God little things are of the greatest importance. I see Jesus washing the disciples' feet; I desire to serve the poor, the sick, the mourning, the ignorant, the aged and the child. . . . Of course the man of the world will say "This is an obscure life." Be it so; it is true that the names of such who labour there will not be inscribed in the Book of Fame; but when its pages are worm-eaten . . . their names will be seen . . . in the Lamb's Book of Life. . . . A few weeks more I am back once more amongst you. . . . Now I desire at my coming no vain display of procession or empty parade to be made. Nothing can give me so much true pleasure as to begin my labours by meeting my dear friends at the prayer meeting at 7:00 on Sabbath morning.[12]

On 3 May 1846, O'Neill came to Baptist convictions and was baptized by Thomas Swan, another of Pilkington's signatories. O'Neill then baptized his entire congregation in three services at each of three key Birmingham Baptist churches. His Chartist Congregation was reconstituted a Baptist church of sixty members on 28 June 1846. In 1847, it united with the Zion congregation in New Hall Street, where Stokes had served as pastor, and O'Neill remained there as minister until his death in 1896. During this long period of ministry, O'Neill lectured widely. He continued to seek realization of Chartist principles such as adult franchise and elementary education. He championed anti-slavery, temperance, diminution of capital punishment, and other causes but devoted himself primarily to the Peace Society.

O'Neill came to prominence as a peace campaigner during the Crimean War. He agitated to stop the war and made concrete proposals which resulted in the insertion of an arbitration clause in the Treaty of Paris.[13] O'Neill became secretary of the Peace Society. Like his Baptist predecessors, this involved lecturing, writing letters, and formulating

---

[12]Arthur S. Langley, *Birmingham Baptists Past and Present* (London: Kingsgate Press, 1939) 152. Arrested with O'Neill was another Chartist, the Baptist pastor Thomas Cooper (1805–1892). Cooper published *Two Orations against Taking Away Human Life under any Circumstances; and in Explanation of the Misrepresented Doctrine of Non-Resistance* (London: Chapman, 1846). Chartism was a working class movement that sought universal male suffrage, vote by ballot, abolition of property qualifications, payment of Members of Parliament, equal electoral districts, and annual parliaments. Dorothy Thompson, *The Chartists* (London: Temple Smith, 1984); Harold Underwood Faulkner, *Chartism and the Churches. A Study in Democracy* (New York: Columbia University Press, 1916).

[13]A. C. F. Beales, *The History of Peace. A Short Account of the Organized Movements for International Peace* (New York: Dial Press, 1931) 99, 139.

petitions for various bodies. When he died, the *Herald of Peace* remembered O'Neill as an "heroic figure."[14]

Did the labours of men like Hargreaves, Stokes and O'Neill reflect currents in nineteenth-century British Baptist life or influence Baptists? Admittedly, this is hard to measure, but the answer seems affirmative. Through sermons, talks, debates, and pamphlets, each contributed to the work of the Peace Society, in part by enlarging its circle of influence among Baptists. Each was recognized as a leader in Baptist life and had an impact on other Baptists. For example, Benjamin Godwin, quoted above, and the Reverend John Jackson (1792–1856), an agent for the Temperance Society, the Anti-Slavery Society, and the Baptist Missionary Society, acknowledged the influence of Hargreaves' preaching for peace. Baptist chapels frequently invited Stokes and O'Neill to speak. Till 1892 O'Neill gave an annual lecture at Cradley Heath Baptist Church, paying a small sum for heat and lighting.

The Baptist press of the day offers another measure of influence. Baptist periodicals regularly reported Peace Society activities, encouraged dialogue on issues of war and peace, and published peace sermons. At least two Baptist editors championed the cause of peace. The first was Joseph Foulks Winks (1794–1866). Raised in the Church of England, Winks joined a congregation of the New Connexion of General Baptists at Killinholme in 1823. As a lay preacher, he served from 1824–1826 at Melbourne Baptist Church; from 1839–1860, at Carley Street Baptist Church, Leicester, where he baptized the Chartist Thomas Cooper; and, at Market Harborough. As printer and editor, he launched at least nine periodicals characterized by concern for "wholesome" children's literature, for bridging divisions among Baptists, for evangelism, and for social reform. These figured prominently in all his periodicals, especially *The Baptist Reporter and Missionary Intelligencer* through which Winks campaigned against "the Three Great Curses—Slavery, War and Intemperance." In many editorials, he advocated abolition of war, arbitration as a means to resolve international disputes, and concurrent disarmament. Winks was not a pacifist. Characteristically he was among those peace

---

[14]*Herald of Peace* 25, n.s. (June 1896): 76.

advocates in Britain and the United States who ultimately supported war as a necessary evil to end slavery.[15]

A second editor who supported the Peace Society was a Pilkington signatory, Benjamin Evans, one of the most popular mid-nineteenth-century Baptist journalists. Like Winks, Evans combined pastoral service with journalism. Through pulpit and press, he supported anti-slavery, anti-poverty, Chartism, the rights of women, mission, and peace. In a pastoral letter, *The Duty of Christians in Relation to War*, written in 1854 as war clouds in the Crimea threatened to bring a period of forty years' peace to an end, Evans denounced war apologists for their pride, ambition, and lust for power. He reminded readers that all war exists simply and alone for the destruction of human life, thus contradicting the Bible and nature of God. He called upon all Christians to exert the influence they possess to avert impending calamity and to mitigate the evil when it comes. When war did come, he criticized the government for secret diplomacy and called for a speedy return to peace.[16]

Strong statements against war by Baptist leaders suggest that the Peace Society influenced Baptist life. In 1846, the Reverend John Stock (1817–1884) of Chatham published a prize-winning essay, *Is It Lawful for a Christian To Fight? and What Is His Duty When Called upon so To Do by the Civil Magistrate?* From the Bible and Christian history, Stock argued that it is the duty of Christians, "when called upon by the civil magistrate to fight . . . firmly and unhesitatingly, to decline obedience, and to persist in this refusal *at any sacrifice*." Stock's anti-slavery views led him to support the cause of the northern States. He joined the Liberal Party and advocated anti-imperialist views.[17]

Charles Haddon Spurgeon opposed the Crimean War and was quoted widely for his anti-militarism. In a sermon entitled "War and the Spread of the Gospel" he stated,

---

[15]Obituary, *Baptist Handbook* (1867) 139; Rosemary Taylor, "English Baptist Periodicals, 1790–1865," (M. Phil. thesis, London University, 1974).

[16]Obituaries, *Baptist Handbook* (1872) 213-18; *Baptist Magazine* (January 1872): 24-36. See also, Kenneth R. Short, "Benjamin Evans, D.D. and the Radical Press, 1826–1871," *Baptist Quarterly* 19 (1962): 243-52.

[17]Obituary, *Baptist Handbook* (1885) 157-59; A. M. Stalker, *Memorial Sketch of John Stock, LL.D.* (London: 1885).

> The great crime of war can never promote the religious of peace. The battle and the garment rolled in blood are not a fitting prelude to "peace on earth; goodwill to men." And I do firmly hold that the slaughter of men, that bayonets, and swords and guns, have never yet been, and never can be promoters of the Gospel.[18]

Spurgeon praised the peace testimony of George Fox and urged, "May the day come when war shall be regarded as the most atrocious of crimes—when for a Christian to take part in it shall be regarded as a most heinous offence! The day may be far distant, but it shall come."[19]

In addition to these occasional words of leading Baptists, Baptist gatherings adopted resolutions on the subject of war and peace. The annual meeting of the Lincoln and Cambridgeshire General Baptist Sunday School Union, held at Fleet on 9 August 1855, resolved unanimously that, "it is the duty of all Sunday School teachers to set before their children the inconsistency of war with the precepts of the New Testament." In 1878 and 1886, Baptist Union assemblies protested against the waste of war and militarism. In 1879, several associations adopted resolutions against colonial wars in Asia and South Africa.[20] As well there were petitions of individual congregations. In 1860, the Mill Yard Seventh Day Baptist Church petitioned Parliament as follows:

> Your petitioners are wholly adverse to the custom and practice of War, believing it to be a combination of the greatest crimes and on the largest scale; and they consider [the proposal of spending £12,000,000 for fortifications] as tending to disturb the peace of the world, to provoke the aggression which it proposes to prevent, and to increase heavy burdens already borne by the nation for military and navy expenditure. Your Petitioners therefore humbly pray . . . not to make any grant of public money for additional Fortifications, nor to sanction any loans or create any annuities for such an unwise and wicked purpose.[21]

---

[18]*Herald of Peace* 4, n.s. (October 1857): 257. In *Baptist Views on War and Peace* (London: Baptist Union, 1969) 11, H. F. Lorkin attributes this statement to Spurgeon's lecture *DE PROPAGANDA FIDEI*.

[19]*Herald of Peace* 9, n.s. (January 1867): 155.

[20]*Herald of Peace* 4, n.s. (April 1856): 4, 16, n.s. (July 1879): 268-69; Lorkin, 11

[21]Cited in *Peace-Beat*, newsletter of the Seventh Day Baptist Peace Fellowship, 5/1-2 (1988) 3.

Resolutions had to do with political sentiments of Baptists towards specific governments. They also revealed widespread pacifist and peace convictions. The Peace Society influenced many Baptists to search both conscience and the Bible. Among those to take up the cause were many Baptist women. An appeal of 1823, renewed in 1836, asked what British women had done actively for this "labour of love." The reply indicated, "with deep sorrow of heart, SCARCELY ANYTHING" and concluded "Christian females, we make a special and affectionate appeal, entreating your immediate, cordial and vigorous co-operation."[22] Some Baptist women formed female auxiliaries of peace societies and peace departments of groups working for temperance, women's suffrage and other reforms. Their activism mirrored that of the broader peace movement: meetings, publications, resolutions, speaking, and writing letters or articles on the subject of peace.

The Peace Society drew support from non-conformist Members of Parliament. Alfred Illingworth, a Baptist worsted-spinner and M.P. for Knaresborough 1868–1874, Bradford 1880–1885 and Bradford West 1885–1895, was a longtime Vice President of the Peace Society. Illingworth criticized aristocracy, royalty and imperialism.[23]

The nineteenth-century peace movement gained international momentum. British Baptists attended foreign peace congresses and reported the activities of Baptist colleagues in North America and elsewhere. Some links were trans-Atlantic. For example, among Pilkington's signatories was Nathaniel Paul (1793–1839). In 1820, Paul became pastor of the First African Baptist Church, Albany, New York. In 1830, he joined the Wilberforce community, the first of several black settlements in Upper Canada (now the Province of Ontario). Paul established himself as a leader in the community and visited Britain as its agent raising funds for schools and churches. He persuaded the abolitionist William Lloyd Garrison (1805–1879) to join him. They championed "the Gospel of Peace" before resuming abolitionist activity in North America. In 1835,

---

[22] *Herald of Peace* 10, n.s. (1836): 17-21.
[23] D. W. Bebbington, "Baptist M.P.s in the Nineteenth Century," *Baptist Quarterly* 29 (1981): 3-24 and "Baptist Members of Parliament, 1847–1914," *Baptist Quarterly* 29 (1981): 51-94. George White (1840–1912), M.P. for Norwich 1900–12, promoted peace. Herbert Dunnico (1876–1953), M.P. for Consett 1922–1931, headed the Peace Society from 1916 until his death. For an obituary, see *Baptist Handbook* (1955) 322-23.

Francis Cox and James Hoby visited the United States to urge Baptists to abandon slavery. Similarly, after the Civil War, John Stock toured the United States where he exchanged views on peace and reconstruction.[24] Recognizing that to work for peace is to work for justice, Baptists like Paul and Stock linked negative and positive peace. Others like Benjamin Evans echoed prevailing sentiments by calling for the healing of the nation.[25]

Conclusion

This chapter helps identify key factors in interpreting the Baptist peace tradition.

During the nineteenth-century, many British Baptists joined peace societies. Motivated by many factors, most came to concern for peace out of their reading of the Bible and their experience in Baptist church life. They argued against war on the basis of scripture and summarized their faith in the gospel of Christ as a gospel of peace. As Baptists, they stressed freedom of conscience, the competence of believers to make decisions for themselves, and the need to manifest the Christian life through responsible social action. At least one, Arthur O'Neill, had a conversion experience that turned him to peacemaking.

Nineteenth-century Baptist peacemakers actively worked for peace in a variety of ways. They preached, lectured, and wrote on behalf of the cause. Many, including O'Neill, William Stokes, and Charles Haddon Spurgeon, opposed the Crimean War. Stokes protested against military spending. John Stock advocated civil disobedience. Many anticipated twentieth-century emphases on positive peace through transforming initiatives in such areas as mission, education, temperance, anti-slavery, and women's rights. They analyzed structural violence, advocated the rights of the powerless, challenged the complacency of the church, and called for spiritual renewal rooted in following Jesus' peaceful ways.

---

[24] K. R. M. Short, "English Baptists and American Slavery," *Baptist Quarterly* 20 (1964): 243-62; M. Ball, "A North American Journey. The Reverend John Stock and the American Churches May–June 1867," *Baptist Quarterly* 33 (1989): 133–45.

[25] *Freeman* 8 (1 January 1862): 9.

By contrast with such figures as John Bright (1811–1889), Richard Cobden (1804–1865) and Henry Richard (1812–1888), the Baptists mentioned in this chapter were not dominant figures of the nineteenth-century peace crusade in Britain. Neither as individuals, nor collectively, did they prevent any war from erupting, bring any war to an end, or break the momentum leading the world to the catastrophe of the Great War. Read today, they were naively optimistic. Why, then, give them attention?

British Baptist peacemakers shared in the nineteenth-century peace crusade, helping to shape its agenda and realize its programme. What began nearly two hundred years ago as the effort of a few individuals and isolated groups grew into an international movement with specific accomplishments: treaties of arbitration, the World Court, and the League of Nations. Determined opposition to the Crimean War by Baptist peacemakers such as Stokes and O'Neill highlighted problems of war, nationalism, and misdirection of resources and ensured that the Treaty of Paris contained an arbitration clause.

As well, British Baptist peacemakers exemplified a religious perspective known as the non-conformist conscience. They resisted any attempt to restrict religion to Sunday morning worship. The chapel became a center for prayer and action, a place to express passionate love of God and to generate public debate. Baptist peacemakers identified in this chapter prepared the way for the sustained effort against the Anglo-Boer War of 1899–1902. In short, nineteenth-century British Baptist peace advocates lived out the biblical vision for healing among the nations. We do well to heed their warnings and to walk their way.

Chapter Four

American Baptists in Nineteenth-Century Peace Societies

North American Peace Crusade

The history of the nineteenth-century peace movement in North America was similar to that in Britain. Formed in the United States after the War of 1812, organized peace societies experienced modest growth. During the 1840s, participation in international peace congresses and formation of the New England Non-Resistance Society and League of Universal Brotherhood gave the movement fresh impetus. Most peace advocates condemned the Mexican War (1846–1848), but they disagreed over how best to oppose the war. The American Peace Society relied on moral persuasion. Members wrote letters, preached, or attended public meetings. More radical groups resisted through conscientious objection and non-payment of taxes. Eclipsed by the Civil War during the middle decades of the century, the peace movement later revived.

Publications of the British and American peace societies reported Canadian activity. In the course of the century, the historic peace churches and a few sectarian groups such as the Children of Peace, formed in Newmarket north of Toronto during the War of 1812, provided the main peace witness. Peace and arbitration societies emerged primarily at the end of the century.[1]

---

[1] Thomas P. Socknat, *Witness against War. Pacifism in Canada 1900–1945* (Toronto: University of Toronto Press, 1987) 19.

For Baptists, questions about Christian involvement in soldiering arose in 1776 and, again, in 1812. As an expression of their yearning for peace amidst the reality of war, Baptists set aside days of public humiliation, fasting, and prayer. On both sides of the United States-Canada frontier, pacifism manifested itself. In Beamsville, Upper Canada (now Ontario), the Baptist church disfellowshiped two members for their pacifist views. Elisha Andrews, pastor of the Templeton, Massachusetts, Baptist Church, opposed taking up arms. Ray Potter, pastor of the Six Principle Baptist Church in Pawtucket, Rhode Island, became convinced that bearing arms contravened Christianity. He resigned from the militia in which he had enlisted, began preaching love, and spent time in debtor's prison rather than pay a fine to provide for someone to take his place in the militia.[2]

After the war, the rise of peace societies had an impact on Baptists. David Low Dodge, a Presbyterian merchant who formed the New York Peace Society in 1815, led Daniel Chessman (1787–1839), a Baptist minister, to re-examine the New Testament basis of peace. He came to the "complete conviction that war in all its forms is contrary to the gospel" and finished a 20,000 word manuscript, "An Essay on Self Defense designed to show that War is inconsistent with Scripture and Reason." While unoriginal in his discussion of the biblical and humanitarian basis for pacifism, Chessman explored wider issues such as the death penalty and the role of government in preserving law and order. For want of funds, Chessman could not publish his essay.[3]

Another Baptist influenced by peace societies was Alexander Campbell (1788–1866), who founded a movement known as the Disciples of Christ. Campbell sought to restore New Testament Christianity and adopted the pacifism of early Christians. In 1848, in an "Address on War," Campbell used arguments put forward by the American Peace Society. Campbell asked, "May a Christian community, or the members

---

[2]Beamsville minutes, 1814, Canadian Baptist Archives. Pierce S. Ellis, Jr., "Baptists and the War of 1812," *Chronicle* 11 (1948): 134; Ray Potter, *Memoirs of the Life and Religious Experience of Ray Potter, Minister of the Gospel, Pawtucket* (Providence: H. H. Brown, 1829) 66-68.

[3]Peter Brock, *Pacifism in the United States from the Colonial Era to the First World War* (Princeton: Princeton University Press, 1968) 466-78. The manuscript is in the Swarthmore College Peace Collection, Swarthmore, Pennsylvania.

of it, in their individual capacities, take up arms at all, whether aggressively or defensively, in any national conflict?" He came down on the side of pacifism, a view he maintained in the Civil War.[4]

Believing that war is incompatible with the life and teachings of Jesus, many Baptists joined peace societies. Continuing the story of the nineteenth-century peace crusade, we now examine Baptist peace witness in North America.

Three Antebellum Peace Advocates

Henry Holcombe (1762–1824) was one of the first Baptists in North America to become active in peace societies. Born in Virginia and raised in South Carolina in a nominally Presbyterian family, Holcombe served during the United States war of independence and attained the rank of captain. In 1784 he was "converted to God." This led him to see war in the new light of the "precepts, life, and whole ministry" of Jesus. Holcombe resigned his command, joined a Baptist church, and began to preach. He served pastorates in Pipe Creek, South Carolina (1785–1791); Eushaw and Beaufort, South Carolina (1791–1799); Savannah, Georgia (1800–1810); and, after recovery from a lengthy illness, First Baptist Church, Philadelphia, Pennsylvania (1812–1824).[5]

Holcombe gained a reputation as a powerful preacher. He also championed political causes and social reform. In 1788, he participated as a representative from the South Carolina lowlands in a convention that

---

[4]Brock, 420-26. Campbell maintained he first opposed war in 1823 when he launched *Christian Baptist*. For his impact upon Baptists, see H. Leon McBeth, *The Baptist Heritage. Four Centuries of Baptist Witness* (Nashville: Broadman, 1987) 375-80; David Edwin Harrell, Jr. *Quest for a Christian America. The Disciples of Christ and American Society to 1866* (Nashville: Disciples of Christ Historical Society, 1966) 141.

[5]John B. Boles, "Henry Holcombe, A Southern Baptist Reformer in the Age of Jefferson," *Georgia Historical Quarterly* 54 (1970): 381-407; William Cathcart, *The Baptist Encyclopedia* (Philadelphia, 1881) 531-32; *Dictionary of American Biography*; David R. Contosta entry in Harold Josephson, ed., *Biographical Dictionary of Modern Peace Leaders* (Westport: Greenwood Press, 1985) 421-22; Roger Hayden, "William Staughton: Baptist Educator and Missionary Advocate," *Foundations* 10 (1967): 19-35; William B. Sprague, *Annals of the American Baptist Pulpit* (New York: Robert Carter & Brothers, 1860) 6:215-20; William D. Thompson, *Philadelphia's First Baptists* (Philadelphia: First Baptist Church, 1989).

ratified the United States constitution. Self-educated, Holcombe promoted higher education. He helped found, and became president of the Beaufort District Society for the Encouragement of Literature, which became Beaufort College. He endowed Mount Enon Academy, an ancestor of Mercer University. At Savannah, Holcombe's congregation set up a permanent committee for the "relief of indigent and distressed persons," while Holcombe and his wife, the former Frances Tanner, established a female orphanage. In Philadelphia, they supported a Female Hospitable Society for the Relief and Employment of the Poor. Holcombe helped organize the Charleston Baptist Association and the Georgia Baptist Convention, but he was no narrow sectarian. In 1802, he launched the *Georgia Analytical Repository*, the first religious periodical in the South. Holcombe printed an announcement that the periodical would be non-partisan. Its purposes were to spread religious knowledge, to discuss literature and theology, and to further Christian unity.

Holcombe did not shy away from contentious issues. Despite adverse reaction, in 1802 he encouraged the growth of several black Baptist churches and participated in the ordination of black preachers. The same year, the first issue of his periodical drew attention to the hanging of a petty thief, John Rice. The case led him to espouse reform of the Georgia penal code. One of the fruits of his campaign was the elimination of the death penalty for certain crimes.

When in 1812 war became a matter of controversy, Holcombe supported the concept of a defensive war. But hesitations about the validity of a Christian taking up arms led him to change his mind. In 1822, he and many members of First Baptist Church, Philadelphia, founded the Pennsylvania Peace Society and two sister organizations, the African Baptist Peace Society in Philadelphia, and a local peace society in Augusta, Georgia. Holcombe published *Advocate of Peace*, which took as its motto "Blessed are the peacemakers." In one sermon, he expressed his conviction that Christians are never permitted to take human life. He believed that if Christians were faithful to the mind of Christ, the entire Christian church would become a great peace society. The result would be universal peace. Holcombe summarized his understanding of peace:

> [Jesus] constantly inculcated patient submission to all natural evils.* Jesus, to his revilers and murderers, manifested no hostility; but, on the contrary, uniform compassion. He opened blind eyes, unstopped deaf ears, healed all manner of diseases, restored cripples to vigour and activity, and raised the dead. . . .

*Behold the Prince of Peace, setting us an example that we should follow his steps! What a different spirit than that of others.[6]

Another Baptist peace advocate was Francis Wayland (1796–1865). After medical studies and a conversion experience, Wayland undertook a career in pastoral ministry. Influenced by his father, a lay pastor who took a special interest in the needs of destitute urban congregations in the Hudson Valley, Wayland championed social causes such as public education, mission, and the abolition of slavery. From 1826–1855 he was professor of moral philosophy and president of Brown University.

Wayland first expressed pacifist sentiments in a sermon on *The Moral Dignity of the Missionary Enterprise*. Preaching before the Boston Baptist Foreign Missionary Society on 26 October 1823, Wayland made a linkage, common to nineteenth-century missiology, between mission and Christian peacemaking:

> Our object is to purify the whole earth from abominations [such as slavery and suttee, or widow-burning]. Our object will not have been accomplished till the tomahawk shall be buried forever, and the tree of peace spread its broad branches from the Atlantick to the Pacifick; until a thousand smiling villages shall be reflected from the waves of the Missouri, and the distant valleys of the west echo with the song of the reaper; till the wilderness and the solitary place shall have been glad for us, and the desert has rejoiced and blossomed as a rose.[7]

Wayland joined the Rhode Island auxiliary of the American Peace Society. As director (1834-1836), vice president (1839–1859, 1861–1866), and president (1859–1861) of the American Peace Society, he gave talks on its behalf, but he made his most important contribution through publication of *The Elements of Moral Science*, which became the most widely used ethics text among Protestants during the antebellum period.[8] In the last section of the book, "practical ethics," Wayland

---

[6]Henry Holcombe, *The Martial Christian's Manual* (Philadelphia: Pennsylvania Peace Society, 1823) 9-11.

[7]Francis Wayland, *The Moral Dignity of the Missionary Enterprise* (Boston: James Loring, 1824) 11.

[8]*Elements of Moral Science* (1835). The first edition of this widely-used textbook sold over 100,000 copies. For biographical information, William H. Brackney, *The Baptists* (New York: Greenwood Press, 1988) 278-79; Thomas E. Frank, "Contending Values: Francis Wayland's Views on War," *Foundations* 21 (1978): 100-12; Jayme A. Sokolow,

articulated his theology of peace under the rubric "the law of benevolence." This law arose from Jesus' command to love one's enemies and overcome evil with good. Wayland explained that humans are under obligation to be instruments of happiness to those who have no claim on them. Without thought of reciprocity, one must extend benevolence to all, including the wicked. Were individuals and governments to adopt the law of benevolence, wars would cease.

From the perspectives of the Bible and natural justice, Wayland concluded that all wars are contrary to the revealed will of God. In the event that wars should break out, one should not take up arms but suffer injury with forgiveness and love. This position led Wayland to oppose the Mexican War, which was, in his view, "wicked, infamous, unconstitutional in design, and stupid and shockingly depraved in its management." Although he stopped short of advocating specific acts of war resistance, he urged citizens to "use all innocent constitutional means" to end the war. "Were the good men of this nation thus to unite, national wickedness among us would be of very limited duration." He also indicated that circumstances such as tyranny and usurpation could arise in which civil disobedience would be permissible.[9]

Another Baptist who identified with the American Peace Society was Howard Malcom (1799–1879). Malcom's career included pastorates in Hudson, New York (1820–1826); Federal Street Baptist Church, Boston (1827–1835); and Sansom Street Baptist Church, Philadelphia (1849–1851). From 1840 to 1849, he was president of Georgetown College, Georgetown, Kentucky. He was president of Bucknell University, Lewistown, Pennsylvania, between 1851 and 1857. Malcom lent his energies to major denominational and voluntary societies. Remembered primarily for his *Travels in South-Eastern Asia*, published by the American Baptist Publication Society in 1839, Malcom also wrote two pamphlets circulated

---

"Francis Wayland," *Biographical Dictionary of Modern Peace Leaders*, ed. Harold Josephson (Westport: Greenwood Press, 1985) 1007-1008; Edson L. Whitney, *The American Peace Society. A Centennial History* (Washington: American Peace Society, 1929).

[9]Francis Wayland [Jr.] and H. L. Wayland, *A Memoir of the Life and Labors of Francis Wayland, D.D., LL.D.* (2 vols.; New York: Sheldon and Company, 1867) 2:55; Francis Wayland, *The Duty of Obedience to the Civil Magistrate. Three Sermons Preached in the Chapel of Brown University* (Boston: Charles C. Little and James Brown, 1847).

in *The Book of Peace*. Malcom denounced war as a criminal activity and believed Christians should not participate in any war. Malcom served various offices in the American Peace Society from 1832 until his death, as did his son, Charles Howard Malcom of Newport, Rhode Island.[10]

In Canada, during the rebellions in Upper and Lower Canada (1837–1838), some Baptists took up arms. Others did not. For example, when the nascent Baptist Mission at Grande Ligne was attacked, the Swiss-born Henrietta Oden Feller (1800–1868), and other Baptist missionaries urged non-resistance. Missionaries experienced persecution but did not retaliate. In Upper Canada, some Baptists questioned taking up arms. At a covenant meeting held at Yarmouth Church on 7 April 1838, Brother Andrew McClure repented of having caused his brothers and sisters grief by going to war under arms. "If it was to do again, he would not do so, as he now thinks it is wrong for Christians to take up arms at any time." The Baptist Church in Dundas went so far as to disapprove the conduct of Brother Hooper, who joined the government forces during the disturbances, because militia duty prevented him from "filling up his place in the house of prayer and preaching to the people."[11]

In the United States, the approaching civil war posed a dilemma for peace advocates. They confronted a clash of two evils. Some, who rejected wars of aggression only, understood war as a tragic necessity in some instances. When war came, most of the leadership of the American Peace Society reluctantly supported it as a means to end slavery.[12] For example, Francis Wayland found that his strong peace stance came into

---

[10]"War Inconsistent with Christianity" and "Criminality of War," in George C. Beckwith, ed, *The Book of Peace: A Collection of Essays on War and Peace* (Boston: American Peace Society, 1845) 129-36, 433-48. For biographical details, Brackney, 223-24; Brock, 622-23; Whitney, 137; and a new biography, Warren P. Mild, *Howard Malcom and the Great Mission Advance* (Valley Forge: International Ministries, American Baptist Churches, 1988). Mild does not mention Malcom's peace activism.

[11]Yarmouth Church Minutes, 7 April 1838; Dundas Church Minutes, 31 December 1837, Canadian Baptist Archives. For other documentation, Paul R. Dekar, "Baptists and Human Rights, 1837–1867," in Jarold K. Zeman, ed, *Baptists in Canada. Search for Identity amidst Diversity* (Burlington: G. R. Welch, 1980).

[12]In addition to Brock's thorough treatment, Dwight Lowell Dumond, *Antislavery Origins of the Civil War in the United States* (Ann Arbor: University of Michigan Press, 1939); Sheldon Richman, "The Anti-war Abolitionists: The Peace Movement's Split over the Civil War," *Journal of Libertarian Studies* 5 (1981): 327-40.

conflict with equally strong convictions regarding slavery. His belief in non-resistance gave way to acceptance of force as a legitimate means to secure the abolition of slavery. In the last edition of *The Elements of Moral Science*, he reiterated his position regarding civil disobedience. He argued that the Creator has provided "terrible sanctions" for removing the evil of slavery. "The Judge of the whole earth will do justice. He hears the cry of the oppressed, and he will in the end terribly deliver them." Wayland went on to qualify his earlier pacifism:

> If a nation in defiance of right, from love of conquest, or desire of territory, or another wicked motive, should resolve on the subjugation of its unoffending neighbor with the intention of overthrowing a just government and establishing in its place the power of brute force: what then is to be done? . . . force must be repelled by force, just so far as it is necessary to resist their evil design.[13]

Not every pacifist joined the flight from the peace camp. Some continued to denounce all war. Rogerene Baptists remained conscientious objectors. Jesse Buckner, a North Carolina Baptist and Confederate Colonel, was a Civil War conscientious objector. Buckner came to the conclusion that "war is contrary to the gospel" and refused to bear arms. He was imprisoned, driven from camp to camp under military arrest, and poorly treated. At the end of the war, he became a Quaker.[14] A few Quakers cited Baptist influence on their peace witness. For example, a Baptist minister named Thorne believed that Baptists ought to adopt the Quaker position.[15]

Women Peacemakers

As the nineteenth-century peace crusade gained momentum, women took up the cause. In a speech delivered on 7 December 1812 before the

---

[13]Wayland revised *Moral Science* between 1859-65; ed. Joseph L. Blau (Cambridge: Harvard University Press, 1963) 396, 412.

[14]Brock, 775-76. Edward Needles Wright, *Conscientious Objectors in the Civil War* (Philadelphia: University of Pennsylvania Press, 1931) 175-76. Brock and Wright mention German Baptists who sought relief from military service.

[15]Fernando G. Cartland, *Southern Heroes of the Friends in War Time* (Cambridge: Riverside Press, 1895) 262-63, 270.

Baptist Female Society for Missionary Purposes, a speaker observed it was a terrible time on earth, a time of war and sin, and exhorted women to pray for repentance, humiliation, and peace.[16] A similar appeal was addressed to a group of women meeting at the Bowdoin Street Chapel in Boston: "Females *can do* as much as the other sex in effecting the desired change in public opinion, no intelligent mind can doubt; that they *will do* as much, all past analogy leads us confidently to expect." Women responded by forming a ladies' peace society.[17]

Baptist women expressed concern for peace in a variety of ways. In 1792 as a teenager, Sally Parsons was swept up in a revival at the village of Westport, New Hampshire. She ran home to tell her family the good news. Her father became angry. "If you're going to become one of those fanatical Freewill Baptists, you can just live somewhere else. You're no longer welcome here!" Thrown out of her house, she prayed that God would forgive her father, change his heart, and protect her mother, brothers, and sisters. In 1797, the New Hampshire Yearly Meeting of Freewill Baptists took notice of her faith and service. Those among whom she ministered encouraged Parsons to become a pastor. She responded by becoming an itinerant preacher up and down the state. The next few years, she worked tirelessly, sharing God's love. Among her converts was her father. He asked for forgiveness. As a sign of reconciliation, he gave her a horse to continue her ministry.[18]

The Civil War led some Baptist women to play a major role in the healing of the nation. In 1863, the American Baptist Home Missionary Society commissioned Joanna Patterson Moore (1832–1916), a recent graduate of a seminary in Rockford, Illinois, to work among freed slaves on an island in the Mississippi River across from Arkansas. In her autobiography *In Christ's Name*, she describes arriving to a great company

---

[16]Ellis, 132.

[17]*Address before the Bowdoin Young Men's Peace Society* (Boston, 1836), cited by Wendy E. Chmielewski, "The Role of Gender and the Role of Women in the Antebellum Peace Movement, 1818–1860," paper presented at the *Celebrating Our Work Conference*, Douglass College, Rutgers University, May 1990. Another example is found in the August 1828 issue of *Harbinger of Peace*, a Peace Society publication. It reported that, "The ladies of First Baptist have subscribed . . . to constitute Mrs. Frances Holcombe a life member of the American Peace Society."

[18]Nancy A. Hardesty, *Great Women of Faith* (Nashville: Abingdon Press, 1982) 67-68.

of 1,100 women, children, and helpless old men. She was the only white there. Family, friends, and classmates considered her crazy to attempt this work.[19]

Moore persisted. She understood that her first task was to love the people. She taught basic literacy skills and led many black soldiers to Christian conversion. One of them, George Gaines of Company B, attested, "I want to do good . . . you are my dearest earthly friend." For the next thirty-eight years Moore worked in six states. She established boarding schools and centers for homeless aging women, and she championed the causes of peace, temperance, and women's suffrage.

Women were central to the post-war recovery of the peace movement. Baptist women responded to the stirring appeal of Julia Ward Howe (1819–1910) to join the crusade for peace:

> Arise, all women who have hearts, whether your baptism be that of water or of tears! Say firmly, "We will not have great questions decided by irrelevant agencies. Our husbands shall not come to us, reeking with carnage, for caresses and applause. Our sons shall not be taken from us to unlearn all that we have been able to teach them of charity, mercy, and patience. We, women of one country, will be too tender of those of another country to allow our sons to be trained to injure theirs. From the bosom of the devastated earth a voice goes up with our own. It says, "Disarm, disarm, the sword of murder is not the balance of justice." Blood does not wipe out dishonour, nor violence indicate possession. As men have often forsaken the plough and the anvil at the summons of war, let women now leave all that may be left of home for a greater and earnest day of counsel.

Mother's Day may have had its origins in this appeal of September 1870. It launched the organization of an international women's peace movement.[20]

---

[19]William H. Brackney, ed., *Baptist Life and Thought: 1600–1980* (Valley Forge: Judson Press, 1983) 237-39; Beverly Carlson, "Servants for Freedom," *Baptist Leader* (January-February 1989) 8-9; A. H. Newman, *A Century of Baptist Achievement* (Philadelphia: American Baptist Publication Society, 1901) 423-24.

[20]Cambridge Women's Peace Collective, *My Country Is the Whole World. An Anthology of Women's Work for Peace* (London: Pandora Press, 1984) 56-57.

Post Civil War Advocacy of Peace

During the last decades of the nineteenth century, peace societies competed with strong currents of imperialism and nationalism. In the United States, many Christians used terms such as "manifest destiny," "muscular Christianity," and "social determinism" to justify expansionism. Despite the crisis of the magnitude of the Civil War, there nonetheless existed sufficient human and spiritual resources for a resurgence in peace activism. New intellectual and religious currents such as the Social Gospel, Marxian socialism, and Tolstoyan groups had an impact.

The older American Peace Society continued alongside movements that pioneered new forms of protest such as organizing anti-war rallies, flying banners, or releasing symbolic peace doves. Annexation of the Philippines in 1898 fueled anti-imperialist activity such as editorials in the Baptist *Watchman*.[21]

George Dana Boardman (1828–1903) was an outspoken critic of the annexation of the Philippines. A stepson of Adoniram Judson (1788–1850), Boardman was born in Burma of missionary parents. At the age of six, he was sent to the United States to be educated. He spent his youth in Maine under the care of his maternal grandparents who were committed to the cause of peace. In 1852, he graduated from Brown University with a career in law in view. A near-fatal illness caused him to respond to a calling to pastoral ministry. Briefly, he served churches in Barnwell, South Carolina and Rochester, New York. In 1864, First Baptist Church, Philadelphia invited Boardman to its pulpit. He served a distinguished thirty-year pastorate. Gradually, in sermon and print,

---

[21]Winthrop S. Hudson, "Protestant Clergy Debate the Nation's Vocation, 1898–1899," *Church History* 42 (1973): 110-18; C. Roland Marchand, *The American Peace Movement and Social Reform, 1898–1918* (Princeton: Princeton University Press, 1972); David S. Patterson, *Toward a Warless World: The Travail of the American Peace Movement, 1887–1914* (Bloomington: University of Indiana Press, 1976); Daniel B. Schirmer, *Republic or Empire. American Resistance to the Philippine War* (Cambridge: Schenkman Publishing Company, 1972); Ivor B. Thomas, "A Baptist Anti-Imperialist Voice. George Horr and *The Watchman*," *Foundations* 18 (1975): 340-57.

Boardman laid foundations for a vocation of peacemaking that by the 1890s saw him active in nine national and international peace societies.[22]

Boardman based his theology of peace on the Bible. While he used the Bible to show that the Christian religion is a religion of peace,[23] he was aware of the difficulties involved. In an address, he noted,

> I would speak advisedly and justly. Devoutly believing as I do in the Bible, I must admit that, in the inscrutable counsels of the Eternal, even war has had its divine office; as, for example, when Jehovah used it as his minister of doom against the Canaanites. . . . No doubt there is a sense in which it is true that the instinct of self-defence is divinely implanted. But self-defence, at least physical, is not one of the ordinary conditions of society; it is an exceptional emergency; and it is manifestly absurd to deduce a rule from an exception.[24]

Boardman was convinced that events were moving towards realization of God's realm on earth. On Easter 1898, he preached a sermon just as the Spanish-American War broke out, in which he confidently affirmed

> that the general trend of the next century will be onward and upward [and] that the spirit of Jesus Christ will be the dominant force in the coming century. I believe . . . that his Mountain Sermon will become more and more the supreme constitution for mankind.[25]

To this end, Christians are to seek to establish better conditions of civilized life and, in particular, to observe "Christ's doctrine of blessedness" by actively reconciling those who are in enmity.[26]

---

[22]Joan Jacobs Brumberg, *Mission for Life* (New York: Free Press, 1980); Janet Kerr Morchane, "George Dana Boardman, Propagandist for Peace," *Foundations* 9 (1966): 145-58.

[23]In his capacity as President of the Pennsylvania auxiliary of the American Peace Society, Boardman published a collection of texts under the title *Scripture Testimony*. On the cover of the copy at Valley Forge, in handwriting, are the words "selected and arranged by Geo. D. Boardman, July 3, 1886."

[24]*Nationalism and Internationalism: or Mankind One Body* (undated pamphlet) 7.

[25]*Christian Outlook for the Twentieth Century*, published as a broadside and as an appendix to Kerr Boyce Tupper, *George Dana Boardman: A Memorial Discourse* (Philadelphia: American Baptist Publication Society, 1904).

[26]George Dana Boardman, *Studies in the Mountain Instruction* (New York: D. Appleton and Company, 1881) 47-49; *New York Baptist Annual* (1904) 74.

In a pamphlet entitled *Disarmament of Nations*, he outlined his main proposals for how Christians should apply the Sermon on the Mount to international relations. He stated,

> Let the weapons of our warfare be spiritual, not carnal; so shall we become mighty before God to the casting-down of strong-holds. In brief, I nowhere read in the New Testament of a beatitude for the warrior. But I do read of the beatitude for the peacemaker: "Blessed are the peacemakers; for they shall be called sons of God." *Peace*—why, it is the very watchword of Christianity itself, its Divine Founder beginning His earthly career with the peace-salutation of Bethlehem, and ending it with the peace-valediction of Olivet.

He based his argument on Paul's image of the church as one body with several members (1 Cor 12). He saw this text as an analogy of relations between nations, according to which each has its own individual mission. Together, all constitute "one common Nation, namely, the Commonwealth of Mankind." He called all wars, domestic and foreign, "suicidal," "social self-maiming," an improper means of settling human quarrels, an institution to be eliminated like polygamy or slavery. He advocated arbitration, disarmament, and an international congress of nations.[27]

Boardman left room for defensive wars in certain situations. It has been impossible to discover his views during the Civil War; later, he called it "a war of principle." As the nineteenth century waned, he came to believe all war to be inhuman and unchristian. He called upon the United States government to terminate its war against Spain as quickly as possible, and he discouraged Baptist clergy from going to the front. When, in 1898, the Czar of Russia appealed for a general disarmament conference, Boardman responded positively.[28]

---

[27]*Disarmament of Nations. Address Delivered at the Annual Meeting of the Christian Arbitration and Peace Society . . . March 4, 1890* (Philadelphia, 1890) 9. In editions published in 1893, 1898, and 1899, Boardman expanded this pamphlet to be used as a vehicle of peacemaking. He distributed it widely, especially to those in positions of influence. Boardman preserved the replies he received (generally positive) in a volume held at the American Baptist-Samuel Colgate Library, Rochester, New York.

[28]Morchaine, 147, 156 and 158, n. 43. Another Baptist peace leader, William Herbert Perry Faunce (1859–1930; president of Brown University in 1899), condemned the Spanish-American War.

Conclusion

Like their British counterparts, North American Baptists who joined the nineteenth-century peace crusade provide a crucial bridge between early Baptist non-resistance and contemporary Baptist peacemaking. As opponents of war, they exhorted Christians to return to the non-resistant teachings of Jesus and early Christians. Generally, they were not radical by temperament or vocation. In the face of prevailing opinion that supported war and imperialism, however, they sometimes articulated genuinely radical positions. This was especially true in the case of conscientious objection. By their advocacy of a disruptive form of anti-war protest, they empowered some to take this course of action during the War of 1812 and the Civil War. Other Baptists may have taken this stand. Pacifism and non-resistance remained options for Baptists.

To a considerable extent, the outbreak of wars served as an indictment of the primary method of peace advocacy adopted by nineteenth-century Baptists in the peace societies. Moral persuasion through published talks and sermons was insufficient to halt the drift to war or to bring wars to a speedy end once they broke out. Nonetheless, by their leadership in the nineteenth-century peace crusade, North American Baptist peacemakers provided an alternative to war. They developed an analysis that made connections between the issues of militarism, nationalism, racism, and war. They developed strategies that could prevent future wars. They struggled with the tension of holding together commitments to justice and peace. North American Baptist peacemakers helped put social reform and internationalism high on the agenda of Baptists. In this century, we would do well to recover their analysis and strategies for promoting healing among the nations.

Chapter Five
John Clifford
(1836–1923)

An Introduction to the Life of John Clifford

John Clifford was born at Sawley, Derbyshire.[1] His parents, Samuel and Mary Stimson Clifford, came from the working class and a line of radical non-conformists. At age ten, Clifford abandoned formal schooling to seek employment. He learned to read while tending machines in a lace factory.

The New Connection General Baptist chapel, Nether Street, Beeston, Nottinghamshire, shaped Clifford's early religious life. Converted at age fifteen, Clifford trained at Midland Baptist College in Leicester (1856–1857) and Nottingham (1857–1858). Moving to London, Clifford studied at University College and received four degrees. He served two pastorates, Praed Street Church, London (1858–1877), and Westbourne Park, London (1877–1915). From 1870–1883, he edited *The General Baptist Magazine*. In 1891, he helped complete amalgamation of New Connexion Baptists and the Baptist Union.

The myriad voluntary associations and committees Clifford headed was remarkable. They included the London Baptist Association (1879), the Baptist Union (1888, 1899), the National Council of Evangelical Free Churches (1898), the Baptist World Alliance (1905–1911), and the World Federation of Brotherhoods (1916–1919), an organization that succeeded

---

[1]*Baptist Handbook* (1924) 288-89; *Baptist Quarterly* 2 (1924): 1-3; H. Edgar Bonsall, *The Dream of an Ideal City. Westbourne Park 1877–1977* (London: Westbourne Park Baptist Church, 1978); G. W. Byrt, *John Clifford. A Fighting Free Churchman* (London: Kingsgate, 1947); James Marchant, *Dr. John Clifford, C. H., Life, Letters and Reminiscences* (London: Cassell and Company, 1924); M. R. Watts, "John Clifford and Radical Nonconformity 1836–1923" (D.Phil. thesis, Oxford University, 1966).

the Pleasant Sunday Afternoons movement promoting healthy recreation for workers.

Clifford came to maturity at the end of a period during which British Baptists generally refrained from engagement in political processes. He rose to prominence in Baptist life and became a leading spokesperson on social issues for all British non-conformity. There were, of course, other voices. Charles Haddon Spurgeon quit the Baptist Union in 1887 because of alleged theological deviations by Clifford and others. After the great preacher died in 1892, many of his former students emphasized personal evangelism. In 1909, George Freeman attacked the formation of the Nonconformist Socialist League, saying, "The ministry that departs from the great mission of saving sinners and making souls is a discredit in the world and a degradation to itself," while Clifford's successor at Westbourne Park, Samuel William Hughes (1874–1954) cautioned against social utopias.[2]

Clifford would have none of this. Evangelical conversion and social action could not be rent asunder. Individual and social religion must be held together. Clifford never left the evangelical camp. He always emphasized the personal side of salvation. For Clifford, redemption in Christ also had social implications. With vigor Clifford addressed the moral concerns of the day and sought to engage Christians in politics.

Clifford gained his reputation primarily as a preacher and orator. He left an imposing literary legacy in the form of newspaper articles and pamphlets. Such themes as democracy, justice, righteousness, peace, and socialism dominated his sermons and writings. The title of an address on 3 October 1888 to the Baptist Union expressed Clifford's approach to ministry: "The New City of God; or the Primitive Christian Faith as a Social Gospel." In the following sections we have explored his efforts to relieve the victims of the industrial revolution, his opposition to imperialism, his campaign for secular public education, and his response to the First World War.

---

[2]Kenneth D. Brown, *A Social History of the Nonconformist Ministry in England and Wales 1800—1930* (Oxford: Clarendon Press, 1988) 212; D. W. Bebbington, *Evangelicalism in Modern Britain. A History from the 1730s to the 1980s* (London: Unwin Hyman, 1989) 211–14.

Social Reform

Clifford passionately believed in social justice. Four factors influenced this commitment: his working class background, the people to whom he ministered, Chartism, and socialism.[3] Looking back on his early years, he recalled,

> I began life in a factory and I have never forgotten the cruel impressions I received there of men and work. Ebenezer Elliott's prayer was on our lips daily—"When Wilt Thou save the people?" Chartists were alive and eloquent. ... So I came to have sympathy with the working classes, of which I was one. ... I have never lost it after 80 years and I feel it stronger to-day than ever. ... I was born in a time of daring social crises and crises of the soul, a time harassed by the restraints of those in authority, but a time of daring aspirations of a struggling faith, permeated by idealistic currents, and also by a growing doubt as to the righteousness of the foundations upon which men may build.[4]

Clifford sought to respond to conditions of the industrial revolution. Regarding the experience of his people, he stated,

> The business of a Christian Church is to find out the real needs of the people in the neighborhood in which it is placed and, as far as it can, supply all that will make for brightness and joy, for strength and service, for manhood and brotherhood. Now thousands of young men and women are in our locality, and we have a direct ministry to them and are responsible to God for discharging it. ... My work is to render any aid I can.[5]

Chartist influences on Clifford were his father and the Baptist pastor, Thomas Cooper. Clifford said,

> The Chartist activities were all directed toward securing opportunity for the development of the individual and specially of the weakest and most wronged

---

[3]Peter d'Alroy Jones, *The Christian Socialist Revival 1877–1914. Religion, Class and Social Conscience in Late Victorian England* (Princeton: Princeton University Press, 1968); David Thompson, "John Clifford's Social Gospel," *Baptist Quarterly* 31 (1986): 199-217.
[4]Marchant, 1-2.
[5]Bonsall, 31.

individual. They aimed at securing a fine and free life for each one. And that I wanted.[6]

Socialism also had an impact on Clifford. Author of two Fabian Tracts and first president of the Christian Socialist League, Clifford believed that industrial life would evolve, free itself from the evils of society, and fulfil its divine mission to enrich the whole of life.[7]

Clifford identified closely with workers. Throughout his ministry, he gave as much attention to issues like inadequate housing and sanitary conditions as he did to national or international concerns. He campaigned against alcohol, gambling, and prostitution. With his encouragement, many social reform groups located at Praed Street and Westbourne Park churches. In 1861, Clifford helped found a Mutual Economical Benefit Society followed by a Mutual Improvement Society. During a strike of London dock labourers in 1889, and again during a strike of miners in 1893, Clifford defended the workers.

Opposing the Anglo-Boer War

British Baptists expressed opposition to the Anglo-Boer War of 1899–1902 more vocally than against any other war. Clifford was one of the most prominent critics. He condemned it as an "unmitigating evil" and spoke frequently of his "implacable loathing" of it. An observer described him as a "windmill in a hurricane; his eyes flash lightnings; he seizes the enemy, as it were, by the throat, pommels him breathless with blows and throws him aside a miserable wreck." Because of his stand, for a few days in 1900 Westbourne Park had to be protected by the police.[8]

On 10 July 1899, before the outbreak of war, Clifford addressed the first public meeting of the Transvaal Committee. Amidst interruptions, Clifford ridiculed government policy:

> It is asserted the Uitlanders have not got the franchise. In a country like ours, is it necessary I should reply to that? [No, no.] Half the people in this country

---

[6]Marchant, 6.
[7]Fabian Tract #78 *Socialism and the Teaching of Christ* (London, 1897) 5; see also Fabian Tract #139 *Socialism and the Churches* (London, 1908); Marchant, 40.
[8]Marchant, 95 (145-54 for the war); Thompson, 205.

> have not got the franchise. [Cheers.] And in my opinion the better half. [Loud cheers.]

Clifford called for arbitration, patience, tact, and justice for all parties. Other speeches followed. The gathering adopted unanimously a resolution supported by Clifford, which protested against "reckless threats of war with the Transvaal."[9] Under Clifford's leadership, the Baptist Union adopted a similar resolution calling for patience, moderation, and negotiation.[10]

Despite public pressure, on 12 October 1899 war broke out. Clifford helped form a "Stop the War" committee. On 1 January 1900, in his annual address to the young people of the congregation, Clifford made a cogent case against the war. He began by expressing kinship with the Boers:

> This is a time of sadness and pain, of division and strife. . . . We are at war with the Boers; that is the outstanding fact of 1899; at war with a people professing the same religious faith as ourselves, and related by ties of race to hundreds of thousands of our fellow-subjects in South Africa. Forty millions of people are at war with a people who number less than the whole of the population of the city of Liverpool; and yet the undeniable fact is that we have been beaten—beaten again and again, and most ignominiously beaten and driven back.[11]

Along with prayers for speedy cessation of the war and conclusion of a peace based on principles of justice and humanity, Clifford expressed sympathy for the bereaved and admiration for the Boers:

> Our defeats are tragic. Our losses are heartrending. . . . Speaking for the greater part of our people, I may say we are one in our sorrow, if not in our judgments. We are one, also, in our admiration of the courage of the men who have gone at the call of the Government to face death on the field of battle. . . . And, I hope I may add, we are one in our respect for the courage of the Boer.

---

[9]Stephen Koss, ed., *The Pro-Boers. The Anatomy of an Antiwar Movement* (Chicago: University of Chicago Press, 1973) 8–11 for text of the address.

[10]*Baptist Magazine* 91 (October 1899): 500.

[11]*Baptist Times and Freeman*, 5 January 1900, 8; *Brotherhood and the War in South Africa* (London: Parlett, January 1900) 3. Subsequent quotations are from this widely distributed pamphlet.

Later, in 1914, identifying with Belgium, another small state struggling for self-government and liberty, Clifford would use similar language to defend going to war. In this case, Clifford spoke of the need to think clearly, feel unselfishly, and talk sanely. Christians "must 'seek *first* the Kingdom of God and His righteousness'—the rule of the eternally good and wise and true—and *His* justice." Clifford identified "abiding principles." First, "wars do not of themselves really settle anything." Inevitably the issues dividing the Boers and the British would be settled by arbitration, use of reason, and judgment. Second, wars violate biblical notions of justice and unity. "The word of the Lord in the last year of the century rings out above the noise of all our strife: Hear, O England and Africa . . . thou shalt love the Lord thy God . . . *and thy neighbor as thyself.*" Clifford could not accept the government's avowal that war expressed "our mission as Britons" (freeing black Africans enslaved by the Boers), self-defence (against Boer aggression), or principle (ending unjust taxation and extending the franchise). Point by point, Clifford refuted each claim and heaped scorn on the government for having blundered into an avoidable war, for lying, and for press censorship.

Speaking and engaging in committee work for the remainder of the war, Clifford maintained his opposition. He called for an end to concentration camps, immediate surrender of all arms, protection of non-whites, and provision of legal rights for labourers. With other peace advocates, he formulated positive recommendations for ending the war. At his instigation, in July 1901, Clifford helped Baptists frame a "constructive policy of peace" including proposals for a generous amnesty and self-government,[12] and a Free Church Manifesto that called for "speedy termination of the war" guided by five principles:

> (1) that there shall be nothing to retard or frustrate the future unity and amity of the peoples of South Africa.
> (2) that every security should be taken to prevent the recurrence of military strife.
> (3) that the invariable policy of the British Empire in the administration of its Colonies should be adopted in the settlement of South Africa, namely, the concession of autonomy and self government, and that there be ultimately the Federation of States.

---

[12]*Baptist Times and Freeman*, 19 July 1901, 479.

(4) that there should be compensation for destroyed homes and farms to all who are able to establish a just claim.

(5) and that there should be an amnesty as generous and far-reaching as possible, on condition of the immediate laying down of arms and breaking up of all military organization.[13]

A thousand Baptist pastors—approximately half of the Baptist Union leadership—and approximately four thousand of nine thousand free church ministers signed the manifesto. As a consensus document it had shortcomings. For example, it failed to condemn imperialism outright, and it made vague recommendations.

The manifesto did not unite Baptists behind Clifford's stance. Some members of his own congregation dissented with his stand on this matter of public policy, but they supported him in his ministry.

Other pastors were less fortunate. In Liverpool, shortly after the outbreak of war, the Reverend Charles Aked of Pembroke Chapel took up the anti-war cause. After one sermon, the local press opined, "Mr. Aked makes a great deal of noise. He tells us that we are murderers. But his is the voice of Charles the Baptist, crying in the wilderness."[14] Aked kept up pressure against the war. On 30 September 1901, he condemned the war as "a crime against humanity, a capitalist war, worked up to by a 'kept' press, initiated by treachery and lying." When, on 2 January 1902, a crowd gathered for an address advertised to deal with Athanasius, Aked denounced "the cowardly war" and proclaimed his sympathies with Boers "rightly struggling to be free." He accepted "the moral responsibility of 'Encouraging the Boer' and all the consequences of my acts." After the speech, Aked had to be smuggled out by a back door. A crowd followed him home, spat upon Mrs. Aked, and broke windows in their home.[15]

Frederick Brotherton Meyer was another prominent Baptist anti-war activist. When war broke out, Meyer was serving as pastor of Christ Church, Lambeth, and as leader of the National Union of Christian Endeavour. Meyer condemned the war, called for days of prayer and

---

[13]*Baptist Times and Freeman*, 26 July 1901, 496.

[14]*Liverpool Review*, 27 January 1900, cited by I. Sellers, "The Pro-Boer Movement in Liverpool," *Transactions of the Unitarian Historical Society* 12 (1960): 69-84.

[15]Ibid., and Arthur Davey, *The British Pro-Boers 1877–1902* (Cape Town: Tafelberg, 1978) 151.

fasting, joined the stop-the-war movement, and helped draft the Free Church Manifesto. A mob broke up a speech by Meyer. Another Baptist pastor was driven from his parish. The anti-war movement had to establish a "pulpit martyr" fund to assist in such cases.[16]

While major sectors of the public manifested violence against critics of the war, the Baptist press steered a middle course. Editorials in the *Baptist Magazine* and *Baptist Times and Freeman* cautioned against excessive outbursts of patriotism, extremism, false optimism, and jingoism.[17] A stream of letters appeared for and against the war. Frank H. Humby of Jersey protested against an "abominable, revengeful, and murderous spirit." With a sense of irony, he recalled that when England refused religious liberty to non-conformists three centuries earlier, ancestors of the Boers protected them. George P. McKay of Stoke Newington hoped that at their annual assembly, Baptists would express unequivocally "that we are for other arbitration than that of the blind and bloody sword."[18] Resolutions called for an end to hostility and urged Baptists to work for peace, to set aside time for fasting or prayer, and to advocate pacific principles necessary for the welfare of nations.[19] The war ended on 31 May 1902. An editorial cautioned that "a sad and gloomy epoch in our history" had ended and warned against instituting peacetime conscription.[20]

---

[16]Hope Hay Hewison, *Hedge of Wild Almonds. South Africa, the "Pro-Boers" and the Quaker Conscience 1890–1910* (London: James Currey, 1989) 108. A deeply spiritual man, Meyer promoted progressive causes, including the Peace Society. There are three, largely hagiographical biographies: W. Y. Fullerton, *F. B. Meyer. A Biography* (London: Marshall, Morgan and Scott, n.d.); A. Chester Mann, *Preacher, Teacher, Man of God* (London: George Allen and Unwin, 1929); M. Jennie Street, *F. B. Meyer, His Life and Work* (London: S. W. Partridge and Company, 1912).

[17]*Baptist Times and Freeman*, 8 December 1899, 837; *Baptist Magazine* 93 (January 1901): 39-40.

[18]*Baptist Times and Freeman*, 1 December 1899, 821; 17 August 1900, 621.

[19]For example, *Baptist Times and Freeman*, 15 December 1899, 865; 16 February 1900, 122.

[20]*Baptist Times and Freeman*, 6 June 1902; Keith W. Clements, "Baptists and the Outbreak of the First World War," *Baptist Quarterly* 26 (1975): 74-92.

Passive Resistance Movement

John Clifford championed the rights of non-conformists. His experience, like that of Baptists since the seventeenth century, had been one of exclusion in the area of education. It is not surprising that Clifford expressed strong interest in the issue.[21]

Adhering to a Baptist principle, church-state separation, Clifford asserted that the state had a responsibility to provide a system of universal, free education. Religious education belonged in the church. The 1870 Education Act provided for the first public primary schools. The Church of England retained a position of privilege. A long struggle ensued, culminating in resistance to the 1902 Education Act. This act attempted to rationalize the elementary school system but fell short of the public control that many Baptists and non-conformists wanted. David Lloyd George (1863–1945), Liberal M.P., Welsh lay preacher and future Prime Minister, and George White (1840–1912), Liberal M. P. from Norwich and Baptist Union President in 1903, headed parliamentary opposition. Clifford headed a wider campaign known as the passive resistance movement.

Clifford believed that the new act failed to abolish religious tests and discrimination. In the view of Clifford and others, the act provided public funds for parochial schools. Clifford demanded an end to privilege, including the end of a two-tier system that favored the privileged. George White advocated resistance through refusal to pay school rates. Clifford helped organize a National Passive Resistance Committee. Participants began refusing to pay their rates in the spring of 1903. Offenders were generally summoned to court. This provided them an chance to state their objection. Often, the courts ordered that some of their personal possessions should be seized and auctioned to defray the rate. Usually, a friend of the refuser was on hand to buy back the goods for him. Court cases could be frequent. By March 1906 at the peak of the campaign,

---

[21]D. W. Bebbington, *The Nonconformist Conscience* (London: George Allen and Unwin, 1982) ch. 7; Marchant, 114-45; J. E. B. Munson, "A Study of Nonconformity in Edwardian England as Revealed by the Passive Resistance Movement against the 1902 Education Act" (D.Phil. thesis, Oxford University, 1973).

there had been 70,880 summonses, 2,568 auctions, and 176 persons had been jailed. Although many Baptists did not support the movement, generally for reasons of respect for the law or non-involvement in politics, many did. By the outbreak of the First World War, Clifford had appeared in court forty-one times.[22]

When delegates gathered in London for the first Baptist World Alliance congress in 1905, the campaign climaxed a long struggle for religious freedom. Amidst thunderous applause, David Lloyd George highlighted the campaign. "You have too few men of Dr. Clifford's sort. [applause] Dr. Clifford instead of leading a brave army of 60,000 passive resisters, as he now is, ought to be leading 600,000 [applause.]" Delegates hailed Clifford as a hero of a world battle against aggression, superstition, and tyranny.[23]

Clifford's tactic of passive resistance served as an early model for Gandhi as he developed strategies of *satyagraha*.[24] Gandhi learned about the passive resistance movement in South Africa from two Baptists, Frederick Brotherton Meyer (1847–1929) and Joseph James Doke (1861–1913).[25] Doke first visited South Africa in the early 1880s, but he returned to England where he served as pastor of Chudleigh Baptist Church (1887–1888) and City Road Baptist Church, Bristol (1889–1894) before undertaking missionary work in New Zealand. In 1901, without a regular charge, Doke returned to Britain and took an interest in the controversy over the Education Act. Although he identified with the movement, it is unlikely that circumstances allowed him to be a passive resister.

---

[22]Bebbington, *Nonconformist Conscience*, 144.

[23]J. H. Shakespeare, ed., *The Baptist World Congress, London, July 11–19, 1905* (London: Baptist Union Publication Department, 1905) vii, 39.

[24]The word means truth force. In *The Story of My Experiments with Truth*, trans. Mahadev Desai (Washington, D.C.: Public Affairs Press, 1948) 389, Gandhi recounts coining the expression to describe nonviolent struggle and briefly mentions learning of the passive resistance movement in England.

[25]F. W. Boreham, *The Man Who Saved Gandhi. A Short Biography of John Joseph Doke* (London: Epworth Press, 1948); William E. Cursons, *Joseph Doke, The Missionary-Hearted* (Johannesburg: Christian Literature Depot, 1929); James D. Hunt, *Gandhi and the Nonconformists: Encounters in South Africa* (New Delhi: Promila and Company, 1986).

In 1903, Doke began a ministry in Grahamstown, Cape Colony. In November 1907, he moved as minister of Central Baptist Church to Johannesburg. Doke's arrival there coincided with one of Gandhi's campaigns. In part out of curiosity, Doke met Gandhi and offered to assist his cause in Britain. This initial encounter led Doke to go to court on 10 January 1908, when Gandhi was convicted for the first time of a capital offense and sentenced to imprisonment. With six other clergy Doke condemned British injustice. A portion of a sermon on the subject appeared in *Transvaal Leader*.[26]

As Gandhi's campaign continued, many acknowledged Doke as Gandhi's leading advocate in the white community. On 10 February 1908, when Gandhi was assaulted, the Dokes took him into their home for a period of convalescence. A few weeks later, the Dokes had another house guest. F. B. Meyer, Baptist Union president in 1906 and at the time President of the Free Church National Council, had come to South Africa on a four-month tour to survey the work of the free churches and Y.M.C.A.s. Doke introduced Gandhi to Meyer, who formed a high estimate of Gandhi. Doke and Meyer shared with Gandhi the story of the passive resistance movement. Later, Doke published the first biography of Gandhi, while Meyer wrote an account of meeting Gandhi.[27] These books introduced Gandhi to British non-conformists and contributed to Gandhi's growing fame.

Towards the First World War and Its Aftermath

While we pick up the story of Baptist response to the First World War in other chapters, we must briefly mention Clifford's peace activism after the Anglo-Boer War. The failure of the "stop the war" movement had a sobering effect on Clifford but did not deter him from engaging in a wide range of peace activity. He warned against materialism and militarism. He protested the martyrdom of missionaries in China, Belgium's atrocities in the Congo, Turkish atrocities in Macedonia, and the loss of

---

[26]Hunt, 104–106, reprints the text in full.
[27]Joseph J. Doke, *M. K. Gandhi. An Indian Patriot in South Africa* (London: London Indian Chronicle, 1909); F. B. Meyer, *A Winter in South Africa* (London: National Council of Evangelical Free Churches, 1908).

franchise by blacks in South Africa. In 1908, Clifford addressed three conferences on the subject of peace. Each speech expressed Clifford's vision of Christians building a more peaceful world based on the pattern of life of Jesus Christ. In May, Clifford concluded his talk to representatives of the churches of Britain and Germany with optimism that the day was at hand when sword shall be turned into ploughshare, the spear into pruning hook, and people shall not learn war any more. In August, Clifford affirmed,

> We are committed to the extermination of war and of the spirit that breeds it. . . . War is directly opposed to the spirit and teachings of Christ. He is the Prince of Peace. His kingdom is the kingdom of peace, and this Baptist brotherhood is pledged in His name and in every land to fight against the spirit of militarism, and whilst nations are everywhere preparing armies and navies, inventing and multiplying new engines of slaughter, we must by prayer and speech and example do our utmost to secure peace on earth and goodwill among men.[28]

As late as 3–4 August 1914, Clifford and James Henry Rushbrooke were in Constance, Switzerland for a meeting of church leaders to discuss peace. The conference collapsed as the war began, but it did give birth directly to the World Alliance of Churches for Promoting International Friendship, an important element in later ecumenical peace efforts, and indirectly to the International Fellowship of Reconciliation.

With the outbreak of war, Clifford concluded reluctantly that the war was necessary. He helped draft a manifesto that supported Britain's war effort while calling on Baptists to pray for a return to peace. Frequently, he defended the war in print.[29] However, he opposed conscription and supported the No Conscription Fellowship. Looking beyond the war to

---

[28] *Baptist Times*, 4 September 1908, 611–14 for Clifford's address to the European Baptist Congress in Berlin. Also, *Peace and the Churches. Souvenir Volume of the Visit to England of Representatives of the German Christian Churches May 26th to June 3rd, 1908* (London: Cassell, 1908) 206; *Official Report of the Seventeenth Universal Congress of Peace* (London: National Council of Peace Societies, 1909) 88-92 for Clifford's address.

[29] *Our Fight for Belgium and What It Means* (London: Hodder and Stoughton, 1914); *The War and the Churches* (London: James Clarke, 1914).

future efforts at reconciliation, Clifford pioneered a movement of brotherhood to ensure that war should never again ravage Europe.[30]

Conclusion

It is impossible in these pages to give a full account of the life of John Clifford. His story is replete with false optimism and spiritual desolation. Did he fail? Given the extent of his exertions against war and for peace, this is a legitimate question. The movements he engendered against the Anglo-Boer War and for Anglo-German cooperation did not prevent the outbreak of any war or hasten the end of hostilities. Clifford's efforts did have some effect. In the case of the Anglo-Boer War, Clifford helped to provoke a widespread reaction against the government, which was defeated in subsequent elections. Politically, the stop-the-war campaign contributed to the re-emergence of the Liberal party as a parliamentary force and to a re-appraisal of Britain's role in the world. As a religious leader, Clifford confronted serious issues at the level of public debate. He rallied conscience against oppression. He steered Baptists into the twentieth century. These were not minor accomplishments.

Baptists and others did not always agree with Clifford, but they paid tribute to him for his moral courage. In an address as president of the Baptist Union, William Cuff (1841–1926) stated, "Was there ever such a Baptist in all our history as Dr. Clifford? We all admire his multitudinous gifts . . . [even] when we are compelled to differ from some things he may hold dear."[31] After his death, he was remembered as a friend of humanity.[32]

---

[30]Clements, "Baptists . . . Outbreak of the First World War."

[31]Koss, xxxviii; Davey, 185; Bentley Brinkerhoff Gilbert, *David Lloyd George. A Political Life* (London: B.T. Batsford, 1987) v. 1, 192; *Baptist Times and Freeman*, 27 April 1900, supplement.

[32]*John Clifford Will Speak. Selections from His Discourses* (1973).

Chapter Six
James Henry Rushbrooke (1870–1947)

An Introduction to Rushbrooke's Life

In Bethnal Green east of London, James Henry Rushbrooke was born on 29 July 1870, the eldest of seven children of Sarah and James Rushbrooke.[1] In 1873, his father became station-master at Thorpe-le-Soken, Essex, where Rushbrooke grew up. Raised in a working-class family, Rushbrooke inherited from his parents a passion for justice and a commitment to radical politics.

From an early age, Rushbrooke had to support himself. In 1875, he went off to London, took an office job, and came under the influence of John Clifford. In a sermon preached at Westbourne Park Baptist Church on the occasion of the centennial of Clifford's birth, Rushbrooke recalled his conversion:

> John Clifford . . . was my "father in God." When I first came to Westbourne Park as a raw country youngster of fifteen, I should not have called myself a Christian, but his preaching gripped me. I recall, as if it were yesterday, the Sunday evening and the very spot where, as I walked down the gallery stairs after the service, the conviction suddenly came that I had made the great surrender and stood in a new relation to Jesus Christ.[2]

---

[1] Basic biographical data are found in the obituary in the *Baptist Handbook* (1948) 286; Ernest A. Payne, *James Henry Rushbrooke 1870–1947. A Baptist Greatheart* (London: Carey Kingsgate Press, 1954).

[2] James Henry Rushbrooke, "John Clifford, Pastor, Social Reformer, National Leader, First President of the Baptist World Alliance," *Baptist Quarterly* 11 (1942): 288; H. Edgar Bonsall and Edwin H. Robertson, *The Dream of an Ideal City. Westbourne Park 1877–1977* (London: Westbourne Park Baptist Church, 1978).

Clifford's courageous witness against social injustice inspired Rushbrooke. He took part in Clifford's institute for men. In 1895, a year after he married Kate Partridge, his young wife died in childbirth along with their infant child. Shattered, he received pastoral care from Clifford, who encouraged Rushbrooke to enter the ministry. Taking up the challenge, Rushbrooke trained first at Midland Baptist College, Nottingham, then, from 1899–1901, at Berlin with Adolph von Harnack (1851–1930), leader in the pre-war German peace movement and in liberal theological circles.[3] During these years Rushbrooke formed a friendship with Newton Marshall (1871–1914), another Baptist peacemaker regarded as a promising scholar.[4]

Rushbrooke returned to England in 1901 and served as pastor of three congregations: St. Mary's Gate, Derby, long a center of General Baptist witness in the Midlands (1902-1907); Archway Road, Highgate, North London (1907–1910); and Hampstead Garden Suburb (1910–1920). People appreciated his preaching and social concern. Already, during his pastorate in Derby, Rushbrooke took up social issues such as temperance and non-sectarian education. During the passive resistance campaign, he helped organize non-payment of school rates.[5] By the 1906 election, he was sufficiently prominent that a local newspaper issued a leaflet that began,

> THE (Rush)BROOK(e)
> With apologies to A. Tennyson.
> A Rushing roaring torrent I
> Abuse can pour out madly,

---

[3]Harnack supported Germany during the First World War. Though not a pacifist, Harnack contributed to recovery of early Christian pacifism through publication of *Militia Christi: The Christian Religion and the Military in the First Three Centuries*, trans. David McInnes Gracie (1905; Philadelphia: Fortress, 1981). Martin Rumscheidt, ed., *Adolf von Harnack. Liberal Theology at Its Height* (London: Collins, 1989); Roger Philip Chickering, "The Peace Movement and the Religious Community in Germany, 1900–1914," *Church History* 38 (1969): 300–11.

[4]Rushbrooke wrote his obituary in the *Baptist Handbook* (1915) 460-62. With Rushbrooke, Marshall helped form a society for fostering friendly relations between Germany and Britain. In one of his six books, *Jesus and the Seekers. The Saviour of the World and the Sages of the World* (London: James Clarke, 1911), Marshall presented Tolstoy as the greatest Christian at the time of his death because of his teaching about non-resistance and righteousness.

[5]*Baptist Times*, 10 July 1903, 481.

All rules and ethics I defy
And go my own way gladly,
For men may come and men may go,
But I go on for ever.[6]

Moving to London in 1907, Rushbrooke continued to give able pastoral leadership and emerged as a rising star in Baptist circles. He became involved in efforts linking British Baptists with Baptists of the world and enabling Baptists to marshal humanitarian responses to the First World War. This culminated in his acceptance of a succession of Baptist World Alliance (BWA) positions: commissioner for Europe (1920-1925); representative to eastern Europe (1925-1928); General Secretary (1928-1939) and President (1939-4197). Most of his publications grew out of these responsibilities.[7] Rushbrooke provided leadership in Baptist efforts promoting Anglo-German friendship. In the following sections we highlight Rushbrooke's contribution to international understanding and reconciliation.

Towards Anglo-German Friendship

Rushbrooke's student years in Germany coincided with the Anglo-Boer War, but other circumstances drew his attention to world affairs. In 1899, a peace congress at The Hague fired his imagination, as did the 1905 London congress of the BWA. The latter event engendered a feeling of unity. Rushbrooke envisioned the dawning of a new era in international cooperation, a coming day when nations would give up their freedom to fight in exchange for the security of global law.

While serving the church in Derby, Rushbrooke married Dorothea Weber, daughter of a German professor. The BWA congress deepened his own commitment to Baptist communities on the continent and exposed the need to strengthen ties among European Baptists. In 1907, he helped negotiate settlement of a dispute among Hungarian Baptists. In 1908, by virtue of having studied in Germany and having a German wife, he was in a unique position to assume a leadership role at the first

---

[6]Payne, 20.

[7]He wrote one book, *The Baptist Movement in the Continent of Europe* (London: Carey Press, 1923). Payne, 87, provides a list of other printed addresses and pamphlets.

European Baptist Congress held in Berlin from 26 August to 3 September 1908. Rushbrooke also helped organize a second European Baptist gathering, held in Stockholm in 1913.

The 1908 gathering drew nearly two thousand delegates. For Rushbrooke, the meetings signalled "Baptist world consciousness," the knitting together of "a holy brotherhood of love," and brightened prospects of universal peace. In a key resolution, the Congress expressed acceptance of the idea that war is contrary to the will of Jesus, urged Baptists to pray for peace and to work against anything likely to cause strife amongst the nations. The resolution concluded by urging Baptists to promote a spirit of unity and love among the nations.[8]

Rushbrooke wanted to involve other British and German churches in the process of promoting international friendship. For some years at various levels, there had been contacts between British and German Christians. Finally, from 26 May to 7 June 1908, 135 representatives of German Lutheran, Roman Catholic, and free churches, including four Baptists, came to the United Kingdom. On the Sunday of the sojourn, Rushbrooke coordinated the opportunity for fourteen delegates to preach from London Baptist pulpits. A resolution adopted in 1908 expressed the resolve of delegates to pursue further contacts.

> We, as representatives of the Christian Churches of Germany and of the United Kingdom, recognising how greatly the world's peace depends upon the amicable relations between our two countries, appeal to all classes in both nations to promote, by their earnest endeavour, a mutual spirit of goodwill and friendship. Our nations are closely allied by the stock from which both nations spring, by the kinship of our Sovereigns, by our history, our long friendship, our mutual indebtedness in Art, Literature and Science, and above all by our common Christianity. We believe that the consciousness of these great traditions is deeply engraved in the hearts of our peoples, and that they endorse

---

[8]Rushbrooke, "The Berlin Congress, Its Significance," *Baptist Times* 28 August 1908, 600-601; *Baptist Times*, 11 September 1908, 631. See Clyde Binfield, *So Down to Prayers. Studies in English Nonconformity 1780-1920* (London: J. M. Dent, 1977) ch. 11; Keith W. Clements, "Baptists and the Outbreak of the First World War," *Baptist Quarterly* 26 (1975): 74-92; Stephen Koss, *Nonconformity in Modern British Politics* (London: Batsford, 1975) ch. 6; Ernest A. Payne, *The Baptist Union. A Short History* (London: Carey Kingsgate, 1959) ch. 10.

our conviction that frank co-operation between us will do much to promote the coming of the kingdom of peace on earth and goodwill among men.[9]

Read today, the text has worrisome features such as its reference to ties of common blood and its undercurrent of nationalism and patriarchy. To Rushbrooke, it signaled a break in momentum leading to conflict. During the reciprocal visit of British Christians to Germany, from 7–20 June 1909, Rushbrooke spoke of the task at hand:

> We . . . resolve to work earnestly and self-sacrificingly for the cause of international friendship . . . we are conscious that when we have worked and testified in the interests of peace, our hope is in God . . . surely our faith is deepened and strengthened knowing Jesus Christ is the King of Peace.[10]

Rushbrooke helped frame resolutions and gave direction to formation of a new organization that took as its name "The Associated Councils in the British and German Empires for Fostering Friendly Relations between the Two Peoples." With the blessing of the Baptist Union, Rushbrooke became a member of the Permanent Committee of the council and editor of the journal published by the British support group. As he launched *The Peacemaker*, Rushbrooke emphasized that the organization had engendered good will and helped prevent the physical horror, economic waste, and irreparable disaster of war.[11]

Over the next three years, the organization claimed modest success, including 4000 members and friendship among those who subsequently created the ecumenical movement and International Fellowship of Reconciliation. In editorial after editorial, Rushbrooke reported encouraging signs such as an enhanced role of the churches in promoting international peace, a growing desire for peace, and strengthened mechanisms to resolve disputes. Ignoring the build-up of arms and the machinations of allies, as well as growing tensions among European states, Rushbrooke anticipated German-British unity, not war.

---

[9]*Peace and the Churches. Souvenir Volume* (London: Cassell & Co., 1908) 139.

[10]James Henry Rushbrooke, in F. Siegmund-Schultze, ed., *Friendly Relations between Great Britain and Germany* (Berlin: H. S. Herman, 1909) 209–10.

[11]*The Peacemaker* 1 (1911): 1-2.

World War I and Its Aftermath

On the eve of the war, Rushbrooke and John Clifford traveled to Constance, Switzerland, for the inaugural conference of the Church Peace Union. Endowed by Andrew Carnegie, the Church Peace Union attempted to unite the churches in their efforts for peace. It was with confidence that Rushbrooke and Clifford returned to the continent for the gathering. Even as threat of war compelled delegates to disperse, they resolved to create the World Alliance of Churches for Promoting International Friendship.[12]

Clifford returned to England. Rushbrooke rejoined his family on the Baltic where they were detained for several weeks. Intervention of influential German friends such as Friedrich Wilhelm Siegmund-Schultze (1885-1969)[13] secured their release. While imprisoned with his family in Germany, Rushbrooke wrote a letter to his congregation expressing his astonishment and sadness at the outbreak of war:

> Pray for me. I need your prayer. Perhaps the shock of this war has fallen on few as heavily as upon me, who had toiled for years on behalf of friendly relations between two nearly-related peoples, and had believed that the Christian faith was strong enough to overcome the suspicions and jealousies that make for war. All seemed but a few weeks ago to promise so well, and now! My personal faith has almost reeled in the presence of the awful fact; and when I exhort you to believe still in the God of peace and love I am exhorting no less my own heart. It is "out of the depths" that we must all cry to Him, whose ways are unsearchable, but who is nevertheless "the God and Father of our Lord Jesus Christ."[14]

---

[12]The next year it changed its name to the World Alliance for Promoting International Friendship through the Churches. For a history, see Charles S. Macfarland, *Pioneers for Peace through Religion* (New York: Fleming H. Revell, 1946).

[13]A founder of the World Alliance, Siegmund-Schultze did social work in German cities. In the 1930s, the government expelled him from Germany for assisting Jews. Failure of the churches to stop the drift to war and inactivity of the World Alliance discouraged him. He devoted his later years to the International Fellowship of Reconciliation. John S. Conway, "Friedrich Wilhelm Siegmund-Schultze," in Harold Josephson, ed., *Biographical Dictionary of Modern Peace Leaders* (Westport: Greenwood Press, 1985) 879-80.

[14]*Baptist Times*, 11 September 1914, 694.

Once they were released, Rushbrooke returned to England. He published a series of articles of his personal experiences under arrest as a "spy." The articles reveal attitudes that would shape Rushbrooke's subsequent approach to the war, including love for German Christians, astonishment at a lack of ethical sensitiveness in German society (evidenced by press censorship) and identification of the Kaiser and other political leadership as responsible for Germany's policies that had brought on the war.[15]

Rushbrooke supported Britain's war effort. He believed that Germany's invasion of Belgium justified Britain's response and blamed the war on Germany's politicians and industrialists. However, he questioned claims that the war was just. Whether the evil engendered would prove a greater or lesser evil had Britain not responded depended on peacemakers redoubling their efforts to ensure realization of the dream of abolishing war. Peace workers must cling to the vision of Isaiah 2 and Micah 4 but confront the fact of human sin with new realism.[16]

Although he was not a pacifist, Rushbrooke supported those who were. He opposed conscription and endorsed the efforts of those in the Fellowship of Reconciliation and No Conscription Fellowship who defended pacifists. Deeply disturbed by war propaganda of the period, he urged Christians resolutely to set themselves against any stimulation of passion or indiscriminate hatred directed against the German people.

Rushbrooke contributed to preparations for the eventual healing of relations between the peoples of Europe as member of the executive of the World Alliance for Promoting International Friendship through the Churches and, from 1915–1920, as editor of its journal *Goodwill*. Early in the war, Rushbrooke concentrated on the causes of war and the misery it engendered. Later, he focused on what he called the "principles of a Christian peace," namely justice, reconciliation, "brotherhood," and "continuous effort to bring all public sentiment and action under the

---

[15]*Baptist Times*, 30 October–11 December 1914. Another British Baptist pastor, Laurance Henry Marshall (1882–1953) was in Germany at the time war broke out. He published an account of his arrest first in the *Baptist Times*, then as *Experiences in German Gaols* (Liverpool: Liverpool Booksellers, 1915).

[16]J. H. Rushbrooke, "Must Wars Continue until the End?," in Basil Mathews, ed., *Christ and the World at War. Sermons Preached in War Time* (London: James Clarke and Co. 1917) 151-59; also in *Goodwill* 2 (1917): 282-86.

control of the mind and spirit of Christ." Through editorials, Rushbrooke urged readers to follow the way of Christ, a way of repentance, prayer, faith, and obedience.

Under his editorship, *Goodwill* gave voice to the thinking of many Christians about conditions necessary for a "just and lasting peace" after the war. "A Creed for Believers in a Warless World" summarized the agenda:[17]

> We believe in a sweeping reduction of armaments.
> We believe in international law, courts of justice and boards of arbitration.
> We believe in a world-wide association of nations for world peace.
> We believe in equality in race treatment.
> We believe that Christian patriotism demands the practice of goodwill between peoples.
> We believe that nations, no less than individuals, are subject to God's immutable moral laws.
> We believe that peoples achieve true welfare, greatness and honour through just dealing and unselfish service.
> We believe that nations that are Christian have special international obligations.
> We believe that the spirit of Christian brotherhood can conquer every barrier of trade, colour, creed and race.
> We believe in a warless world, and dedicate ourselves to its achievement.

Despite optimism manifest in his war-time pronouncements, Rushbrooke and his German-born wife suffered personally during the war. He enjoyed the confidence of most members of his congregation and most leaders of the denomination, but some succumbed to prevailing anti-German sentiment and made life difficult for them. Rushbrooke persevered and helped lay the foundations for post-war relief and reconstruction efforts.

Baptist World Alliance

By the end of the war, Rushbrooke had extensive contacts on the continent. It was natural that the BWA turned to him to undertake a relief mission. For nine weeks in early 1920, he crisscrossed the devastated areas of Europe. The BWA then asked him to act as Commissioner for

---

[17]*Goodwill* 3 (1918): 71; 4 (1921): 172.

Europe (1920–1925). While reluctant to leave his pastorate, he accepted the appointment and, later, other BWA positions. During the 1920s, he administered funds and distributed supplies, encouraged struggling churches (sometimes negotiating on their behalf), and demanded greater freedom of worship and evangelism wherever Baptists experienced persecution.

Elected president of the Baptist Union of Great Britain and Ireland in 1926, Rushbrooke used this opportunity to stress the need for vigilance in three main areas. In his presidential address, he urged that Baptists continue to relieve the victims of disaster, with no denominational bounds to helpfulness; that Baptists recognize their continuing global responsibilities; and that Baptists continue to defend religious liberty at home and in nations that often had only recently become free.

Rushbrooke's efforts in Russia and Rumania took on special significance. During this period, he visited Russia seven times, building up contacts that proved essential later, when the Soviet Union restricted travel to and from the country. Because Russian Baptists held strong pacifist convictions at the time, Rushbrooke ensured that their perspective found a voice within BWA circles.[18]

Organization of relief to Rumania proved especially challenging to Rushbrooke. He undertook several visits there. In 1921, he met Rumanian Prime Minister Take Jonescu and won assurances of religious freedom for Romanian-speaking and other minority Baptist communities. Over a period of many years, the government consistently ignored these guarantees. Rushbrooke never ceased to protest violations of human rights. In many circles, his name came to be synonymous with the struggle for religious liberty in Rumania. For many years, no country figured more prominently among the records of the BWA than Rumania.

After completing a term in Europe, Rushbrooke's exertions on behalf of Baptists increasingly took on a global dimension. This included assisting blacks in southern United States, negotiating the return of German Baptist missionaries to Cameroon, worshiping among the young Christian communities of Asia and South America, and, in 1934, at the fifth BWA congress held in Berlin, helping reintegrate German Baptists into the

---

[18]For example, a commission which studied matters of war and peace gave considerable place to pacifism and conscientious objection. James Henry Rushbrooke, ed. *Sixth Baptist World Congress* (Atlanta: Baptist World Alliance, 1939).

larger Baptist family. During these years of service, Rushbrooke provided wise leadership to the Baptist cause and to that of international peace and reconciliation.

As war again loomed on the horizon, then broke out, Rushbrooke upheld in word, deed, and spiritual strength a vision of healing among the nations. Abandoning plans for retirement, he did not allow his British nationality, nor the death of his wife to undermine his vision of a more peaceful world. "We must restore as speedily as possible the interrupted fellowship," he wrote. Rushbrooke continued to have a prominent role in Baptist and wider ecumenical circles, contributing to a far more restrained response to the war by Christians than had characterized World War I, and helping to formulate peace terms and plans for the post war international order.[19] For nearly two years after the war, until he took ill and suffered a stroke in early 1947, Rushbrooke travelled on the continent, helped initiate the vast relief efforts needed, and ensured that contacts among Baptists and the wider Christian community be restored and strengthened.

Conclusion

How are we to assess this gentle man of peace? James Henry Rushbrooke personally experienced the peace Jesus brings those wounded by sin and war. From his perspective, the sickness of Europe was due to the apostasy of what was Christendom from its master and savior. He called for repentance and amendment of life. He encouraged all Christians to bring good news of physical and spiritual healing to all, Christian and non-Christian alike. Throughout his life, he overcame divisions that artificially separate people. He bridged barriers of class, culture, race, and nationality. He balanced individualism with community. For Rushbrooke, no Christian was an island, and no Christian denomination could stand aloof from the wider Christian community. Unflinching in the face of modern trends such as growth of secularism and the rise of ideologies hostile to the gospel of Jesus Christ, Rushbrooke taught and lived a simple message, summarized as follows: Jesus is our peace and has entrusted to us a ministry of healing and reconciliation.

---

[19]Payne, *Rushbrooke*, 66; *Baptist Union*, 266-67.

Rushbrooke challenged Baptists to ignore neither their wider citizenship among the family of nations, nor their citizenship in God's realm. For Rushbrooke, this dual citizenship defined for the Christian the cost of discipleship in a world ablaze with hatred and tyranny: to accept responsibility for the whole human community; to care for the exiled, imprisoned, harassed, and threatened; and to love one's enemy. While the prophetic vision of Isaiah and Micah will find fulfilment in God's time and way, we are to live as though God's realm of righteousness, peace, and joy is to be established here and now.

Rushbrooke's dream of a warless world collapsed as a result of having to live through two great wars. He recognized that progress towards peace could never be other than tentative. During a lifelong ministry of reconciliation, Rushbrooke never wavered in his commitment to give practical expression to it. Baptists of his day loved Rushbrooke as they loved no other Baptist. He received many awards including honorary doctorates from McMaster University (1921) and Acadia University (1939). Throughout his life, he remained true to sentiments shared before the second BWA congress, at Philadelphia in 1911. He stated that our liberty as Christians is a liberty to become through love, bondslaves of all. Such a love shall yet under God make the church of which we are members "a glorious church, not having spot or wrinkle or any such thing. Father, Thy kingdom come—through Thy church! Thy will be done on earth as in heaven!"[20] We give thanks for Rushbrooke's ministry of love. God needs more Baptist peacemakers like him working for healing among the nations.

---

[20]*The Baptist World Alliance Second Congress, Philadelphia June 19–25, 1911. Record of Proceedings* (Philadelphia: Harper, 1911) 312.

Chapter Seven
Douglas Clyde MacIntosh (1877–1948)

An Introduction to MacIntosh's Life

Douglas Clyde MacIntosh was born on 18 February 1877 and raised in Breadalbane, in rural Ontario.[1] His father, Peter McIntosh, came from Scottish stock and served in a Baptist church as deacon. His mother, Elizabeth Everett, descended from John Cotton, the Puritan divine (1584–1652). As a youth, in the absence of Sunday School, he received religious instruction from his mother. On Sundays, she permitted only Bible stories, *The Pilgrim's Progress*, and similar "Sunday reading." He looked forward to Sundays "as the happiest [day] of the week."[2]

In the summer of 1886, MacIntosh attended a revival meeting in a nearby Presbyterian church. Experiencing "a certain sense of awe and a feeling that it would be very wrong of me not to respond to the invitation," he went forward at the altar call. Soon, he felt he had been manipulated. His "decision" did not give MacIntosh a sense of being

---

[1] Biographical file, Canadian Baptist Archives; D. C. MacIntosh Papers, Manuscript Group No. 30, Special Collections Library, Yale Divinity School, New Haven, Connecticut. MacIntosh wrote two autobiographical essays: Douglas Clyde MacIntosh, "Toward a New Untraditional Orthodoxy," in Vergilius Ferm, ed., *Contemporary American Theology. Theological Autobiographies* (vol. 1, New York: Round Table Press, 1932) and the first chapter of *Personal Religion* (New York: Charles Scribner's Sons, 1942). See also S. Mark Helm, "The Path of a Liberal Pilgrim: A Theological Biography of Douglas Clyde MacIntosh," *American Baptist Quarterly* 2 (1983): 236-55 and 4 (1985): 300-20; Preston Warren, *Out of the Wilderness: Douglas Clyde MacIntosh's Journeys through the Grounds and Claims of Modern Thought* (New York: Peter Lang, 1989).

[2] "Toward a New Untraditional Orthodoxy," 279.

Christian. His newfound Christianity gave way to the "group-spirit and standards of playfellows."

When MacIntosh was fourteen, a student pastor named James Cross,[3] came to the Breadalbane Baptist Church and elicited an interest among young people, including MacIntosh. Later, as MacIntosh recounted the story of his conversion, he recalled a conversation with his mother. MacIntosh wondered if he was a Christian, to which she responded, "If you are a Christian you ought to know it." The narrative continued in his own words:

> [I]mmediately it occurred to me that I was not a Christian at all; I had no inner assurance and I had to admit to myself that there was nothing noticeably Christian about my manner of life. Being now convinced that I was not a Christian, I felt I ought to seek a genuine experience of Christian conversion without further delay. So I decided to go to the meeting that night. But I was extremely anxious to avoid any repetition of the failure which I now felt my first "profession" had been. I was not going to take my stand as a Christian until I could be very sure of my ground.

That night, MacIntosh listened to a sermon on John 3:16. During the meeting, an older person said, "Perhaps there is someone here who is waiting until he feels saved before he will take Christ as his Saviour; but he has no right to expect to feel saved until he is saved, and he cannot be saved until he takes Christ as his Saviour." That was what MacIntosh wanted to hear. He gave the matter no further thought. "I said in my heart, 'I do now take Christ as my Saviour.' I felt that it was a momentous transition, and as I walked home after telling the young minister about it, my heart was full of joy." He called this experience "right religious adjustment."[4]

With restored faith, MacIntosh read the Bible with new interest. He found a circle of Christian friends. By age sixteen, he resolved to enter the ministry. After completing high school, MacIntosh worked for six years on his family's farm. For two years, MacIntosh taught in a one-room school, followed by two years as pastor of a Baptist mission at

---

[3](1858–1922), *Baptist Yearbook* (1922) 90; brother of the theologian George Cross (1862–1929), a close friend of MacIntosh during a teaching career at Rochester Theological Seminary.

[4]"Toward a New Untraditional Orthodoxy," 281-82; *Personal Religion*, 157-62.

Marthaville, near Petrolia in western Ontario. At this stage of his theological journey, he shared major elements of Baptist evangelicalism: the Bible as the revealed Word of God, certainty of God's existence and of the knowledge of God in Christ, religious liberty, democratic polity, mission, and social concern.

MacIntosh began to explore empirical philosophy, the subject on which his intellectual reputation rested. In 1899, he undertook formal studies, first at McMaster University, from which in 1903 he received a Master's degree, and later at the University of Chicago, which in 1909 awarded him a doctorate. For a year, he taught at McMaster. Although MacIntosh served summer pastorates at Thornbury Baptist Church in the Owen Sound Association, it was not until 1907 that he was ordained into Christian ministry at Hyde Park Baptist Church, Chicago. From 1907–1909, he launched departments of Bible and systematic theology at Brandon College, Manitoba. Called in 1909 to Yale University, New Haven, Connecticut, MacIntosh spent the balance of his career there, first as assistant professor and, from 1916–1942, as Dwight Professor of Theology and Professor of Philosophy.

Through his publications, teaching, and care for students, MacIntosh became one of the most prominent and loved theologians in North America.[5] He helped shape a future generation of scholars, including Roland Bainton, H. Richard Niebuhr, Reinhold Niebuhr, and Albert Outler. Sixty of his former students became professors of philosophy.[6] Yale church historian Roland Bainton summarized his legacy in these words:

> Douglas MacIntosh was one of the giants of the faculty in my days as a student and junior colleague. As the teacher of systematic theology he combined the

---

[5]In addition to books discussed elsewhere in this chapter, MacIntosh wrote *The Reaction against Metaphysics in Theology* (Chicago: University of Chicago, 1911; his Ph.D. dissertation); *The Problem of Knowledge* (New York: Macmillan, 1915); *Theology as an Empirical Science* (New York: Macmillan, 1919); *The Reasonableness of Christianity* (New York: Charles Scribner's Sons, 1925); *The Pilgrimage of Faith in the World of Modern Thought* (Calcutta: University of Calcutta, 1931).

In *Yale and the Ministry* (New York: Harper and Brothers, 1957) 233, Roland Bainton made MacIntosh come alive as a "student's teacher." He related to students as "three thousand" favorite sons and daughters.

[6]Warren, Preface.

three strands which have been woven into the fabric of instruction in this school: pietism, rationalism and social concern. In accord with the pietism of his Baptist heritage he would go with students on evangelistic tours and regularly taught a Bible class in the First Baptist Church.[7]

World War I

After the outbreak of World War I, MacIntosh voluntarily sought appointment in the Canadian Army. At the time, he believed in the justice of the Allied cause and the necessity of fighting a "war to end war." In 1916, he saw service at the front as a chaplain. He exhorted the men to do their duty for their country and for the future welfare of humanity, even when it meant making the supreme sacrifice of giving and taking life. Returning to Yale in 1917, he spoke in support of the Allies. In 1918 he returned to the front in France as a Young Men's Christian Association worker and ministered to United States forces.[8]

By the end of the war, MacIntosh was deeply troubled. During the war, he had talked with soldiers who, in their fidelity to duty or superstition, seemed to abandon ideals that had led MacIntosh to serve. In a book written after the war, MacIntosh wrote,

> There are two kinds of religion . . . first, devotion to the divine Ideal, that is to an ideal of such absolute value that it is worth living for, and may even prove on occasion worth dying for; and second, dependence upon the divine Being or Power, that is, upon the superhuman reality which man has a right to regard as the ultimate objective Factor in his experience, that upon which he is absolutely dependent. Devotion to the divine Ideal we may call *fundamental religion*, and dependence upon the divine Being with reference to some desired experience, *experimental religion*.[9]

---

[7]Roland H. Bainton, "Reflections on the Life and Work of Professor MacIntosh," Yale Divinity School, 13 February 1980 (program). In *Yale and the Ministry*, 228, Bainton recalled a contest among the Yale faculty to determine who knew the English Bible the best. MacIntosh achieved the highest score.

[8]MacIntosh, "Toward a New Untraditional Orthodoxy," 307.

[9]Ibid, 309, *ital* in text. *God in a World at War* (London: George Allen and Unwin, 1918) 58.

MacIntosh concluded that war was incompatible with transcendent values of experimental, or experiential, religion. War made it impossible to live out the Golden Rule.

MacIntosh pondered issues such as the problem of evil, the nature of human freedom, and how to live responsibly. Gradually, he came to believe that killing one's "enemy" was not Christian, that wars never settled anything, and that it was highly immoral for an individual "to promise beforehand to support what he may have to regard at the time as an unnecessary and immoral war."[10] Disillusioned, he repented his ready advocacy of the war. A decade later, these hesitations catapulted MacIntosh into a struggle over the issue of conscientious objection to war.

Citizenship and Conscience

As early as 1910, MacIntosh declared his intention to become an American citizen. War prevented MacIntosh from completing the process. On 18 February 1925, he filed a declaration of intent to become a citizen. Two years later, he submitted in district court a petition for naturalization accompanied by the proper certificates, affidavits of witnesses, and answers to questions. To question 22, "If necessary, are you willing to take up arms in defense of this country?" MacIntosh wrote on the form, "Yes, but I should want to be free to judge of the necessity."[11] Finally, on 10 June 1929, MacIntosh had a preliminary hearing before a naturalization examiner. On 24 June 1929, MacIntosh submitted additional information, including a memo of his war record and elaboration of the interpretations that he put to the question. The judge, a patriotic Baptist named Burrows, asked what MacIntosh meant by his statement. MacIntosh testified:

> I said I was not a pacifist. . . . I said that even if my country were to engage in what I had to regard as an unjustified war, I would be anxious not to do anything that would injure my country, but rather to serve in some other way than by bearing arms or supporting and defending the bearing of arms.

---

[10]"Toward a New Untraditional Orthodoxy," 308-309.
[11]Oversize scrapbook, MacIntosh Papers, Boxes 88-91.

Asked what would happen if people generally took the same stand, MacIntosh replied:

> I said I thought it would not be a bad thing for the country if people generally were to put first allegiance and obedience to God (that is to what is morally right and for the highest well-being of mankind) and next to that and before private interests, their allegiance to their country.[12]

That day, there were 186 applicants for citizenship. Of these, 180 were admitted while six were debarred. Of the latter, one had not been long enough in residence, another had failed to bring two competent witnesses and three, in answer to questions, had been previously arrested. The sixth was MacIntosh.

Immediately, his principled statement stirred public attention. Harry Emerson Fosdick, then pastor of Park Avenue Baptist Church, New York, wrote MacIntosh that he considered the petitioner's views "as worthy of the best traditions of old-fashioned American independence and patriotism." Roger Baldwin of the American Civil Liberties Union wrote, "Your position strikes squarely for the right of a citizen to have a conscience at all." Not all comment was positive. An American Legion post questioned the fitness of MacIntosh to teach American youth.[13]

At the time, there were provisions of some state laws and constitutions, as well as various acts of Congress, which gave United States citizens the right to be excused from bearing arms or from military service based on conscientious religious scruples. Judge Burrows based his ruling on the Naturalization Act of 29 June 1906, which required an applicant for citizenship to declare under oath, before admission, that he or she would support and defend the Constitution and laws of the United States against all enemies. He concluded that MacIntosh was not "attached to the principles of the Constitution of the United States" and

---

[12]*Ibid.* In a supplementary statement for the information of the judge, MacIntosh stated, "I am willing to pledge full loyalty, as I understand loyalty, to my country. By this I mean that I recognize the duty of placing the true well-being of my country above all private and selfish interests, and that I would strive to act in accordance with this ideal. But I do not recognize any duty to place the outward prosperity or military success of my country above the true well-being of humanity."

[13]Letters and newspapers clippings, MacIntosh Papers. As the case proceeded through the courts, it generated documentation, which MacIntosh meticulously filed.

that the oath MacIntosh was willing to take, as he interpreted it, was not the oath required of him by law.

MacIntosh sought legal counsel. During the proceedings that followed, John William Davis (1873–1955), 1924 Democratic Party Presidential candidate and one of the outstanding lawyers in the country, represented MacIntosh. Davis saw Judge Burrows' decision as a "damn absurdity." Davis stated,

> The idea that a priest in his cassock, a nurse in her gown, a woman with her children hanging to her skirts, and a paralytic in his chair must all swear to bear arms before they become citizens reduces the process of naturalization to an absurdity.[14]

Along with parallel cases involving Marie Averill Bland and Rosika Schwimmer,[15] MacIntosh's legal battle generated enormous interest. By virtue of advancing age, MacIntosh was not likely ever to be conscripted into the armed forces. By virtue of temperament, MacIntosh was not likely ever to threaten the United States. A Circuit Court of Appeals of three federal judges upheld MacIntosh on the grounds that the rights of conscience are unalienable, which a citizen need not surrender and a legislature or society cannot take away.[16]

On appeal by the government, the United States Supreme Court agreed to hear the case. On 28 May 1931, by vote of 5-4, the Supreme Court sustained the original decision of Judge Burrows. Justice George Sutherland (1862–1942) wrote the majority opinion denying MacIntosh the right of citizenship. Sutherland argued that MacIntosh offered to take the oath of allegiance with an unacceptable qualification that the question whether the war is necessary or morally justified must, so far as his support is concerned, be conclusively determined by reference to his own opinion. Sutherland argued,

---

[14]William H. Harbaugh, *Lawyer's Lawyer: The Life of John W. Davis* (New York: Oxford University Press, 1973) 291. Harbaugh discusses the case on 281-97, 410–11.

[15]Editorial, "Conscience versus Citizenship," *Literary Digest* June 6, 1931; Edith Wynner, "Rosika Schwimmer," in Harold Josephson, ed., *Biographical Dictionary of Modern Peace Leaders* (Westport: Greenwood Press, 1985) 862-65.

[16]MacIntosh v. United States, 42 F. (2d) 845 (C.C.A., 2d, 1930).

> When he speaks of putting his allegiance to the will of God above his allegiance to the government, it is evident, in the light of his entire statement, that he means to make *his own interpretation* of the will of God the decisive test. . . . We are a Christian people according to one another the equal right of religious freedom, and acknowledging with reverence the duty of obedience to the will of God. But, also, we are a nation with the duty to survive; a nation whose Constitution contemplates war as well as peace; whose government must go forward upon the assumption, and safely can proceed upon no other, that unqualified allegiance to the nation and submission and obedience to the laws of the land, as well those made for war as those made for peace, are not inconsistent with the will of God.

Chief Justice Charles Evans Hughes (1862–1948), a Baptist layperson, wrote the minority opinion. He maintained that freedom of conscience implies respect for an innate conviction of paramount duty. He continued,

> The battle for religious liberty has been fought and won with respect to religious beliefs and practices which are not in conflict with good order. . . . There is abundant room for enforcing the requisite authority of law as it is enacted and requires obedience, and for maintaining the conception of the supremacy of law as essential to orderly government, without demanding that either citizens or applicants for citizenship shall assume by oath an obligation to regard allegiance to God as subordinate to allegiance to civil power.[17]

In many quarters, the outcome of the case elicited outrage. Tersely John Davis wrote, "Dear Dr. MacIntosh: I blush for my country." In cooperation with much of the religious press of the time, *Christian Century* lobbied unsuccessfully for remedial action.[18] Editorial sentiment was divided. For *The New York Times*,

> The MacIntosh case addressed the principle, contained in the law, that naturalization cannot be granted to an alien who professes the slightest scruple about ever doing military duty. This is the law, but whether under Chief Justice

---

[17]*Ital* in text; United States v. MacIntosh 283 U.S. 605, 51 Sup. Ct. 570 (1930). Joseph Tussman, ed., *The Supreme Court on Church and State* (New York: Oxford University Press, 1962) 51-64; Anson Phelps Stokes, *Church and State in the United States* (vol. 3, New York: Harper, 1950) 271-73.

[18]Davis to MacIntosh, 26 May 1931, MacIntosh Papers; "Citizenship and Conscience. What Shall American Citizens Do with the Supreme Court's Decision in the MacIntosh Case?," *Christian Century* (20 January 1932).

White's famous "rule of reason" it ought to be applied to a man like Professor MacIntosh is still open to doubt.[19]

The New York Evening Post gave another reading of opinion:

> The citizens of this republic must rejoice that its Supreme Court has denied citizenship to . . . MacIntosh and Marie A. Bland, a war nurse. They were barred because they refused to bear arms in defense of the United States unless they approved of the war in which she happened to be engaged. These people seem to us most undesirable citizens. They may not consciously be a spearhead for a pacifistic attack upon the military defense of this country, but their respectability lends itself admirably to that purpose. . . . Under the arrogant plea of the two Canadians, we would be utterly helpless to defend ourselves.[20]

Prohibited by Davis, as a condition of his taking on the case, from commenting on the case in public, MacIntosh had said or written little about the litigation. Once the highest court in the country rendered its decision, MacIntosh could express himself more freely. He supported campaigns for disarmament, and wrote on pertinent issues.[21] In one article, MacIntosh asked:

> Is there any state in the world to-day which can be said to have definitely adopted as its guide in international relations this obvious ethical principle of the greatest and highest good of all concerned and especially of the future of humanity? And even if governments were honestly to give this principle public endorsement, would they and future administrations always strive faithfully to be true to it? And even if they did, would they always use good judgement as to what true well-being is and how best the well-being of humanity may be secured? In each instance the obvious answer must be No, or at least, Most probably not.

MacIntosh also raised fundamental questions about peace and war.

> I hesitate to pledge myself to an absolute or unconditional pacifism. I have a good deal of respect for absolute pacifism when it is the expression of the guess that the most effective way of working for the future peace of the world is to make an absolute declaration beforehand that under no possible circumstances

---

[19] 26 May 1931.
[20] Ibid.
[21] "Professor MacIntosh Believes Disarmament Both a Personal and a Scientific Problem," *Yale News*, 23 November 1931.

will one bear arms or support the bearing of arms. But I have never been able to feel sure that under no possible future circumstances will the use of military or naval force be necessary for the welfare of humanity.

Nonetheless, he observed, there are guiding principles.

> There is a vast difference between a just cause and a just cause *for war*. It does not necessarily follow, because China has a just cause for complaint against Japan, that she is or would be morally justified in declaring war or committing acts of war against Japan. A war may be morally unjustified for any one of several reasons. (1) Its cause may be unjust; or (2) while its cause may be just all possible ways of securing justice without going to war may not have been exhausted; or (3) it may be improbable that justice will be secured by war; or (4) it may be better to suffer many an injustice rather than to cause the injustice and other dread consequences that would be involved in going to war. In fact, modern war being what it is, a tremendous burden of proof must rest upon an individual who advocates or any government which undertakes in our day the waging of even a so-called "defensive" war.[22]

I have quoted this article at length because it provides a rationale for a position known as "selective conscientious objection." Within the framework of just war thought, this position encourages objection to specific wars on grounds of conscience. From Augustine to Hugo Grotius, proponents of just war theory had shared with pacifists concern for moral reform, for limiting war, and for rendering the conduct of war more just. They did not intend to endorse all wars. Yet governments on every side in every war consistently defended their cause as just. MacIntosh now challenged this abuse of just war theory.

By experience and study, MacIntosh had come to recognize the bankruptcy of debate as to whether wars are just or not. He recognized that he—and virtually everyone else—had justified the First World War too easily. Now he sought a middle ground between absolute pacifism and blind nationalism.

In 1939, MacIntosh explored these ideas at length. In a book on ethics entitled *Social Religion*, he wrested with the question, was Jesus a pacifist? He concluded that Jesus repudiated a messianic war, not merely because he was convinced that any military attempt against Rome

---

[22]*Ital* in text. Douglas Clyde MacIntosh, "Conscience and War," *Religion in Life* 1 (1932): 163-68; also in *Crozer Theological Seminary Bulletin* 24 (1932): 133-40.

would end in failure but because he regarded war as inherently evil, a violation of the command to love one's neighbour as one's self. MacIntosh wrote that at the heart of Jesus's proclamation of God's messianic realm was forgiveness and love of enemy. Writing at a time of growing menace of war, he believed that there was a need for strengthened instruments of collective security. His suggestions for an "American peace program" included a call for a radically reconstructed League of Nations and for a conference at Geneva to initiate creation of an international police force, disarmament, a programme of economic or military sanctions against aggressors and global economic justice.[23]

At least twice during World War II, MacIntosh returned to these themes. In the preface to *The Problem of Religious Knowledge*, he wrote of the "present darkly ominous world situation." He hoped that religion at its best would be able to contribute to an ultimate solution of the world's problems. However, he expressed scepticism whether the use of force in international relations in order to "put an end to the use of force in international relations" would prove any more effective in 1940 than the rhetoric of a "war to end war" between 1914–1918. Rhetorically, he asked, "Must we not have recourse to something better than the attempt to overcome evil with evil?" MacIntosh responded by quoting Bunyan's *Pilgrim's Progress*: "He who would valiant be, 'Gainst all disaster, Let him in constancy, Follow the Master."[24]

In his last published work, *Personal Religion*, MacIntosh continued to steer a middle course between pacifist renunciation of the war and unthinking support for war. He focused on the need for Christians to find alternatives to war. War was a dangerous means if the welfare of humanity is ultimately to be served and conserved. Christians must offer themselves as agents of God's reconciling love.[25]

The MacIntosh ruling established legal history. On a number of occasions, other defendants challenged to have it overturned. For fifteen years, judicial opinion did not change. Then, in 1946, a case came before the United States Supreme Court involving James Louis Girouard, a

---

[23]*Social Religion* (New York: Charles Scribner's Sons, 1939) 67-77 on the pacifism of Jesus; 129-30 on eschewing vengeance and loving one's enemy; Section 4, 133-91, on prevention of war.

[24]*The Problem of Religious Knowledge* (New York: Harper and Brothers, 1940) viii.

[25]*Personal Religion*, esp. 358-62.

Canadian Seventh-Day Adventist who was willing to enter the army but only as a non-combatant. The court reversed its earlier rulings. With three justices dissenting, Justice William Orville Douglas (1898–1980) wrote a majority opinion stating that the precedents of the Schwimmer, MacIntosh, and Bland decisions "do not state the correct rule of law."[26]

John Davis, who never ceased to take an interest in the case, immediately contacted MacIntosh to inquire if he still desired United States citizenship. His wife replied that because of a stroke MacIntosh suffered in 1942, he could not pursue the matter again. Moreover, he was at heart a Canadian. The ancient loyalty prevailed. A year later, Roger Baldwin proposed that a private member bill should be introduced in Congress to grant Schwimmer, MacIntosh, and Bland citizenship. Again, Mrs. MacIntosh indicated that her invalided husband was not in a position to follow up. MacIntosh died on 6 July 1948. A recent attempt to have Congress grant MacIntosh citizenship posthumously did not succeed.[27]

Conclusion

Douglas Clyde MacIntosh stood for freedom of conscience. Judging from many letters he received critical of his stand, one observes that he suffered for his convictions. Editorials and letters that vilified him deeply hurt him. The Supreme Court decision disappointed him and shocked his supporters. United States officials harassed MacIntosh during some visits to and from Canada.[28]

At the same time, MacIntosh derived satisfaction from public support and a simple fact. Of the thirteen federal judges who passed judgment on his case, seven decided in his favour. He lost his case by virtue of the quirk in which these thirteen judgments were distributed. Many honoured him for his courage through his three-year ordeal.[29]

---

[26] Girouard v. United States 572 (1945) 7.

[27] Porter Chandler to D.C. MacIntosh, 3 May 1946; Hope Conklin MacIntosh to Chandler, 7 May 1946 (cited by Harbaugh); Roger Baldwin to D. C. MacIntosh, 22 January 1947; Hope Conklin MacIntosh to Baldwin, 29 January 1947; Warren, 39 n. 15.

[28] Interview 29 July 1988, former student Dr. Frank William Waters (1889–1989).

[29] To judge from letters and articles about the case in the MacIntosh papers, he elicited regard from theological friend and foe alike. For example, in a letter of 18 April 1935,

Not a pacifist, MacIntosh believed World War I to have been justified at the time he volunteered for service. War service made MacIntosh a war resister. He had the courage to rethink his views. He came to loathe war. Previously, a few governments recognized in law if not always in practice the principle of conscientious objection, but no government was prepared to adjust conscription laws to the conscience of those who insist in interpreting just war criteria strictly or in giving loyalty to a higher law than the laws of state. By defending himself in the highest court of the land, MacIntosh prepared the way for fundamental changes in United States law and empowered others to yet more far-reaching war resistance and legal challenges.

Moved by the experience of war to resist tides sweeping over and over again nations to war, MacIntosh exemplified two aspects of the Baptist heritage: defence of religious liberty and work for the coming reign of God. At an ordination council shortly before his debilitating stroke, MacIntosh offered this prayer: by word and life, may we rededicate every power to the coming of the Kingdom of God in the world.[30] This is his prayer to those who follow in his footsteps, seeking healing among the nations.

J. Gresham Machen expressed "sorrow for the sake of my country. . . . I feel profoundly humiliated and saddened by the disgrace that was brought upon America through that decision of our highest court. Sad days, I am afraid, are in store for lovers of free institutions."

[30]Ordination Service of Alvin D. Johnson, 17 May 1942.

Section Two

Voices Against War: Positive Peace

In the preceding chapters, we have examined aspects of the Baptist peace heritage through the category of negative peace. We have noted examples of non-resistance, pacifism, and conscientious objection to war. We now explore the heritage of Baptist peacemakers through the category of positive peace. This classification enables us to identify Baptists who have sought to eliminate conditions that engender war, such as human rights violations, illiteracy, infected drinking water, poverty, racism, and slavery. The chapters in this section identify Baptists who extended God's love and reconciliation within a broken world.

Chapter eight introduces pioneers of religious freedom, including two Baptists regarded as pioneers of contemporary concern for human rights. Roger Williams (ca. 1603–1684) was the first pastor of the first Baptist congregation in North America. In England, Gerrard Winstanley (1609–1676) began the Digger movement around 1650.

Chapters nine and ten present anti-slavery campaigners. George Liele (ca. 1750–1828) and William Knibb (1803–1845) contributed to liberation of Jamaica's blacks. Others worked to create a better world for blacks as slavery came to an end. Among blacks who followed the north star to freedom in Canada are those who established the Amherstburg Association of Baptist churches. These churches have empowered women such as Elizabeth Shadd Shreve (1826–1890) and Jennie Johnson (1868–1967) fully to exercise their gifts for ministry.

Missionaries figure prominently in Chapter eleven. Two hundred years after William Carey (1761–1834) inspired the modern missionary movement, it is appropriate to identify aspects of Baptist witness in India, where Dr. Pearl Chute and Dr. Zella Clark pioneered women's medical mission outreach and Dr. Ben Gullison (1905–1987) brought sight to many. Adoniram Judson (1788–1850) began North American Baptist work in Burma (renamed Myanmar in 1989). Isabel Crawford (1865–1961) defended the rights of native Americans and migrant farmers in the

United States and Canada. These missionaries understood Christian mission in holistic terms and sought to heal wounds of both sin *and* injustice.

The Baptist family is global. Chapter twelve acquaints readers with Baptists in Africa, Latin America, and Asia who have animated service, spiritual vitality, and peacemaking. Black missionaries pioneered work in Africa: David George (ca. 1743–1810) in Sierra Leone; Lott Cary (ca. 1780–1828) in Liberia; Joseph Jackson Fuller (1825–1908) and Mammie Johnson (d. 1888) in Cameroon; and Mary Tule (1860–1923) in South Africa. Others who have engendered Baptist peacemaking initiatives include Justino Quispe (1926–1971) in Bolivia; L. Kijungluba Ao (1907–1981) in Nagaland, North India; Matthew Limma in Orissa state, India and Mandakini JeeJatchuch in Andhra Pradesh state, India.

Chapter thirteen recalls the life of a pastor, teacher, and writer, Howard Thurman (1900–1981). In words now quoted on many Christmas greeting cards, Thurman described how he sought to find the lost, heal the broken, feed the hungry, release prisoners, rebuild the nations, and bring peace among people. These remain goals for contemporary Baptist peacemakers.

Chapter Eight
Champions of Liberty

Introduction

In discussing origins of Baptist thinking about peace, war, and non-resistance, we have noted the importance of religious liberty as an essential component of positive peace. In this chapter, we examine two champions of religious liberty, Roger Williams (ca. 1603–1684) and Gerrard Winstanley (1609–1676). As Baptist peacemakers, they provide a link between the vibrant dissent of early Baptists like Busher, Helwys, and Smyth, and that of Baptists who opposed war during the nineteenth century.

The early seventeenth century was a revolutionary period in English history. Hope loomed large. Religious and social idealism were at their height. To many it seemed God was about to accomplish something glorious and marvellous. Roger Williams and Gerrard Winstanley were swept up in the maelstrom. Both drank from a common source of ideas. Both called for complete separation of church and state. Both criticized formal religion as a bulwark of the existing social order. Both helped create parallel but independent Baptist movements in North America and Great Britain. Even though both left the Baptist denomination and became Seekers, they contributed significantly to Baptist life.

Williams taught that salvation was not simply a personal matter but also a catalyst for responsible action in the world. Williams stood unwaveringly for freedom of conscience. He defended ideas at the heart of all peacemaking: religious liberty, democracy, and toleration of Native Indians and non-Christian religions.

Like Williams, Gerrard Winstanley stood unwaveringly for freedom of conscience. Winstanley also advocated economic justice for all. Through his writings on behalf of the "True Levellers," or Diggers, Winstanley envisioned the complete transformation of society. His synthesis of radical economic and political ideas later found expression in Marxist thought.

Roger Williams

Roger Williams was born around 1603 in London.[1] His parents were James Williams, a merchant tailer, and the former Alice Pemberton. At Cambridge, Williams became acquainted with Puritanism. Whatever dissatisfaction he may have felt with the state of religion in the Church of England, Williams did not immediately adopt the dissenting views of his later years. Upon graduation with a Bachelor of Arts degree, he received ordination, served as a chaplain, and, in December 1629, married Mary Barnard.

By that time, Williams had come to a rigid position regarding the need to separate from the Church of England. On 1 December 1630, Williams went into exile to escape certain imprisonment. With his wife, Williams fled to North America. After periods of residence in Boston, Salem, and Plymouth, Williams found himself in trouble with authorities because of his views on the magistracy and ministry. Banished from Massachusetts Bay Colony on 15 October 1635, Williams again found himself in flight. Williams wrote:

> I was unmercifully driven from my chamber to a winter's flight, exposed to the miseries, poverties, necessities, wants, debts, hardships of sea and land in a banished condition. . . . I was sorely tossed for one fourteen weeks in a bitter

---

[1]There are uncertainties regarding details of Williams' life. In 1666, a London fire destroyed his birth record. Many letters are lost. Contemporaries ignored his legacy for fifty years. Primary sources include *The Complete Writings of Roger Williams* (6 vols.; Providence: Publications of the Narragansett Club, 1866–1874; reprinted 1963 in 7 vols, with an introduction by Perry Miller and tracts not in the original collection (New York: Russell and Russell, 1963); Glenn W. LaFantasie, ed., *The Correspondence of Roger Williams* (2 vols.; Providence: Published for the Rhode Island Historical Society by Brown University Press, 1988). Secondary sources include William H. Brackney, *The Baptists* (New York: Greenwood Press, 1988) 282-83; Samuel Hugh Brockunier, *The Irrepressible Democrat, Roger Williams* (New York: Ronald Press Company, 1940); W. Clark Gilpin, *The Millenarian Piety of Roger Williams* (Chicago: University of Chicago, 1979); Edmond S. Morgan, *Roger Williams. The Church and the State* (New York: Harcourt, Brace and World, 1967).

winter season, not knowing what bread and bed did mean . . . exposed to a winter's miseries in a howling wilderness of frost and snow.[2]

Roger and Mary Williams found protection among Native Americans who enabled them to survive. By June 1636, with several friends, they formed the nucleus of a new colony, Providence Plantations.

In 1639, the Salem church officially excommunicated Roger and Mary Williams. Around then, Williams came to Baptist convictions and was baptized "by one Holyman, a poor man late of Salem. Then Mr. Williams rebaptized him and some ten more. They also denied the baptizing of infants and would have no magistrates."[3] Williams helped found the Baptist church in Providence and became its first pastor. Soon, he had doubts about the haste with which he and the others had proceeded. Since only God could act to restore the apostolic church, it was incumbent upon believers to wait patiently until Christ's return. Then Christ would commission new agents and establish the true church. Williams became a Seeker. While he remained theologically a Calvinist, he adhered to no creed or communion.

In 1643, Williams returned to England and received a charter for Providence Plantations. From 1644–1647, he served as its chief officer. From 1648–1649, he was deputy president. Following another sojourn in England, Williams served from 1654–1657 as president of Rhode Island. Subsequently, although he held no official position in the colony, he remained active in its affairs for the rest of his life.

This brief chronology of Roger Williams' life identifies two crucial areas to be considered in greater depth: (1) religious and political views that led to the banishment of Williams from Britain and Massachusetts Bay Colony, and (2) his attitudes towards Native Americans and non-Christian peoples more generally.

By October 1635, when specific charges were lodged against Williams, he had become a strong advocate of views that the authorities found objectionable. First, he denied that the kings of England had any

---

[2]In H. Leon McBeth, *The Baptist Heritage. Four Centuries of Baptist Witness* (Memphis: Broadman Press, 1986) 129.
[3]John Winthrop, *Journal* (James Savage edition, Boston, 1853) I:352-353. Winthrop (1587–1649) was the first governor of Massachusetts Bay Colony. As a contemporary and correspondent of Williams, his *Journal* is an important source.

right to land in British North America. The Native Americans were the true owners. If others desired the land, they had to purchase it from the natives. Secondly, he refused to take oaths in God's name. Thirdly, he urged Christians to withdraw from the Church of England and to shun others who failed to withdraw, even a member of one's own family. Finally, he denied that any civil authority could punish offenses from the first table of the Ten Commandments, which prescribe one's duties to God.[4]

Williams spelled out these views in his most sustained treatise, *The Bloudy Tenent of Persecution, for cause of Conscience, discussed, in A Conference betweene Truth and Peace*, written in haste while Williams sought a charter for Rhode Island in England.[5] In the book, Williams explored twelve propositions, making strong pleas for peace and for separation of church and state. He protested, "first, that the blood of so many hundred thousand soules of *Protestants* and *Papists*, spilt in the *Wars* of *present* and *former Ages* . . . is not required nor accepted by *Jesus Christ* the *Prince of Peace*" and that, "fifthly, All *Civill States* with their *Officers* of *justice* in their respective *constitutions* and *administrations* are proved *essentially Civill*, and therefore not *Judges, Governours or Defendours* of the *Spirituall* or *Christian state* and *Worship*" (3). He concluded that persecution for the cause of conscience is entirely contrary to the Gospel of Jesus, the Prince of Peace (425).

Roger Williams did not concern himself exclusively with his own human rights. With regard to Native Americans, his early experience among them led him to protest against their mistreatment. He did not idealize or romanticize Native Americans. Indeed, he despised their religion and customs. Still, he was prepared to live with them in peace, on equal terms as humans with rights denied to them by some of the more squalid settlers. In a poem, he wrote:

> When Indians hear the horrid filth
> Of Irish, English men;
> The horrid oaths and murders late,
> Thus say these Indians then:

---

[4]*Ibid.*, 128-29.

[5]1644; references are from the text as printed in vol. 3 of *The Complete Writings of Roger Williams*, ed. Samuel L. Caldwell (Providence, 1867).

> "We wear no clothes, have many gods,
> And yet our sins are less;
> You are barbarians, pagans wild,
> Your land's the Wilderness."
>
> Oft have I heard the Indians say,
> "These English will deceive us;
> Of all that's ours, our lands and lives,
> In the end they will bereave us."[6]

In dealing with Native Americans, Williams won their confidence. He mastered several of their languages. He preached to them frequently, entered into mutually favorable trading ventures with them, and sought arbitration when there were disputes. He protested the enslavement of the Pequot Indians and, when he helped formulate the statutes of Providence Plantations adopted in 1652, ensured their freedom even though he did not take similar action with respect to blacks.[7]

With regard to the rights of women, Williams exemplified a progressive stance. He proffered women an independent social status and recognized their religious and civil liberties. Providence became the first government in North America to guarantee constitutionally the rights of women. Once, Williams barred from worship a man who beat his wife severely to prevent her from attending public worship.[8]

Williams was a near pacifist, but he was not a pacifist. As early as the writing of *The Bloudy Tenent* (45) Williams indicated that all carnal weapons should be abandoned in the days of the gospel, as envisioned by the prophets and taught by Jesus and Paul. He wrote that it was impossible "for any Man or Men to maintain their *Christ* by their *Sword*, and to worship a true Christ." He believed adamantly that there could be *no* rationale for imposing religion by force.[9] War was a plague

---

[6]Cited by J. H. Rushbrooke, "Roger Williams: Apostle of Soul-Freedom," *Baptist Quarterly* 8 (1936): 27, originally an address at a tercentenary celebration organised by the American Baptist Historical Society in Philadelphia.

[7]William Warren Sweet, *Religion on the American Frontier. The Baptists 1783–1830. A Collection of Source Material* (New York: Henry Holt, 1931) 77.

[8]McBeth, *The Baptist Heritage*, 130.

[9]Williams to John Endicott, ca. August 1651, LaFantasie, 344. For a fuller treatment of Williams on peace and war, Morgan, 120-26; Arthur H. Buffinton, "The Puritan View of War," *Colonial Society of Massachusetts Publications* 28 (1935): 67-86; and Timothy

of God, along with famine and pestilence, one of the three most dreadful judgments upon humans.[10] Williams rejected misuse of scripture to justify crusades against heretics and infidels. For Williams, this was further evidence of the extent to which Christianity had departed from Christ and inflicted disaster upon humanity.

Williams believed that the state had a responsibility to protect the well-being of its citizens. It was legitimate for the state to engage in defensive war, such as the Indian wars that occurred at the end of his life. Williams reacted bitterly to attacks by Indians on Providence and accepted military action against them.

Williams also believed in a limited right to bear arms. In 1654, while Williams was the colony's president, Rhode Island prepared to institute compulsory militia service because of concern that nothing should disturb the "civil peace." Some members of the congregation Williams had once served as pastor adhered to an absolute prohibition of bearing arms. The issue came to a head when several members of Providence Baptist Church wrote a letter of protest.[11] This letter may have prompted Williams to write his well-known letter comparing human society to a ship at sea. On such a ship, he argued, Protestants, Catholics, Jews, and Turks might exercise liberty of conscience and worship as they pleased. But if the vessel itself became imperiled, the need to save the ship itself superseded individual rights of conscience. In such a case, none of the passengers would have the liberty to exempt themselves from service.[12]

When Roger Williams advanced his ideas about religious freedom and separation of church and state, these were radical ideas, passionately defended and bitterly attacked. He advanced his ideas, believing that they would engender peace, truth, and tranquillity while preventing war.

More than most early Baptist writers, Williams did not promote these ideas simply to further the status of religion. He considered carefully how governments should govern. He was an able administrator. Rhode Island did not become the New Jerusalem of his dreams. Contention and war remained too much a part of society about him. He left to his successors

---

George, "War and Peace in the Puritan Tradition," *Church History* 53 (1984): 492-503.

[10] Williams to John Winthrop, Jr., 17 October 1650, *ibid.*, 325.

[11] See Chapter 1; Brockunier, 225.

[12] LaFantasie, 419-25.

the task of realizing fully his dream of a free church in a free land. He left to God the working out of the healing of the nations.

Gerrard Winstanley

Gerrard Winstanley was born in Wigan, Lancashire. He was baptized on 10 October 1609.[13] His father, Edward Winstanley, dealt in textiles and held Puritan sympathies. In 1605, he faced court charges with his wife for irregular assemblies.

Although biographical details are sketchy, probably Gerrard Winstanley attended grammar school. He learned Latin but eschewed university training to become apprenticed in April 1630 to Sarah Gater of Cornhill, widow of a businessman. In 1637, he became a freeman of the Merchant Taylors' Company. In 1640, he married Susan King and lived as a tradesman in the parish of St. Olave's in Old Jewry. Within three years he was bankrupt. He moved to Cobham, or Walton-up-Thames, where he farmed the estate of his father-in-law, William King. Hard economic times and the political troubles of the time undermined his career as a farmer, as they had his business career.

During the 1640s, Winstanley joined a Baptist congregation and faithfully attended church. Probably, he became a lay Baptist preacher. By the late 1640s, however, he left the main streams of English Baptist life. Winstanley wrote of having gone through the "ordinance of dipping, which the letter of the Scripture doth warrant" but of having come to believe that it is not "the materiall water, but the water of life . . . in

---

[13]From an extensive bibliography, see especially the anthologies edited by Christopher Hill, *Winstanley. The Law of Freedom and Other Writings* (Cambridge: Cambridge University Press, 1983) and by George H. Sabine, *The Works of Gerrard Winstanley* (New York: Russell and Russell, 1965). Among secondary sources, I have drawn from H. N. Brailsford, *The Levellers and the English Revolution* (Stanford: Stanford University Press, 1961); R. E. E. Harkness, "Gerrard Winstanley-An Unknown Baptist," *Chronicle* 9 (July 1946):137-43; T. Wilson Hayes, *Winstanley the Digger. A Literary Analysis of Radical Ideas in the English Revolution* (Cambridge: Harvard University Press, 1979); Christopher Hill, "The Religion of Gerrard Winstanley," *Collected Essays*, v. 2: *Religion and Politics in 17th Century England* (Brighton: Harvester Press, 1986) 185-252.

which soules are to be dipped."[14] He rejected infant baptism as a practice not enjoined by scripture.[15]

Winstanley expressed dissatisfaction with all outward forms of religion.[16] He identified with groups—those reproached as "roundheads, Anabaptists, and Independents" and persecuted by "scoffers" who seek to destroy God's people—within which like-minded seekers explored radical religious ideas. Initially, he did not formally join any movement. In early religious treaties, he expressed the conviction that an invisible communion of Saints had been commanded to observe God's laws of righteousness with the assurance that they would be redeemed by God.[17]

Gerrard Winstanley announced his vision of a coming new age of righteousness and peace in a treatise entitled *The New Law of Righteousness*, which he received in a trance. Responding to an inner voice compelling him to announce God's truth by word of mouth and pen, Winstanley articulated a primitive communitarianism in which the people would work together, eat together, and share together in the fruit of their labour. Among key ideas, he called for equality and an end of privilege, or slavery, including ecclesiastical privilege in such form as mandatory tithes.

In *The New Law of Righteousness*, Winstanley proclaimed a gospel of liberation of the poor. "Know that the cries of the poor, whom thou laieth heavy oppressions upon, is heard." He saw the private accumulation of land in the hands of a few as a source of misery and exploitation and, ultimately, of war. "The poor people by their labours in this time of the first *Adams* government, have made the buyers and sellers of land, or rich men, to become tyrants and oppressors over them." To protect property and preserve privilege, governments form armies, kill, and wage wars.[18]

Winstanley envisioned the perfection of God's realm on earth. The landed poor would receive land and benefit from the fruit of their labour. In poetic language of power and vision, Winstanley wrote of Christ, the restorer, establishing the new heaven and new earth, filling the whole

---

[14]*Truth Lifting Up Its Head above Scandals* (1648) in Sabine, 141.
[15]*Ibid.*, 143-44.
[16]*The New Law of Righteousness* (1649) in Sabine, 162.
[17]*The Saints Paradice* (1648) in Sabine, 93-96.
[18]*The New Law of Righteousness* (1649) in Sabine, 159, 190, 222; cf. Brailsford, 661.

Creation with a "sweet complyancy of love in him, and with him" and of a tree of life bringing forth abundant fruit.[19]

In response to this vision, on 1 April 1649, a group appeared on the common land at St. George's Hill, which lies to the south of the Thames in Surrey. A little later, a second community began at Cobham. These were the first manifestation of the coming new age of peace and righteousness. Inspired by Winstanley, the little band styled itself "The True Levellers," or Diggers. In the broad spectrum of political and religious movements of the day, the Diggers were never more than of negligible size. The group initially numbered approximately a dozen men with their families. The movement grew to over fifty men and their families on eleven acres of waste land.

The Diggers challenged the rights of two manorial lords in the area by squatting on the commons, digging the waste land (hence their name), planting crops, and felling trees from surrounding woodlands. They invited others to join in a common venture to cultivate the land in support for the needy. On 20 April, Winstanley and another leader of the movement, William Everard, appeared before government authorities. Insisting that they recognized no distinctions of rank, they refused to remove their hats. They pleaded that the Diggers did not intend to interfere with private property but rather to empower the poor to provide sustenance for the distressed. Initially, the government did not intervene, but the local populace sought to drive the Diggers off the land. Subsequently, troops were sent twice to suppress them, twice they went to court, and twice they returned. By 1651, the movement ceased to exist.

During that period, however, in a remarkable outpouring of pamphlets, Winstanley gave substance to his understanding of the coming peaceful realm that would bring oppression to an end. Central to Winstanley's understanding of this coming utopia was economic justice for all. He declared that private ownership of land was "rebellion and high treason against the King of Righteousness . . . let this word of the Lord be acted amongst all; work together, eat bread together Acts 4.32."[20]

---

[19]*Ibid.*, 169, 235-36; cf. Hayes, chapters 4-5 on Winstanley's vision of a utopian community in which the earth becomes paradise for all.

[20]*The New Law of Righteousness* (1648) in Sabine, 201.

He declared that it is not possible to be fully human so long as anyone is hungry.[21]

> True Religion, and undefiled, is this, To make restitution of the Earth, which hath been taken and held from the Common people, by the power of Conquests formerly, and so *set the oppressed free*. Do not All strive to enjoy the Land? The Gentry strive for Land, the Clergie strive for Land, the Common people strive for Land. . . . But I affirm, It [the Land] was made for all; and true Religion is, To let every one enjoy it. Therefore, you Rulers of *England*, make restitution of the Lands which the Kingly power holds from us; *Set the oppressed free*; and come in, and honour Christ, who is the Restoring Power, and you shall finde rest.[22]

As conceived by Winstanley, a "Peacemaker" works for justice, endeavours to reconcile hostile parties, preserves the common peace, and, when the laws of peace are broken, shows mercy. He wrote that actions and conversations of the Diggers were based on Jesus' precept, "'Love your enemies, and doe to all men, as you would they should do to you, for this is the very Law and the Prophets.' This is the New Commandement that Christ left behind him. Now if any seem to say this, and does not do this, but acts contrary, for my part I owne not their ways, they are members that uphold the curse." Winstanley envisioned a world in which former enemies would live in peace.[23]

Winstanley abhorred violence. Citing biblical texts, he appealed to free men and women actually to turn swords into ploughshares and spears into pruning hooks. He expected that his communal society would be brought about through passive resistance. He went to prison for nonviolent civil disobedience when he trespassed on lands that he considered common land. No doctrinaire pacifist, Winstanley accepted the need, once a free commonwealth should be established, for an unprofessional militia of citizens in arms to protect the common peace and to resist or

---

[21]*The Law of Freedom, or True Magistracy Restored* (1651) in Sabine, 222.

[22]*A New yeers Gift Sent to the Parliament and Armie* in Andrew Hopton, ed., *Gerrard Winstanley. Selected Writings* (London: Aporia Press, 1989) 81.

[23]*A New-yeers Gift for the Parliament and Armie* (1650) in Hopton, 74; Hill, "Religion of Gerrard Winstanley," 222.

destroy "all who endeavour to keep up or bring in Kingly Bondage again."[24]

Winstanley envisioned the coming of the biblical realm of peace. A new heaven and a new earth were coming, for "the present state of the old World . . . is running up like parchment in the fire, and wearing away."[25] Winstanley's Godly commonwealth did not come to be. After 1660, records indicate that by trade he was a corn farmer and candlemaker. Probably, he died a Quaker. Winstanley and the Diggers left a legacy for peacemakers. Inspired by their vision, Leon Rosselson, a contemporary songwriter, penned verses to "The World Turned Upside Down," which have been used in by campers at Greenham Common and Molesworth in the United Kingdom, and by others:

> In sixteen forty-nine to St George's Hill
> A ragged band they called the Diggers
>   came to show the people's will.
> They defied the landlords, they defied the laws;
> They were the dispossessed reclaiming what was theirs.
>
> We come in peace, they said, to dig and sow.
> We come to work the land in common
>   and to make the waste land grow.
> This earth divided, we will make whole
> So it will be a common treasury for all.
> . . . .
>
> They make the laws to chain us well,
> The clergy dazzle us with heaven or they damn us into hell.
> We will not worship the God they serve,
> The God of greed, who feeds the rich while poor folk starve.
>
> We work, we eat together, we need no swords.
> We will not bow to masters or pay rent to the lords,
> We are free now, though we are poor,
> You diggers all, stand up for glory, stand up now.
>
> From the men of property the orders came.
> They sent the hired men and troopers
>   to wipe out the Diggers' claim,

---

[24] *Law of Freedom*, in Sabine, 573.
[25] *The True Levellers Standard Advanced* (1649) in Sabine, 252.

Tear down their cottages, destroy their corn.
They were dispersed. Only the vision lingers on.

You poor take courage, you rich take care.
This earth was made a common treasury for everyone to share.
All things in common, all people one;
We come in peace. The orders came to cut them down.[26]

Conclusion

Roger Williams and Gerrard Winstanley did not set forth a comprehensive religious system or set of proposals for a better world. Nonetheless, their conception of human rights spread among Baptists and among others in England and New England, influenced eighteenth-century Enlightenment thought, and shaped modern ideas about democracy and freedom.

As part of their legacy, Williams and Winstanley passionately affirmed fundamental freedoms, including freedom of religion. They neither restricted human rights to religious liberties nor confined religious liberties to those of Christians. They understood that freedom includes economic, political, and social freedoms for all.

As Baptists and religious Seekers, Williams and Winstanley believed that we live in an ordered universe with the mandate to bring the world into conformity with biblical teaching. To bring about the necessary transformation, they affirmed that Christians must be active in the world. The power of the state rests upon the will of the people. Properly, the people invest governments with authority, and governments must serve the people as a whole.

In today's world, Williams and Winstanley probably would be surprised to find so much attributed to them. Based on our brief examination of their lives and literary legacy, we may conclude that they would be pleased with the progress made towards realization of their ideas. Still, they would have something to say about our failure fully to realize positive peace.[27] They would still champion the cause of those who struggle

---

[26]*Gentle Angry People. Songs of Protest and Praise* (Stafford: Alliance of Radical Methodists, 1987) 44.

[27]See the suggestive essay by Tony Benn, "The Levellers and the English Democratic

against tyranny of any sort. They would still not confuse any earthly political arrangement with their vision of God's coming realm of peace with justice. They would still affirm the role of non-violent mass movements in achieving change.

In concrete ways, Williams and Winstanley contributed to broad movements of social change. Their writings helped shape modern political theory. Their advocacy of human rights helped bring about a better world. Their defence of economic rights and toleration helped achieve healing of divisions of society. We should not merely celebrate their legacy. Let us seek to perfect the work that they began and which has fallen into our hands.[28]

Tradition," in Rex Ambler and David Haslam, eds. *Agenda for Prophets. Towards a Political Theology for Britain* (London: Bowerdean Press, 1980) 49-60.

[28]See Hill, "The Religion of Gerrard Winstanley," 229.

Chapter Nine
Freedom at Midnight

Although they have not always spoken with one voice, moral clarity, and prophetic power concerning slavery, or involuntary servitude, Baptists have addressed the issue. For some, it was a legal practice forbidden nowhere in the Bible. For Robert Robinson, Roger Williams, and others, slavery was barbarous and unjust. In the nineteenth century, many Baptists came to regard slavery as a matter for condemnation, repentance, and change.

This chapter describes the movement against slavery principally in Jamaica. Chapter Ten explores anti-slavery advocacy in North America with particular reference to blacks who pioneered Baptist witness in Ontario, Canada. In Chapter Eleven, free blacks who established Baptist work in Africa receive attention.

George Liele (ca. 1750–1828)

During the United States War for Independence, many slaves recognized that there was no immediate prospect of liberty and threw their lot in with the British. Among black loyalists, George Liele distinguished himself as a founder of churches in South Carolina and Jamaica and for abolitionist activity.[1]

---

[1] "An Account of the Jamaica Baptists, with Memoirs of Mr. George Liele," *General Baptist Repository* 1 (1802): 229-40; Clement Gayle, *George Liele, Pioneer Missionary to Jamaica* (Kingston: Jamaica Baptist Union, 1982); Edward A. Holmes, "George Liele: Negro Slavery's Prophet of Deliverance," *Baptist Quarterly* 20 (1964): 340-51, 360 and *Foundations* 9 (1966): 333-45; Mary Turner, *Slaves and Missionaries. The Disintegration of Jamaican Slave Society* (Urbana: University of Illinois Press, 1982); Ellen Gibson Wilson, *The Loyal Blacks* (New York: G. P. Putnam's Sons, 1976). For a photograph, see Edward D. Smith, *Climbing Jacob's Ladder. The Rise of Black Churches in Eastern American Cities, 1740–1877* (Washington: Smithsonian Institution, 1988) 32. Some sources spell the name Leile, Lisle.

Liele was the son of Virginia slaves, Nancy and Liele, "the only black person who knew the Lord in a spiritual way in that country."[2] Born into slavery, George Liele belonged to Henry Sharpe, who, prior to 1770, moved to Burke County, Georgia. Sharpe joined the Big Buckhead Creek Baptist Church, where he became a deacon and allowed Liele to attend worship.

In 1773, Liele heard a sermon by the Reverend Matthew Moore. For months he remained under conviction of sin until Moore baptized Liele and accepted him into the predominantly white congregation at Big Buckhead Creek. Moore and Sharpe encouraged Liele and gave him "freedom papers." This allowed Liele to exercise his ministerial gifts. Liele joined a group of believers. They organized a black Baptist church at Silver Bluff, South Carolina, along the Savannah River. The first black congregation in the Americas, the congregation drew up a covenant with twenty-one points, including provision that, "We hold not to shedding of blood; and think ourselves forbidden to go to law with another before the unjust, but settle any matter we have before the saints."[3] Liele never abandoned non-resistance.

Between 1775 and 1778, Liele preached at a number of locations along the Savannah River. After United States troops evacuated Savannah, Georgia, Liele took refuge there and served as pastor of the First African Baptist Church and the First Bryan Baptist Church. After the war, the Sharpe family attempted to reclaim Liele and had him jailed. He produced his emancipation documentation and, with the help of a British officer, purchased one-way passage to Jamaica for himself and his family. He left his ministry in Georgia in the hands of converts Andrew Bryan, Abraham Marshall, and Jesse Peter, who ministered at Augusta, Savannah, and Silver Bluff.[4]

In Jamaica, Liele found employment and began preaching in the evenings in a private home. He thus became the first Baptist foreign missionary—several years before Carey's appointment to India.[5] Liele began

---

[2] Liele to John Rippon, 18 December 1791, Holmes, 340.

[3] "An Account of the Jamaica Baptists," 235; G. W. Rusling, "A Note on Early Negro Baptist History," *Foundations* 11 (1968): 363-64.

[4] Walter H. Brooks, "The Priority of the Silver Bluff Church and Its Promoters," *Journal of Negro History* 7 (1922): 172-96.

[5] Holmes, 344; G. A. Catherall, "Baptist War and Peace. A Study of British Baptist

preaching around Kingston, St. Thomas, St. Mary, and St. Thomas-in-the-Vale. With four refugees from the United States, including his wife and George Gibbs, Liele formed a church at Kingston. During the next few years, Liele baptized over 500 converts and encouraged co-workers Thomas Nicholas Swiggle and Moses Baker, himself converted by Liele's group, to undertake Baptist work elsewhere on the island.

The finances of the Baptist congregations were precarious. Slaves had little money and could barely feed themselves. Liele summarized: "Out of so small a sum we cannot expect anything that can be of service from them; if we did, it would soon bring scandal upon religion."[6] Liele wrote the newly formed British Baptist Missionary Society (BMS) to request monetary support. The prominent pastor John Rippon (1751–1836) responded by collecting and forwarding money for construction of a Baptist meeting house on the island. In 1793, the first non-conformist meeting house opened at Windward Road, Kingston.

For a time, the work prospered. Liele and his congregation made several wise decisions. They bound themselves "to do duty to our King, Country, and Laws, and to see that the affixed Rules [the covenant] are duly observed." They admitted into membership no slaves but those who obtained permission from their owners. The congregation used a bell on the church steeple to call members to worship and give notice to slave owners where their slaves gathered and when they might be expected to return.

Despite such measures, undertaken to allay possible fears of slave owners, Liele experienced maltreatment including verbal abuse, insult, and imprisonment. Seized by authorities in 1797, he spent three years, five months, and ten days in jail. Charged with preaching sedition, he was tried, "But no evil could be proved against him, and he was honourably acquitted." Officials regarded Liele with suspicion and threw him into debtor's prison until members paid off loans incurred for building the chapel.

In 1802 and 1805, the Jamaican legislative assembly passed repressive laws forbidding dissenters, or non-conformists, to preach to

---

Involvement in Jamaica 1783–1865" (Ph.D. thesis, University of Keele, 1990); Leonard Tucker, *"Glorious Liberty." The Story of a Hundred Years' Work of the Jamaica Baptist Mission* (London: Baptist Missionary Society, 1914).

[6]Holmes, 345.

slaves. The Jamaican government did not always enforce the laws vigorously. Abolition by Britain of the slave trade in 1807, blamed on "fanatics and enthusiasts in Great Britain,"[7] however, enraged Jamaica's planter community. Severe persecution took place in the form of whipping and murder. Liele's church closed. Moses Baker's church became a hospital. Liele held his congregation together until 1814 when his persistent entreaties were rewarded by the arrival of the first BMS missionaries. By that time, Liele was responsible for a network of Baptist congregations whose membership numbered around 8,000.

Cooperating with the missionaries, Liele continued his preaching and educational ministry. In 1822, Liele visited Britain and may have met future missionaries to Jamaica, including Thomas Burchell (1799–1846), James M. Phillippo (1798–1879), and William Knibb (1803–1845), destined to become the leading BMS anti-slavery advocate. When Liele died in 1828, Knibb attended his funeral.[8]

BMS Missionaries and the "Baptist War"

As early as 1791, Liele interested British Particular and New Connexion General Baptists in Baptist witness in Jamaica. He was instrumental in recruiting to Jamaica, in 1814, the first British Baptist missionaries. They encountered struggling Baptist congregations, a "native" Baptist element that combined Christian and traditional African religious practices, the opposition of planters, and a hostile climate. Several pioneer workers died of yellow fever, malaria, and other diseases. Gradually, however, the work progressed as the mission established churches and schools at, among others, Kingston, Falmouth, and Spanish Town.

In Britain, the movement against slavery was gaining ground. Having achieved the end of the slave trade on 1 January 1808, abolitionists turned their attention to the issues of enforcement and, ultimately, of

---

[7]Turner, 16.

[8]John Clarke, *Memorials of Baptist Missionaries in Jamaica including a Sketch of the Labours of Early Religious Instructors* (London: Yates and Alexander, 1869) 11. Clarke and other British missionaries acknowledged Liele's role in launching Baptist work in Jamaica. James M. Phillippo, *Jamaica: Its Past and Present State* (1843; London: Dawsons of Pall Mall, 1969) 279-80.

slavery itself. Thomas Fowell Buxton (1786–1845) assumed the role of leader of the cause in Parliament. In 1823, he introduced a resolution that slavery ought to be abolished gradually. An anti-slavery society formed with the object of putting an end to the system.

Although BMS missionaries received instructions forbidding political and secular activity, they stood in a radical tradition of principled resistance to oppression. In Jamaica, they regarded slavery as an evil but initially remained aloof from political involvement. Gradually, they began to advocate reform. After the December 1831 insurrection, they threw themselves fully into the anti-slavery cause.

The career of Thomas Burchell illustrates this progression. Burchell arrived at Montego Bay on 15 January 1824. He found conditions of slavery on the island deplorable and an impediment to evangelism. When, in 1826, health reasons prompted him to return on a visit to Britain, Burchell publicized the situation in Jamaica. He urged the BMS to change its ban on secular activity and preached against an act of the Jamaican House of Assembly, the Consolidated Slave Act, passed on 22 December 1826, which prohibited slaves, "as anabaptists or otherwise," from preaching and teaching. Resolved to ignore restrictions in religious matters and to campaign for amelioration of the system, Burchell asked, "When the laws of men are opposed to the laws of God, which are we to obey?" Failing that, he worked for full emancipation.[9]

In 1824 and again in November 1831, the British government issued Orders-in-Council directing an end of abuses and improvement of the condition of slaves in the West Indies. In Jamaica, planters and the local assembly predictably resisted these measures. The planters objected to any changes. Some renewed talk of calling up the militia and placing the island under United States control to ensure that slavery might continue indefinitely.[10] They charged non-conformist missionaries, including Baptists, with interference. In August 1831, a public meeting resolved,

---

[9] William Fitzer Burchell, *Memoir of Thomas Burchell, Twenty-Two Years a Missionary in Jamaica* (London: Benjamin L. Green, 1849) 121-22; G. A. Catherall, "Thomas Burchell, Gentle Rebel," *Baptist Quarterly* 21 (1966): 352; John Howard Hinton, *Memoir of William Knibb, Missionary in Jamaica* (1847; 2d ed., London: Houlston and Stoneman, 1849) 87.

[10] *Report from the Select Committee on the Extinction of Slavery Throughout the British Dominions* (London: J. Haddon, 1833) 256.

> His Majesty's Ministers . . . truckle to the power of the Sectarians, the enemies of the Colonies, and of that mad and irresponsible party denominated Saints, and listen with too ready an ear to the calumnious falsehoods which are eternally fabricated and disseminated by them against the West Indies.[11]

For their part, slaves wanted emancipation, not improved conditions. Throughout the West Indies, slave resistance took various forms including illegal meetings, revolts, strikes, and acts of insubordination. In Jamaica, unrest broke out in 1807, 1823–1824, and 1831. The last was by far the most serious slave uprising.[12] Conditions were ripe for action. The material circumstances of slaves, already unbearable, had worsened because of drought and outbreaks of smallpox and dysentery. Slaves saw missionaries as their allies in the cause of freedom and responded to a gospel that was profoundly liberating.[13] In July, when ill-health again forced Burchell to return to Britain, he vowed, "I'll tell a tale. Slavery! Accursed slavery! That infernal system! From my inmost soul I detest and abhor it! I'm tired of living in its midst."[14] Naturally, his return to Britain aroused hopes among slaves that an end to slavery was imminent.

Ignoring warnings that Burchell had not secured an end to the evil system, slaves began planning in August a strike for the end of the year. Slaves used missionary activity—teaching, worship, and prayer meetings—to organize socio-economic self help and for planning. They did not tell the missionaries their plans because they knew missionaries would attempt to dissuade them as, indeed, happened on 27 December 1831 when the uprising broke out.

At this point, we discern the divergent paths of missionaries and slaves. The missionaries did not know about the planned strike and dissociated themselves from it. When Knibb learned of it on 26 December, he urged slaves to go home and to resume their masters' work.[15]

---

[11]Cited, Alan Burns, *History of the British West Indies* (London: George Allen and Unwin, 1965) 620-21.

[12]See Hinton, ch. 9, "The Insurrection," and Catherall, "Baptist War and Peace" for careful accounts.

[13]Philip Curtin, *Two Jamaicas, The Role of Ideas in a Tropical Colony 1830–1865* (Cambridge: Harvard University Press, 1955) 32-35; Ernest A. Payne, *Freedom in Jamaica. Some Chapters in the Story of the Baptist Missionary Society* (London: Carey Press, [1933]) 21-22.

[14]Catherall, "Burchell," 352.

[15]Hinton, 115.

To the extent that there was an ideologue and organizer of the revolt, a Baptist named Samuel Sharpe assumed the mantle of leadership. Sharpe envisioned a nonviolent uprising in the form of a strike and urged that violence not be inflicted on the planters or their families. In the event, and in the face of efforts by Sharpe to prevent violence, the militia reacted excessively to the strike and provoked slaves, who set the Kensington-St. James plantation on fire. Other plantations went up in flames, which destroyed most of the island's sugar harvest. Briefly tasting freedom, one slave cried out to a proprietor and missionary, "The life we live is . . . the life of a dog, we wont be slaves no more; we wont lift hoe no more; we wont take flog no more. We free now, we free now, no more slaves again."[1]

The revolt involved large numbers; according to one estimate, 50,000 participated.[2] Once violence began, leaders could not contain it. The slaves had inadequate organization, were poorly armed, and lacked agreement as to objectives. Largely spontaneous, the rebellion was quickly and brutally suppressed by the Jamaican militia. Officially, fourteen whites died during the uprising. Two hundred slaves died (the number was certainly greater). Of 634 persons tried by court martial or civil courts on charges arising out of the rebellion, 312 slaves were sentenced to death and 285 sentenced to other punishments. Although he had opposed violence, Samuel Sharpe was among those executed on May 23, 1832. Nearly a hundred and fifty years later, in 1975, he was declared a National Hero of Jamaica.[3]

Most of the planters regarded the insurrection as clear confirmation of what they had been saying for many years about the subversive influence of the Baptist missionaries. They called it the Baptist war even though Knibb later testified that not a single estate on which he had a church member was burnt and that many slaves defended their masters and masters' properties. Three of his congregation of a thousand members numbered among those punished (not capitally) by the government.

---

[1] Quoted by Turner, 160.
[2] Burns, 621.
[3] C. S. Reid, *Samuel Sharpe. From Slave to National Hero* (n.p.: Bustamante Institute of Public and International Affairs, 1988); Philip Wright, *Knibb, "the Notorious" Slaves' Missionary 1803–1845* (London: Sidgwick and Jackson, 1973) 92; Turner, 157.

Among leaders of the strike, only Sharpe was a member of a Baptist church.[4]

Planter vandals reacted by destroying at least thirteen non-conformist chapels; the total damage to Baptist properties was estimated at £14,000. Along with William Whitehorne and Thomas Abbott, Knibb was imprisoned. Burchell, returning from Britain on 2 January 1832, was confined on board ship for a month. His release from confinement permitted officials to arrest him, charged with having told slaves that freedom was theirs and that they should fight for it. In court, a slave named Samuel Stennet testified that he had been bribed to accuse Burchell. Burchell was released. So were Knibb, Whitehorne, and Abbott. One BMS missionary, Francis Gardner of Savanna-la-Mar, had to stand trial. He was acquitted and set free.

While the rebellion played a crucial role in hastening the end of slavery, its immediate failure and brutal suppression led Burchell, Knibb, Phillippo, and other Baptist missionaries to act more vigorously against slavery. Previously, they had rejected a political role, preached against violence, and cautioned patience. Now they took up the cause. Chief among them was William Knibb.

William Knibb

William Knibb was born on 7 September 1803, one of twins.[5] Knibb's father Thomas was a tradesman. His mother, the former Mary Dexter, attended an independent chapel. Raised in Kettering, where in 1792 William Carey had inspired formation of the BMS, Knibb joined a Sunday school at age seven. After three years of grammar school, he apprenticed as a printer. With his elder brother Thomas (1799–1823), Knibb removed to Bristol in 1816.

---

[4]*Report of the Select Committee*, 538. Also, *Narrative of Certain Events Connected with the Late Disturbances, and the Charges Proffered against the Baptist Missionaries in that Island* (London: Holdsworth and Ball, 1832).

[5]In addition to Hinton and Wright, Austen Kennedy de Blois, *Fighters for Freedom: Heroes of the Baptist Challenge* (Philadelphia: Judson, 1928); C. Fell Smith, "William Knibb," *Dictionary of National Biography*, v. 22 (supplement) 70-71.

William Knibb attended Broadmead Baptist Chapel and was baptized in 1822 by the missionary leader John Ryland. He began to preach in an area of Bristol called "Beggars Opera," a rough neighbourhood known popularly as "Beggars Uproar." His brother, Thomas, went to Kingston, Jamaica as a schoolmaster. In 1823, Thomas Knibb joined the long list of missionaries who died in tropical climes. William Knibb resolved to take his place.

Accompanied by his bride, the former May Watkins, Knibb arrived in early 1825. He reported, "I have now reached the land of sin, disease, and death, where Satan reigns with awful power, and carries multitudes captive at his will. True religion is scoffed at."[21] The latter phrase carried a double meaning.

On the one hand, Knibb discerned an unhealthy spiritual situation among Jamaican Baptists. Many had not accepted the authority of the missionaries. Free "coloureds" and slaves were divided, and, from Knibb's point of view, heterodox beliefs, practices carried over from traditional African religions, and immoral behaviour characterized both communities.

On the other hand, Knibb encountered the opposition of the planters. Among provisions of the 1826 Consolidated Slave Act were bans against sectarian ministers or teachers of religion using their homes for instruction and training an indigenous clergy. It was inevitable that the strong-willed Knibb would come into conflict with authorities.

Knibb had moved from Kingston to Savanna-la-Mar in the south-east of the island but was preparing to set up a station on the north coast, in Falmouth. During his absence, Knibb allowed church members to assemble in his home for prayer. They gathered for prayer Easter Sunday evening, 1830. Deacon Sam Swiney was in charge. Officials intervened and charged him with preaching, teaching, and causing a disturbance. Punished by flogging, Swiney had not broken the law. In accord with the Consolidated Slave Act, Swiney had received permission from his owner to attend the meeting. Knibb protested in vain that there was a difference between preaching and praying. He then found himself accused (falsely) of interfering between master and slave. Knibb took his case, with that of Swiney, to the local press. After a second, similar incident, he reported

---

[21]Hinton, 1849 ed., 46.

the two cases to superiors in Britain. After several months of agitation, the colonial adminstration launched an investigation. Vindicated, Knibb could take some satisfaction in the outcome. Knibb had stirred up fresh concern for slave welfare and launched his own career as a slave emancipator. Sympathizers in Britain raised funds enabling Swiney to purchase his freedom from slavery.

In Jamaica, powerful interests organized to preserve the institution of slavery. Denouncing Knibb and his ilk as enraged lunatics, they threatened to kill slaves rather than ever to free them. While Knibb threw himself into the new work at Falmouth, he laboured under a cloud of suspicion. Many slaves regarded him as an agent of the planter system. As for the planters, opinion oscillated. On the one hand, some planters found converted slaves to be their best workers. On the other hand, they were driven to blame missionary activities every time pressures mounted for amelioration of conditions or for full emancipation.

In the light of this atmosphere, Knibb and his colleagues were successful. Between 1827–1831, they reported an increase in the Baptist churches from eight to twenty-four. Membership doubled from 5,000 to 10,000. There were 17,000 inquirers.

Knibb had no direct influence on the December 1831 uprising and tried to stop it. Until that time, Knibb had avoided direct political involvement. His major role in the campaign against slavery lay ahead. He soon returned to England, where he learned that a Reform Bill had passed, easing legal disabilities against Baptists and contributing ultimately to bringing an anti-slavery majority into the British House of Commons. "Thank God," he declared, "now I'll have slavery down. I will never rest, day or night, till I see it destroyed, root and branch."[22]

The December 1831 insurrection sounded the death knell of slavery. Non-political before his visit to England, Knibb now mounted pressure against slavery. He undertook an extensive round of speaking and preaching, sometimes accompanied by Eustace Carey, a nephew of William Carey and himself a missionary in India. According to published reports, Knibb acquired skill as a speaker and excited intense interest throughout Great Britain. An excerpt provides insight into his approach and impact.

---

[22]Hinton, 140.

Africa, thou shalt be free. Britons, Patriots, Fathers, Females, join me in my endeavors to rid my country of this Moloch of iniquity. . . . If we are united, the bonds of the slave will be broken, his fetters will be snapped, the tears of the female African shall cease to flow. The trumpet of jubilee shall sound. The banner of freedom shall be unfurled; and, beneath its life-giving shade, Africa shall arise and call you blessed. Anarchy and confusion shall be banished from the earth, peace shall be restored, joy shall beam in every eye, happiness reign in every heart, and plenty shall open her stores to bless mankind, while the God and father of the oppressed shall smile upon the work which justice demanded, and which Britain has achieved. Remember that I plead for liberty, for liberty for those who have never forfeited it by any crime they have committed, and that without this blessing, Africa must be miserable.

Knibb caused a stir by producing an iron collar with spikes ten inches long, "a nice plaything, one of the blessings of slavery." As he concluded, the room resounded, "three cheers for Knibb."[23]

As events unfolded, freedom came in two stages. First, in May 1833, the Secretary of State for the Colonies introduced legislation into Parliament abolishing slavery throughout the British colonies, promoting the industry of the emancipated slaves, and compensating those previously entitled to their services. Realizing that they had lost this phase of the struggle, Jamaican planters sought as generous a settlement as possible and other aspects of their privileged position. The bill received royal assent on 28 August 1833. On 1 August 1834, slaves received partial freedom under an apprenticeship system.

The apprentice system proved nearly as odious as that which had ended. Planters thwarted attempts by apprentices to buy manumission and extracted as much as possible out of free coloureds by paying low wages and withholding various allowances customary under slavery. Punishment such as flogging continued. Knibb urged ex-slaves to insist on better working conditions. He assisted them to leave the estates and settle in free villages, which were complete with churches and schools. He used personal resources and funds raised by Joseph Sturge (1793–1859), a Birmingham Quaker who visited Jamaica on behalf of the Anti-Slavery

---

[23]*Colonial Slavery. Defence of the Baptist Missionaries from the Charge of Inciting the Late Rebellion in Jamaica; in a Discussion between the Rev. William Knibb and Mr. P. Borthwick, at the Assembly Rooms, Bath, on Saturday, December 15, 1832* (London: Tourist Office, 1832) 31.

Society leader, to buy land for settlers. Through his instrumentality, premises were purchased for a training institution.

Knibb campaigned for full emancipation. In letters to Britain, he condemned the system in such words as this: "Oh! this thrice-accursed apprenticeship! nothing but blood, murderous cells, and chains!"[24] In part because of these efforts, a Jamaican Emancipation Act brought what remained of slavery to an end. At midnight, 1 August 1838, freedom came. Knibb addressed a rally. Pointing to a clock, he said, "The hour is at hand, the monster is dying." The clock struck twelve, he shouted, "The monster is dead: the negro is free."[25]

A further stage to full freedom took much longer. Former slave-owners preserved planter society until 1866 when, after decades of tension between Jamaican and British assemblies, Jamaica became a Crown Colony. Political independence came only in 1962.

Immediately after emancipation, Knibb continued his ministry in Jamaica and turned his sights on slavery in the United States and elsewhere. Knibb envisioned a new society based on the potential he believed existed among the former slaves. At the heart of a free Jamaica would be a Christian community growing materially, numerically, and spiritually. He aimed at establishing self-supporting, self-governing, and self-propagating churches and encouraged the formation of a Jamaican Missionary Society in 1842.

In part through his friendship with Joseph Sturge, Knibb became a proponent of peace views. He wrote,

> In all our opposition, we wish it to be understood, that we use no weapons but those of calm reason and of deliberate thought, and the putting out (as men have a right to do) the free expression of our opinions. We wish not to obtain the alteration of anything by physical force; we wish only to establish in all their omnipotence the eternal principles of justice, assured that they will do the work.[26]

In 1842, the BMS celebrated its fiftieth jubilee. In Jamaica, Knibb and other Baptists celebrating by singing,

---

[24]Hinton, 232.
[25]*Ibid.*, 261. *Freedom in Jamaica* (pamphlet, London, 1838).
[26]*Ibid.*, 484.

> God bless our native land,
> May heaven's protecting hand
> Still guard our shore.
> May strife for ever end,
> Foe be transformed to friend,
> And Britain's power depend
> On WAR no more.[27]

Knibb died on 15 November 1845 of typhoid fever in Kettering, a small town in Trelawny District named for his birthplace. A hundred and forty years later, on 1 August 1988, he received the Order of Merit of Jamaica posthumously. The citation read,

> [Knibb] envisioned a society that would not exploit the weak and down-trodden, but be a democracy run by the people. He believed that competent leaders could be found among the people who could make that society a success. We today are inheritors and beneficiaries of that vision, which inspired those who followed him.[28]

Conclusion

Emancipation of Jamaican slaves followed a long struggle initiated by black leaders like George Liele and Moses Baker and supported ultimately by Knibb, Burchell, and other BMS missionaries. After 1831, leaders in the movement for abolition, including Knibb and Sturge, recognized that perpetuation of slavery would engender more violence. They sought to encourage peaceful change through the broad transformation of society. Implicit in their analysis was an understanding of the interrelationship between negative and positive peace.

Shortly after the event, members of the Falmouth Baptist Church erected a tablet recalling the moment freedom came. It featured the figure of Justice holding in her left hand the balances of equity and in her right hand a sword. Beneath this figure were likenesses of Knibb, Sturge, and

---

[27]*Baptist Herald* (Jamaica) 9 August 1843, quoted by Wright, 218.
[28]*Civil List of the 1988 Independence Day National Honours and Awards* (Kingston: Jamaica House, 1988) 5.

two other anti-slavery advocates, Granville Sharpe (1735–1813) and William Wilberforce (1759–1833), in bas relief. The inscription read,

> DEO GLORIA!
> Erected by emancipated Sons of Africa, to commemorate the birth-day of their freedom, August the first, 1838. Hope hails the abolition of slavery throughout the British colonies as the day-spring of universal liberty to all nations of men, whom God "hath made of one blood." "Ethiopia shall soon stretch out her hands unto God." Psalm lxviii.31

Under the inscription were two blacks in the act of burying the broken chain and useless whip and waving the Bible. Associated with them, a fond mother joyously caressed the infant that, for the first time, she could call her own.[29] They have bequeathed to successor generations a compelling mandate, that one day all should be free from every scourge.

---

[29]Hinton, 310; photo in Tucker, opposite 37.

Chapter Ten
Following the North Star

Introduction

Slavery had a part in New France and British North America from the time of settlement in the seventeenth century. Baptist voices against slavery were rare before the late eighteenth century. Then, slowly, slavery became a moral issue for Baptists. By the 1830s, anti-slavery advocacy intensified, divided the denomination in the Untied States, and shaped the Canadian church.

One can document the growth of anti-slavery opinion from the end of the United States war of independence when agitation against the system followed in the wake of democratic and enlightened idealism. In 1785, the Baptist General Committee of Virginia declared slavery "contrary to the word of God." In 1787, the Ketocton Association called slavery "a breach of divine law" and proposed gradual emancipation. Several congregations protested; the association took no further action. In 1790, Virginia Baptists revived the issue and appointed a committee to frame a policy. John Leland (1754–1841), pastor in Virginia (1776–1791), drafted a resolution calling slavery "a violent deprivation of the rights of nature and inconsistent with a republican government; and therefore (we) recommend it to our brethren to make use of every legal measure, to extirpate the horrid evil from the land."[1] The resolution passed but failed to win the approval of state associations.

These moves grew out of the ethos of the second great awakening that engendered Baptist growth in Virginia, Kentucky, and elsewhere in the South. Some congregations permitted blacks to join or to form their

---

[1] H. Shelton Smith, *In His Image, But. . . : Racism in Southern Religion, 1780–1910* (Durham: Duke University Press, 1972) 47–48.

own congregations and associations. Baptist success among slaves elicited protest within and outside the denomination. In Virginia, some non-Baptists urged creation of an Established Church. One reason was the fact that Baptists allowed meetings of slaves for religious instruction without the consent of their masters. This produced "very bad consequences."[2] In Kentucky, some congregations forced their pastors to resign because of their anti-slavery views. Nonetheless, during the nineteenth century, more and more Baptists took up the anti-slavery cause.

Friends of Humanity Association

Among the earliest Baptists to organize anti-slavery activity in the United States were Kentucky pastors William Hickman (1747–1834) and David Barrow (1753–1819). In September 1807, Hickman declared non-fellowship with slave holders and preached against slavery at the Forks of Elkhorn Church. Nineteen years after Hickman had become pastor of the congregation, it severed its ties with him. Also in 1807, the North District Association expelled Barrow because of his anti-slavery views. He helped form the Friends of Humanity Association.[3]

The inaugural meeting of the Friends of Humanity took place from 26–28 September 1807 at Ebinezer, Mason County, Kentucky. The gathering adopted "Tarrant's Rules," named after the moderator of the meeting, Elder Carter Tarrant. These rules provided that no person should be admitted to any of their churches, (1) whose practice appears friendly to perpetual slavery, or, (2) who holds slaves. Tarrant exempted those holding young slaves (to be emancipated at an age agreed to), women whose husbands opposed emancipation, widows lacking the means to liberate their slaves, and those who, by reason of insanity, old age, or any debility of body could not support themselves. Afterwards, Tarrant circulated a letter to "our former brethren." The letter condemned the

---

[2]William Warren Sweet, *Religion on the American Frontier. The Baptists 1783–1830. A Collection of Source Material* (New York: Henry Holt, 1931) 77-78.

[3]*Ibid*, 564–607. Sweet cites a fifty-page pamphlet by Barrow entitled *Involuntary, Unmerited, Perpetual, Absolute, Hereditary Slavery Examined on the Principles of Nature, Reason, Justice, Policy and Scripture* (Lexington: Printed by D. and C. Bradford, 1808); also, Smith, 48-52.

oppressive system and urged Baptists to join in professing their "abhorrence to unmerited, hereditary, perpetual, absolute unconditional Slavery."

The next year, the Friends of Humanity adopted a motion that stated that "the present mode of association or confederation of churches in their relation to slavery is unscriptural and ought to be laid aside." This led to formation of the Kentucky Abolition Society.[4]

The Friends of Humanity and Kentucky Abolition Society began with a few ministers and churches. By 1812, their numbers included twelve churches and three hundred members, but in 1816 only six churches were affiliated. Dearth of leadership contributed to the decline. Tarrant died shortly after he became an army chaplain in 1812, while Barrow died in 1819 on the eve of the awakening of the great anti-slavery movement.

The Friends of Humanity never became numerically strong in Kentucky. Gradually, however, the movement spread to Illinois, Missouri, and elsewhere. Circular letters and itinerant preaching served as the main means for propagating anti-slavery views. Members stressed the Bible as the pillar of faith and stressed separation, the denying of union and communion with all persons accepting slavery.

By 1833, the association grew to thirty-nine churches with 1347 members. It helped defeat efforts to introduce slavery into Illinois and condemned slavery strongly. Increasingly in the North, other Baptists took up the cause. In Illinois, the Edwardsville Association adopted at its 1838 assembly a resolution that testified against slavery, offered prayers for those who held slaves, and urged that means be devised to remove slavery and "all kinds of oppression from our country and the world." The Freewill Baptists and two smaller denominations, the Seventh Day Baptists and German Baptists, also took up the anti-slavery cause. These bodies barred slaveholders from membership. For example, in 1839, the Freewill Baptists excluded 5,000 Carolina Baptists for their pro-slavery views.

In the 1840s, the Friends of Humanity merged into the wider abolitionist cause. As was true for many early abolitionists, these pioneer Baptists agreed in principle to reject violence in their own, strictly abolitionist activity. Many adhered to the Declaration of Sentiments,

---

[4]Sweet, 84.

drafted by William Lloyd Garrison and adopted by the Anti-Slavery Society in 1833. Garrisonian Baptists rejected carnal weapons for deliverance of slaves from bondage and chose to rely solely upon those means that were spiritual. "Ours shall be . . . the opposition of moral purity to moral corruption—the destruction of error by the potency of truth—the overthrow of prejudice by the power of love—and the abolition of slavery by the spirit of repentance." Baptists discouraged slave revolts and sought emancipation by traditional methods such as speaking, publishing, and political action, and new means as well. The underground railroad became the most important form of nonviolent resistance. In 1849, for example, a Providence, Rhode Island, congregation of abolitionist Freewill Baptists claimed it helped sixteen blacks to escape north.[5]

Following the North Star to Canada

As noted in the previous chapter, during the war of independence, many blacks in the United States supported the British cause and emigrated at the end of the war. Some accompanied British loyalists to the Caribbean. Others went north to Nova Scotia. During the early part of the nineteenth century, Upper Canada, or Canada West (as Ontario was called between 1841–1867) became a second destination of black immigrants.

In 1793, slavery was barred from Upper Canada and, gradually thereafter, throughout the rest of British North America. Successive waves of black refugees emigrated to Upper Canada after the War of 1812 and the legislative end of slavery in 1838. In 1850, the United States passed the Fugitive Slave Act, with provisions such as Section Seven that made it unlawful to hinder anyone from recapturing escaping slaves. What had been a trickle became a flood.

At first few in number, blacks settled primarily in the black neighborhoods of growing towns. They worked at menial jobs or, less frequently, in commerce or the professions. Later, black refugees became farmers. In the years after 1829, many opted to live in one of three

---

[5]Carleton Mabee, *Black Freedom. The Nonviolent Abolitionists from 1830 through the Civil War* (London: Macmillan Company, 1970) 23, 231, 272.

utopian settlements founded near Chatham, Wilberforce, Dawn, and Buxton.

Among those who fled to Canada was William M. Mitchell, born free but taken in slavery in North Carolina. In 1843, he escaped to Ohio, where he became a "notorious Negro-stealer." After passage of the Fugitive Slave Act, he moved to Toronto, where he became pastor of the First Baptist Church and a missionary in service of the American Baptist Free Mission Society, formed by Boston Baptists in 1840. Mitchell claimed he helped transport 1,200 slaves to Canada each year after 1850. In his account of the underground railroad,[6] he depicted the flight of a slave mother, her daughter, and grand daughter:

> But God, whose eye never sleeps, and whose ears are never dull of hearing, mysteriously guided the fugitive unto freedom. He heard and answered her prayers. Trusting in the God of Israel, her trembling limbs bore her feeble body Northward; subject to rain, hail, snow and tempestuous storms; a Pilgrim, not to the Holy Land, to bow to the Popish Shrine, but to Freedom's Land, to worship God, and enjoy the boon of liberty.

Although statistics are not entirely reliable, by 1852 there were several tens of thousands of blacks in Canada. Initially, whites helped blacks fleeing to freedom, but the welcome soon vanished. Developments within the church, and in particular Baptist churches, illustrated this progression.

Not all blacks in Canada were Baptist, but Baptists dominated for three reasons: (1) many of the fugitives already were Baptist, (2) Canadian Baptists undertook evangelistic efforts among fugitives, and (3) Baptists were known for their anti-slavery advocacy elsewhere. In fact, Ontario Baptists were among the first to speak out against racism in Canada and continued slavery in the United States. In February 1841, the Ottawa Baptist Association passed an anti-slavery motion that urged congregations to refuse communion to slave owners. Other associations adopted the resolution. Leading pastors, notably Robert Alexander Fyfe (1816–1878), served pastorates in Canada and the United States, spoke forcefully against discrimination and slavery.

---

[6]W. M. Mitchell, *The Under-ground Railroad from Slavery to Freedom* (London: William Tweedie, 1860) 31.

Initially, most Baptist congregations admitted people of color. The first predominantly black congregations began on an interracial basis. However, segregation separation soon appeared. Baptist congregations in Dundas, Jerseyville, and North Cayuga resisted the trend. However, the historian Robin Winks observed, "Most Negroes were Baptists and Methodists, and so too were the whites who wished to exclude them."[7]

Blacks resented forms of discrimination they encountered and responded to the growing threat of segregation. In 1841, three black congregations—First Baptist, Amherstburg (nineteen members); First Baptist, Sandwich (eleven members); Second Baptist, Detroit (seventeen members)—formed a new association of Baptist churches, the Amherstburg Association.

In a way, the primary focus of the Amherstburg Association was religious, not racial. Members of the three congregations saw God as Lord over all of life. They organized temperance societies, Sabbath schools, and other moral agencies. They promoted evangelism. They disciplined members who failed to maintain high standards of Christian living. They provided for the needs of those outside their membership.

At the same time, creation of the Amherstburg Association represented a move to counter the growing racism blacks encountered. Delegates at the first meeting resolved, "that we ought to form ourselves into an Association because *we cannot enjoy the Privileges we wish as Christians and with the White Churches in Canada.*"[8] Subsequently, association members expressed alarm at the dilly-dallying by Baptists on the issues of color-phobia and slavery. In 1846, for example, Elder Hosea H. Hawkins denounced a resolution passed by the (white) Long Point Association, which had failed to sever ties with slave owners to the south.

---

[7] Robin W. Winks, "Negro School Segregation in Ontario and Nova Scotia," *Canadian Historical Review* 50 (1969): 178.

[8] Amherstburg Association Minutes, 8 October 1841, 1, Canadian Baptist Archives, my emphasis. Published sources are James K. Lewis, "Religious Nature of the Early Negro Migration to Canada and the Amherstburg Baptist Association," *Ontario History of Coloured Baptist Churches, 1820–1865, in What Is Now Known as Ontario* (New York: Arno, 1980); Dorothy Shadd Shreve, *Pathfinders of Liberty and Truth* (Amherstburg: Merlin, 1940); Robin W. Winks, *The Blacks in Canada. A History* (New Haven: Yale University Press, 1971).

Year after year, the Amherstburg Association repeated anti-slavery resolutions. It denounced "the deformed evil of slavery." However, members were not of one mind on the question of relationships with white organizations, which generally were based in the United States. In 1849, some members of the association formed a separate Canadian Anti-Slavery Baptist Association. Their principle concern at the time was to establish an institution of learning for ministerial candidates at one of the three major black settlements, the Dawn community founded in 1842. However, the anti-slavery association soon became embroiled in controversy.

The disagreement centered on the fund-raising practices of the leader at Dawn, the Reverand Josiah Henson (1789–1883).[9] Henson obtained material and spiritual aid from white supporters in the United States. This engendered a reaction on the part of black leaders who accused the leadership of Dawn of "begging," accepting support from churches that did not condemn slavery and undermining black self-sufficiency.

For twenty years, Dawn was a relatively successful venture. Even though he was not a Baptist, Henson encouraged formation of a Baptist congregation at Dawn, and many Baptists throughout the world supported his work. In 1856, the two Ontario black Baptist associations reunited. They continued to support Henson but criticized Baptist bodies with proslavery members.[10]

Others had their doubts. Among those who condemned begging and separatist organizations were two sisters, Mary Ann Shadd Cary (1823–1893) and Elizabeth Shadd Shreve (1826–1890), born free in the large family of Abraham Doras and Harriet (*nee* Parnell) Shadd. Born in Wilmington, Delaware, by the mid–1830s the Shadds were living in West Chester, Pennsylvania. In 1851, they joined other blacks in following the north star to freedom in Canada.

Mary Shadd emerged as a prominent leader and spokesperson for the immigrant black community.[11] She settled initially in Windsor, where she

---

[9]Henson was the celebrated Uncle Tom of Harriet Beecher Stowe's novel *Uncle Tom's Cabin*, first serialized in 1851–1852.

[10]For the text of a resolution adopted in 1857, see *The Black Abolitionist Papers. Volume 2: Canada 1830–1865*, ed. C. Peter Ripley (Chapel Hill: University of North Carolina Press, 1986) 364-66.

[11]Jim Bearden and Linda Jean Butler Shadd, *The Life and Times of Mary Shadd Cary*

opened a school for blacks and wrote *Notes on Canada West* (1852), a guide for fugitives fleeing to Canada. In March 1853, she launched the publication of the *Provincial Freeman* with Samuel Ringgold Ward (1817–1866). Shortly thereafter, Ward went to Britain on behalf of the American Missionary Association and subsequently settled in Jamaica where he served Baptists as a pastor. As a result, Shadd became the first black woman newspaper editor in North America, a position she held until 1858. She used the paper to express her commitment to integration and her condemnation of self-segregated black Canadian communities. (Ultimately she left the church and never renewed membership because of segregation.)

In 1855, Mary Shadd moved a few miles east to Chatham, in the heartland of black settlement. In January 1856, she married Thomas J. Cary, a Toronto businessman and antislavery activist who joined her in publishing the *Provincial Freeman*. They had two children. After his death in 1860, Mary Cary operated a black school in Chatham and continued writing. In 1864, she returned to the United States, living first in Detroit, then in Washington, D.C., where she was principal of a black grammar school from 1872–1884. She also took a law degree and continued her reform activities as a lawyer, suffragette, and advocate of black economic self-sufficiency and economic justice for poor whites.[12] A number of abolitionists, including Frederick Douglas and W. E. Burghardt Du Bois, cited her continuing influence.

For many years, Mary worked with her sister Elizabeth Shadd.[13] They threw themselves into the work of settling the sudden influx of black refugees. They served as a catalyst for nonviolent resistance when efforts were made to return slaves to their owners in the United States. On one occasion, a slave-hunter overtook a boy who had fled without hat, coat,

---

(Toronto: NC Press Ltd, 1977); Harold B. Hancock, "Mary Ann Shadd: Negro Editor, Educator, and Lawyer," *Delaware History* 15 (1973): 187-94; entries by Elsie M. Lewis in Edward T. James, ed., *Notable American Women 1607–1950* (Cambridge: Harvard University Press, 1971) 300-301, and by Robin W. Winks in R. W. Logan and M. R. Winston, eds., *Dictionary of American Negro Biography* (New York: W. W. Norton, 1982) 552-53.

[12]*Black Abolitionist Papers*, 388-91, for a sermon preached on 6 April 1858, which expresses concern for justice for all, in every aspect of life.

[13]The main source is E. Alexander, "Biography of Madam E. W. Shreve," in Shreve, 65-66.

or shoes to Chatham. Seeing what was happening, the two women intervened, tore the boy free, ran to the court-house, and had the bell rung to arouse the community. According to reports, with commanding form, piercing eyes, and stirring voice Mary Shadd denounced the assailant who fled from the crowd and headed south empty-handed.

In an important way, Elizabeth Shadd Shreve had a greater impact on Baptist life than did her more famous sister. Born into a Roman Catholic family and trained by Quakers, in 1867 Shreve joined the Baptist church in Buxton. At the time of her baptism, she and another black woman gave their testimonies. They inspired "a male professor" to plunge into the water crying, "Baptize me, too!"

Like her sister, Elizabeth Shreve contributed to the abolitionist cause by helping settle the influx of black refugees who fled to Canada after passage of the infamous Fugitive Slave Law. After the Civil War she exerted influence on Ontario Baptists by nursing the sick, collecting and distributing clothing for the needy, delivering food to the hungry, and preaching the gospel. In 1882, she helped to organize the Women's Home Missionary Society of the Amherstburg Association. As its first president and a powerful speaker, she was in great demand. On her last missionary journey, her horse stumbled. She never recovered from her injuries. At her funeral, Mary Branton, whom we meet in chapter eleven, called Elizabeth Shreve her "dearest sister" who did God's will.

Jennie Johnson (1868–1967)
Pioneer Woman Baptist Pastor

The Amherstburg Association began in 1841 with three churches and forty-seven communicant members. By 1861, it grew to nineteen churches and 1,060 communicant members. After the Civil War in the United States, many blacks returned south. In a pioneering study, Ida C. Greaves observed,

> For the large number who remained in Canada, conditions were difficult. Their welcome vanished with the cause in which it originated; the people who had regarded the abolition of slavery as an urgent moral task had no interest in the

future of the Negro as such, and the race found in Canada as elsewhere that there are more subtle and pernicious forces of hostility than legal slavery.[14]

For Baptists who remained, the Amherstburg Association stayed active. It became a stabilizing factor for descendants of those who fled to freedom in Canada and for newer black immigrants. The Reverend Jennie Johnson was one of the outstanding leaders of the association.[15] Born on 20 July 1868 in Dresden, Ontario, Johnson descended from runaway slaves who followed the north star to Canada. Her father came from Maryland, her mother from Kentucky. At age ten, Johnson accepted Christ as Lord and Savior and joined an integrated church in Chatham. She became active in a mission band of which she was made an honorary life member in 1945. Somewhat later, she experienced a call to ministry and was led to study at the Wilberforce Seminary in Ohio. She returned to Chatham and founded the Prince Albert Baptist Church.

In 1909, Johnson was ordained and inducted into the ministry of Prince Albert Baptist Church. The Reverend Johnson's ordination and church planting did not go unnoticed. In her memoirs, she explained that she found a certain amount of prejudice against the ordination of women. This made it difficult for her to carry on. She observed, "No crime had I committed against the laws of God, rather had I encountered the coldness of man-made rules and regulations."[16] Nonetheless, she persevered. During nearly twenty years as pastor of the Prince Albert Baptist Church she regularly conducted revival services and encouraged the missionary enterprise. She gained a reputation as a powerful preacher and was used by God to win Christian converts.

In 1928, Johnson moved to Flint, Michigan, where she opened a mission. During the depression years that followed, thousands of unemployed blacks, Mexican-Americans, and poor whites received meals and spiritual encouragement from her. Johnson continued a vigorous ministry, serving congregations in Ontario and Michigan. Just before her death on 11th December 1967, she received letters of commendation from the United States President Lyndon Johnson and Michigan Governor George

---

[14] Ida C. Greaves, "The Negro in Canada," *McGill University Economic Studies 16* (Orillia: Packet-Times Press, 1930) 43.

[15] The most important source is Jennie Johnson, *My Life* (undated pamphlet).

[16] *Ibid.*

sets aside a Sunday to remember her role as founder and pastor of the congregation.

Conclusion

As long as wars produce prisoners, politics produce tyranny, economics produce poverty, and patriarchy produces exploitation, slavery, or involuntary servitude will never disappear. As a result, slavery remains today the fundamental factor characterising the abuse of many millions of men, women, and children, particularly in Asia, Africa, and Latin America—continents called the two-thirds world.

Resistance to the trans-Atlantic slave trade began centuries ago. Only slowly and painfully did the slaves' long march to freedom gain momentum in Africa, the Caribbean, British North America, and elsewhere. In 1807, Great Britain abolished the slave trade. In 1838, slavery ended in British realms. In 1863, President Lincoln's Emancipation Proclamation marked another stage in the struggle.

In this chapter, we have explored opposition to slavery and racism during two periods in two societies. Before slavery ended during the Civil War in the United States, Baptist anti-slavery advocates in both the United States and Canada prodded white churches on the matter of race, developed nonviolent means of resistance, and cared for fugitive slaves. After the war, many Baptists continued a ministry of healing and reconciliation. In Canada, black congregations offered asylum for the sick or any in need and championed liberation, including the end of oppression of women. In these ways, those who followed the north star to freedom in Canada modeled the love of Christ and established a tradition of Baptist work for positive peace.

Blacks expressed their gratitude for freedom in prayer and song. In 1851, the following "prayer of the slave" linked the notions of spiritual and temporal peace:

> Holy Father, God of Love,
> Send thy Spirit from above;
> Help us thy great name to sing,
> God of mercy, heavenly King.
> For the burdened slaves would we
> Ask the gift of liberty;

> Ask the gift of liberty;
> For the weary souls oppressed
> We would ask thy peae and rest.
>
> In thy gracious love arise,
> See our burdens, hear our cries.
> Rend the fetters, set us free
> From oppression's tyranny.
> They our voices we will raise
> Songs to thee of grateful praise
> Thy great love shall be our theme,
> We will own thee, Lord, supreme.[17]

Oppression had not ended. For those who grapple with the institution of war, it may be a hopeful sign that the institution of slavery, once accepted as just and lawful, did come to be regarded as oppressive and a term of opprobrium. Nearly two hundred years passed before large numbers of Baptists took up the anti-slavery cause. But Baptists did, in fact, take up the cause.

Nearly another two hundred years have passed. Only recently have significant numbers of Baptists acted on issues such as threatened ecological and nuclear destruction, systemic human rights violations, and economic injustice. As they join others in promoting peace, justice, and the integrity of creation, they inspire hope that one day, this dream of Martin Luther King, Jr., will become reality:

> One day, youngsters will learn words they will not understand. Children from India will ask: What is hunger? Children from Alabama will ask: What is racial segregation? Children from Hiroshima will ask: What is the atomic bomb? Children at school will ask: What is war? You will answer them. You will tell them: Those words are not used any more, like stage-coaches, galleys, or slavery, these words are not longer meaningful. That is why they have been removed from dictionaries.[18]

---

[17]*Voice of the Fugitive*, 26 March 1851.
[18]Quoted in *Reconciliation International* 6 (Spring 1991): 2.

Chapter Eleven
The Missionary as Peacemaker

Introduction

Until the late eighteenth century, Baptists rarely expressed concern for the spiritual condition of non-Europeans. In 1792, amidst a general awakening of Christian humanitarian and missionary activity, the publication by William Carey (1761–1834) of *An Enquiry into the Obligations of Christians, to Use Means for the Conversion of the Heathens*, and the subsequent formation of the British Baptist Missionary Society (BMS) led to a massive initiative by Baptists to bring salvation to the heathen.

Responding to the command of Jesus to "go . . . and make disciples of all nations" (Matt 28:19), Baptists served in many capacities, as home and foreign missionaries, as executives and members of mission boards, or as part of the domestic support network. Many Baptists proclaimed a whole gospel for whole people in transformed societies. They exercised their mandate in many ways. They preached, translated the Bible, formed churches, inveighed against such injustices as slavery, and opposed through constructive programs illiteracy, infected water, or poverty.

Few Baptists used the words "peacemaker" or "positive peace" to describe their missionary self-understanding. Yet, these concepts were implicit in their vocation as ministers of reconciliation. Seeking to bring about a state of the universe in which humanity and nature together reflect the unity and love of God, Baptists campaigned against conditions that contributed to war. At times, they opposed war itself.[1]

---

[1] R. Pierce Beaver, *Envoys of Peace: The Peace Witness of the Christian World Mission* (Grand Rapids: Eerdmans, 1964).

In the following sections, we explore peacemaking as a central dynamic of Baptist outreach. We use two case studies, protest against oppression of Native Americans and medical work in India.

Missionaries and Peace

During the nineteenth-century explosion of missionary activity, peacemaking often emerged out of the encounter with religious practices and social structures that missionaries regarded as barriers to personal and societal change. Many issues demanded attention, including what was perceived as immoral domestic arrangements (for example, polygyny in Africa), violation of human rights (for example, slavery in Jamaica), illegitimate commerce (for example, the African slave trade or opium trafficking in China), race prejudice, and atrocities in Macedonia, Armenia, and the Congo. Missionaries condemned evil in many forms, and they developed strategies to introduce cultural forms that facilitated the expansion of Christianity. Often, missionaries displayed ignorance of their own cultural assumptions, but some did hesitate to reproduce western cultural patterns in their converts.

During the first decades of BMS work in India, missionaries focused on several issues, such as caste, *sati* (the custom of burning Hindu widows on the funeral pyres of their dead husbands), infanticide, and the lack of educational opportunities for women. In evaluating India's social ills, they concluded that caste was at the root of all problems. William Carey denounced the system as a "noxious weed" and an accursed engine invented by the devil to enslave humanity, as did other missionaries.[2]

More than any other issue, the practice of *sati* seized the conscience of Baptists and fueled concerted action. On grounds of humanity, BMS missionaries attacked the practice. To contradict the claim that it was rare, Carey compiled statistics. In 1803, he found 438 occurrences within a thirty-mile radius of Calcutta.[3] Despite the charge that they were challenging the customary status of women and interfering with the Hindu religion, missionaries launched a crusade against the custom, even risking

---

[2] S. Pearce Carey, *William Carey* (1923; London: Carey Press, 1934) 211; *Periodical Accounts Relative to the Baptist Missionary Society* 1 (1800): 126.

[3] Carey, 222.

expulsion from India. In particular, the writings of Carey, his colleague at Serempore William Ward (1769-1823), and the General Baptist missionary in Orissa, William Peggs (1793-1850), contributed significantly to the successful campaign to legislate an end to the practice of *sati*. In 1829, the government of Bengal prohibited the custom, followed the next year in Madras and Bombay.[4]

While missionaries found at home a ready audience, including parliamentary allies for their challenge against specific customs, they had a harder time developing models for mission sensitive to more durable cultural patterns. For example, it was nearly fifty years before a strategy of effective evangelism among women emerged. This was to be a contribution of several women missionaries including Elizabeth Sale (*née* Geale; 1818-1898), who adopted Baptist convictions at age sixteen, was baptized, and joined Blandford Street Baptist Church, London. She married John Sale (1818-1875). In 1849, the BMS appointed the Sales to India. After language training, they served in Barisal (1850-1854, 1868-1874), Jessore (1854-1858), Calcutta (1858-1861), and Lal Bazaar (1864-1868). Elizabeth Sale pioneered *zenana* visitation, which entailed calling on caste women in the secluded quarters of their homes. She introduced potential converts to the rudiments of Christianity; identified families in need of food, clothing, or medicine; and recruited children for schools. In Britain, she helped form the Baptist Zenana Mission and London Indian Association. This domestic base supported expanding educational work among "neglected and despised" women of India and Ludhiana Medical College. At the time of her death, the Baptist Zenana Mission employed 67 female missionaries in five countries.[5]

---

[4] J. C. Marshman, *The Life and Times of Carey, Marshman, and Ward* (London: Longman, Brown, Green, Longmans, and Roberts, 1859) I:182, 442-44, II:412-13; J. Peggs, *The Suttees' Cry to Britain* (London: Seely and Son, 1827; rev. ed., 1828). For a general discussion, Sunil Kumar Chatterjee, *William Carey and Serampore* (Calcutta: Ghosh, 1984) 53-66; Kenneth Ingham, *Reformers in India, 1793-1833* (Cambridge: University Press, 1956); E. D. Potts, *British Baptist Missionaries in India 1793-1837* (Cambridge: University Press, 1967); Brian Stanley, *The Bible and the Flag. Protestant Missions and British Imperialism in the Nineteenth and Twentieth Centuries* (Leicester: Inter-Varsity Press, 1990) 100-102.

[5] O. M. Coats, "Elizabeth Sale," in A. S. Clement, ed., *Great Baptist Women* (London: Carey, 1955); *Freeman* 18 March 1898, 131-32; E. A. Payne, *The Great Succession* (London: Carey, 1938); [Marianne] Lewis, *A Plea for Zenanas* (pamphlet, London, 1866);

Sometimes missionaries dealt directly with the issue of war. Carey opposed war and called the New York Peace Society "a society with whose object my heart most cordially coincides."[6] Peggs declared peace a "benevolent and truly Christian principle" and looked forward to the coming day when "Nation shall not lift up sword against nation, neither shall they learn war any more."[7]

During the Burmese-British war in 1824–1825, the Burmese government held Adoniram Judson (1788–1850) captive eighteen months. After his release, he helped draft the Treaty of Yandabo, which ended the war. Judson joined the Massachusetts Peace Society from Burma, stating:

> I repent of whatever expressions or acts in my past life may have cherished the war spirit, in myself or others. I repent that I have so long delayed to enter my protest against the practice of war, by some overt act—a measure, which appears to be, in the present state of things, the indispensable duty of every Christian; and I resolve, that hereafter I will endeavour to diffuse the sentiments of peace, as far as lies in my power.[8]

In chapter nine we noted the support for peace offered by William Knibb. When the first general peace convention met in London in 1843, Knibb and nine other BMS missionaries to Jamaica sent a message expressing their view "that all war is contrary to the spirit and precepts of our holy religion, and detrimental to the best interests of the human race."[9] Like Carey, Peggs, and Judson, they expressed the conviction that it was no longer optional for Christians to remain silent on the issue of

---

Sunil Kumar Chatterjee, *Hannah Marshman, The First Woman Missionary in India* (Calcutta: S. K. Poddar, 1987).

[6]Carey, 299; cited, *Friend of Peace* 1/9 (1815): 36-37.

[7]James Peggs in George Pilkington, *Testimonies of Ministers of Various Denominations, Showing the Unlawfulness to Christians of All Wars . . .* (London: G. Eccles, 1837) 15.

[8]*Friend of Peace* 3 (April 1822) 121-22; Courtney Anderson, *To the Golden Shore. The Life of Adoniram Judson* (1956; Grand Rapids: Zondervan Publishing House, 1972) 351-62. For the role of Ann Hasseltine Judson (1789–1826) during his period of captivity and a photograph of Adoniram Judson, see Joan Jacobs Brumberg, *Mission for Life* (New York: Free Press, 1980) ch. 4.

[9]J. J. [John Jefferson], ed., *The Proceedings of the First General Peace Convention Held in London, June 22, 1843 and the Two Following Days* (London: Peace Society, 1843) 11.

war. Another early missionary who worked for the International Peace Society was John Casimir Rostan, the first missionary to France under American Baptist appointment.[10]

Some Baptist women came to see war as incompatible with a call for people to turn to Christ. Typically, they combined advocacy for mission and peace. For example, Mrs. Allsop, wife of a Baptist pastor and supporter of mission, became a leader of the Burton-on-Trent Local Peace Association in the 1880s. In addition to organizing meetings in her home, she became a local correspondent, writing letters and articles and speaking on the subject of peace. She helped distribute *Peace and Goodwill*, which routinely called women to peace work. One issue featured an "Alphabetical Scripture on Peace," which went as follows:

> Acquaint thyself with God, and be at peace. Job 22.21
> Be at peace among yourselves. 1 Thess 5: 13.
> Chastisement of our peace was upon Him. Isa 53:5.
> Depart from evil and do good; seek peace and pursue it. Ps 34:14.
> End of the upright man is peace. Ps 37:37.
> Follow peace with all men. Heb 12:14.
> Great peace have they who love Thy law. Ps 119:165.
> He shall speak peace to the heathen. Zech 9:10.
> In the peace thereof shall ye have peace. Jer 29.7.
> Jesus said, "Peace I leave with you." John 14:27.
> Kingdom of God is righteousness, peace, and joy. Rom 14:17.
> Let the peace of God rule in your hearts. Col 3:15.
> My covenant was with him of life and peace. Mal 2:5.
> No peace, saith the Lord, to the wicked. Isa 48.22.
> On earth peace, goodwill toward men. Luke 2:14.
> Pray for the peace of Jerusalem. Ps 122:6.
> Quietness and peace unto Israel. 1 Chron 22:9.
> Rahab received the spies with peace. Heb 11:31.
> Solomon had peace on all sides round about him. 1 Kings 4:24.
> The Prince of Peace. Isa 9:6.
> Unto Darius the King, all peace. Ezra 5:7.
> Very God of peace sanctify you wholly. 1 Thess 5:23.
> What hast thou to do with peace? 2 Kings 9:18.
> Xerxes, king of kings, unto Ezra perfect peace. Ezra 7:12.

---

[10] J. H. Rushbrooke, *The Baptist Movement in the Continent of Europe* (London: Carey Press, 1923) 176. For other examples, see Reid Trulson, "Baptist Pacifism: A Heritage of Nonviolence," *American Baptist Quarterly* 10 (1991): 199-217.

Ye shall be led forth with peace. Isa 55:12.
Zimri, peace, who slew his master? 2 Kings 9:31.

Isabel Crawford (1867–1961)

Known by her Indian name Ge*e-ah-ho-an-go-mah* ("she gave us the Jesus way"), Isabel Alice Hartley Crawford was born of Baptist parents who immigrated to Ontario from Northern Ireland.[11] Her father John Crawford (1819–1892) was a pioneer missionary and educator. Because of the demands on his time, he frequently called upon 'Belle to teach Sunday School, lecture or preach. At age seventeen, she came down with consumption. Bedridden for six months, "parched with fever and racked with pain," she recovered but was left nearly deaf for life. During this time of testing, 'Belle Crawford decided upon a career as a missionary.

There had never been enough money to provide the Crawford children a formal education. In order to attend the Baptist Missionary Training School in Chicago, Crawford raised her own tuition by teaching and selling her own paintings. From 1891–1893, she enrolled in the program. As part of her training, she took food, clothing, and the message of Christian love to the poor in an area called the "Black Hole." She focused on hardships children faced such as alcoholism, child labour, and starvation. "Am I really and truly in Christian America?" she asked. She went on to contrast the wealth encountered during a visit to Chicago's Board of Trade with the poverty of the Black Hole: "What a fine illustration of Dante's *Inferno*."

Attending a women's convention in 1893, Crawford intensified her sense of calling. Impressed by Susan B. Anthony, Julia Ward Howe, and others, Crawford concluded that women, who did not oppress the poor, had a special opportunity to better their condition. The realities she subsequently encountered sharpened this analysis and elicited a passion for justice.

---

[11]Isabel Crawford, *Joyful Journey: Highlights on the High Way* (Philadelphia: Judson Press, 1951). Salvatore Mondello, "Isabel Crawford, the Making of a Missionary," *Foundations* 21 (1978): 323-39; "Isabel Crawford and the Kiowa Indians," 22 (1979): 28-42; "Isabel Crawford, Champion of the American Indians," 22 (1979): 99–115.

After her studies, the Women's American Baptist Home Mission Society assigned Crawford to work among the Kiowas at Saddle Mountain, Indian Territory, Oklahoma. Over the next thirty years, she encountered repeated patterns of injustice. Whites encroached upon the land of Indians, exterminated their game, and stole their resources. An incident revealed her growing outrage. A thief sold a stolen horse to Paudlekeah and then took off with it during the night. At her urging, Paudlekeah reported the theft. When the guilty white was caught and charged, Paudlekeah's credibility was on trial. Despite Crawford's testimony, the court dismissed the case for insufficient evidence. She observed,

> The prisoner went free, the owner of the horse lost it, and the Indian lost his money. Justice had been satisfied! Had the Indian been the prisoner accused of the horse-stealing, the evidence given would have been so overwhelming that the verdict might have been 99 years in the penitentiary, the sentence once given in a local court to an Indian woman accused of being drunk.... I left the court with no desire to be "civilized."[12]

Another incident concerned her initiative to form a Baptist church at Saddle Mountain. On one occasion, the church voted that in the absence of its minister, Crawford's Indian assistant, Lucius Aitsan should administer the ordinance of the Lord's Supper. Crawford assisted him in this first communion service held by the congregation in the new church building. The local Commissioner of Indian Affairs and some local Baptists objected to such independent action by a woman and expressed "grave apprehension and disapproval." Mary G. Burdette (1842–1907), secretary of the Women's American Baptist Home Mission Society, wrote Crawford, "You certainly would not have made so radical departure from Baptist usage as that while bearing the commission of the Society without the approval of the Board." Crawford replied, saying that Indians had the right and duty "to partake of the Lord's Supper and I could not tell them otherwise with an open Bible before me. Do not Baptist Churches that are pastorless celebrate the Lord's Supper?" She and the church were found faultless. Crawford felt "boycotted" and left the field.

---

[12] *Joyful Journey*, 74-75.

From 1917–1921, Crawford worked among Native Americans of western New York, where she found conditions of migrant workers appalling. Frustrated, she resigned from the mission society in order to devote her years before retirement to lecturing, writing, and teaching on behalf of Indian causes.

For Crawford, the root cause of injustice was the theft of Indian land. In addition to teaching the rudiments of Christianity, she taught them to fight for their rights. After retirement, she continued to champion Indian causes. At their request, after she died at age ninety-six, she was buried in the church cemetery at Saddle Mountain. Her gravestone bore the words, "I dwell among mine own people."

Medical Missionaries to India

With the world's second largest population and eighth largest land mass, India is a complex civilization of great peoples, cultures, and revolutions. The origins of this greatness, as well as of most of India's manifest problems, are found in the distant past. For centuries India has experienced wave upon wave of invasion and empire-building. What is perhaps most surprising about the most recent invaders and empire-builders, the British, is that they were there for so short a period of time and left in 1947, primarily as the achievement of a revolution based on principles of non-violent struggle.

Christianity can claim only partial responsibility for the revolution. Foreign missionaries and native Christians did not design or teach it, but, as early as 1921, a non-Christian judge of the high court of Bombay, Narayan G. Chandavarkar, concluded that "ideas which lie at the heart of the gospel of Christ are slowly but surely penetrating every phase of Hindu thought."[13] Reginald Miles Bennett, who served in India with the Canadian Baptist Foreign Mission Board (CBOMB) from 1929–1958, observed,

> The gospel of Jesus is the most explosive ideology in the world and contains far more spiritual dynamite than do the teachings of Karl Marx. We have proclaimed the freedom of the soul; we have inveighed against poverty,

---

[13]Eleventh Annual Report of the Canadian Baptist Foreign Mission Board, 1922, 14.

ignorance, want, misery and disease, and have tried to give practical expression to our belief. We have stood against injustice and inequality. We have brought education, both to the social outcast in the village, and to others in the big city college. We have fought caste and race pride. And God forgive us that there have been times when our own deeds militated against the work done.[14]

During the early decades of Baptist missionary presence in India, missionaries undertook such evangelistic functions as preaching, catechizing, and visitation, as well as vital work in agriculture, education, industry, medicine, public health, self-help, translation, and women's training. Whatever their task, whether agriculture, medicine, education, or pastoral work, they saw a dual function: evangelism and extending God's love in service.

In some respects, women were better able than men to function within this holistic framework. Given the complex nature of the relationship between missionaries, British authorities, and Indian princes, their work often appeared innocuous and safe. As a result, women's work began with a strong social service orientation but functioned in such a way that it facilitated realization of the broad missionary mandate.

The contribution of women to medical services in India illustrated the close relationship between evangelism, social ministry, and peacemaking. Initially, mission boards resisted sending out doctors.[15] In the case of Canadian Baptists, the mission board gradually came to acknowledge that spiritual and physical healing could not be separated. Canadian Baptists developed five medical institutions in Andra Pradesh and Orissa: Vuyyuru, Akividu, Pithapuram, Serango, and Sompeta. Along with an extensive network of out-patient and dispensary work, these have been administered since 1947 as an autonomous medical council. Briefly we examine the origins of the Star of Hope Hospital at Akividu and Arogyavaram Eye Hospital at Sompeta.

In 1895, Dr. Pearl Smith Chute, a graduate of the Toronto Women's Medical College, followed her brother Everett Smith, also a CBOMB medical doctor, to India. Married to a rural evangelist, Jesse Chute, Dr. Chute began her medical work on the veranda of her home. In 1898, she

---

[14]Reginald M. Bennett, *The Church in India. A Canadian Viewpoint* (Toronto: Canadian Council of Churches, 1954) ix.

[15]R. Fletcher Moorshead, *"Heal the Sick." The Story of the Medical Mission Auxiliary of the Baptist Missionary Society* (London: Carey Press, 1929) 20.

opened the Star of David Hospital, which consisted in two good sized rooms for in-patients and a dispensary. She focused especially on the needs of women patients, providing them with medical care and instruction in improved hygiene procedures and prophylactic measures such as digging wells and prenatal health care.[16]

During her thirty-five year career, Dr. Chute sent promising girls to the training hospital for women founded by Dr. Ida Scudder at Vellor. By 1930, most of the Canadian Baptist hospitals had at least one Indian woman doctor on staff. Along with her brother and two other women doctors, Dr. Chute was among nine Canadian Baptist missionaries to receive the Kaiser-i-Hind award, instituted by Queen Victoria in 1900 to honour those, irrespective of race, sex, position, or occupation, who served in India by personal devotion, large-minded charity, ameliorating suffering, and improving the conditions of others.[17]

Two sisters from Prince Edward Island, Martha Clark (in India 1894–1928) and Dr. Zella Clark (in India 1906–1944) started work at Sompeta. They provided education and medical care first at the Good Samaritan Hospital for women and children at Chicacole, 1908–1911, and from 1911–1934 at Sompeta, where they established a girl's boarding school, a dispensary, and day schools. They sought to break down caste and mistreatment of women. Recognizing the need for an eye specialist, Dr. Zella Clark called for someone to build on foundations she and her sister had laid.

Appointed as their successors were Dr. Ben Gullison (1905–1987) and his wife, Mary Evlyn Erb Gullison (1906–1991).[18] Like the Clark sisters, both had roots in the Maritime provinces, although Dr. Gullison was born in India of missionary parents. He trained at Acadia University and Edinburgh; she trained as a teacher and attended the mission school at Gordon College, near Boston.

---

[16]Gordon Carder, "Poured Out," *Enterprise* no. 303 (Winter 1983–1884) 29-32; Orville E. Daniel, *Moving with the Times* (Toronto: CBOMB, 1973) 43; Caroletta Hacker, *The Indomitable Lady Doctors* (Toronto: Clarke, Irwin Company) 118-23.

[17]*British Orders and Awards* (rev. ed., London: Kaye and Ward, 1968); Lawrence L. Gordon published a version in 1959.

[18]Based on William H. Jones, *The Eye Openers. Operation Eyesight. A Study Guide on the Work of the Arogya Varam Eye Hospital* (Toronto, 1977). I have benefited from interviews with Dr. Gullison, as well as staff people with Operation Eyesight Universal, including Harold Cowie, Tom Balke, and the staff at Sompeta.

Upon arrival at Sompeta in 1933, Dr. Gullison surveyed 200 villages. He found 200,000 persons with cataracts or other curable eye disorders: trachoma, glaucoma, and vitamin A and C deficiency. As well, he found other medical problems that could be treated such as cholera, malaria, maternity disorders, and leprosy.

Stories of his fame as a doctor multiplied. Once, seven blind people came led by a seven-year old girl. They had begged during their 200 mile journey. Seeing the emaciated girl, Dr. Gullison ran to her, picked her up, and cared for her.

In 1938, the Gullisons opened a dispensary, Arogyavaram, from two sanskrit words *Arogya* (health restored) and *Varam* (God's gift). Dr. Gullison wrote, "In our hospital, through the very name, we ascribe all honour and praise to God, for restored health—be that sight or whatever the process of healing may be."

Dr. Gullison gave priority to training native workers. John Coapullai, a converted Hindu, had a lucrative private practice. On a visit to Sompeta, he responded to Dr. Gullison appeal for help in an emergency. They attended to the victim of an attack by a bear. Bonds of love and trust knit them together, with the result that Dr. Coapullai joined the staff.

The hospital came to be known as Shanti Sadanam, Abode of Peace in Telugu. Anne Catherine Munroe, missionary in India between 1920–1957 and recipient of the Kaiser-i-Hind medal, wrote,

> A building fitly framed and joined together.
> Peace shall be within its walls
> Peace, upon its portal.
> Sick and suffering though they come,
> Sorrow laden and bowed down,
> Peace shall fill their hearts and lives.
> My peace, for every mortal;
> For I walk with thee, my son.
> Sing and serve, serve and sing,
> For I show thee a new thing.
> Exceeding magnifical shall this building be,
> For thou buildest unto Me.

A missionary in her own right, Mary Evlyn Gullison taught, nursed, and resolved personal problems. With a team of Bible women, she provided effective outreach that helped identify patients for operations. By the time of their retirement in 1970, the Gullisons had treated hundreds of thousands of patients, including 120,000 blind restored to sight. They treated all, irrespective of religion or caste. One Hindu, born blind because his mother contracted measles during the first three months of pregnancy was among those cured through their ministry. As a result of Christian teaching he received after the operation, he confessed he had a false conception that blindness had been the result of his sins in a previous life. "Being given eyesight is like having all my sins freely forgiven."

In the 1960s, as retirement neared, Dr. Gullison organized Operation Eyesight Universal with some Calgary, Alberta, business leaders. Flourishing, it works in fourteen countries. Over a quarter of a million persons a year are treated, including 40,000 operations on curably blind. It also provides emergency relief, for example, after the 1977 cyclone and 1984 Bhopal gas leak.

Conclusion

Missionaries provided a comprehensive ministry of spiritual and physical healing. They incarnated Christ in a broken world among victims of sin and evil by extensive work in such areas as education, care for lepers, medicine, and, in India, breaking down caste. They ministered to the poor and set in motion the transformation of personal lives and social structures. In her poem "Oh Touch," Anne Catherine Munroe stressed that missionary peacemakers followed the model of Jesus in bringing personal and collective freedom and healing to the people:

> Oh, touch the seamless robe of Jesus!
> Press through and touch it now!
> His power is there,
> He answers prayer,
> Press through! Reach out!
> Oh, touch His seamless robe!
> And know He heals today,
> Heals now![19]

---

[19] *A Second Book of Poems* (privately printed, 1971).

Chapter Twelve
Voices from the Developing World

Introduction

As previous chapters have documented, many Baptists have experienced the Spirit of God motivating them to respond to human need, to extend Christian love and compassion, to bring millions to knowledge of God in Christ, and to form new churches. During four hundred years of denominational history, Baptist witness has spread from Britain and North America, where Baptist witness first took root, throughout the world.

In this chapter we focus on work for positive peace on the part of Christians in the younger churches of Asia, Africa, and Latin America. Whether they have been actively involved in missionary efforts in a land other than their place of birth or primary residence or have functioned as Christian ministers in their homelands, work for peace with justice has been integral to their calling.

Four North American Missionaries to Africa

We begin with black missionaries who established Baptist churches as they returned to Africa from the Americas. David George (ca. 1743–1810) launched Baptist work in Nova Scotia and Sierra Leone. Lott Cary (ca. 1780–1828) initiated Baptist work in Liberia. Mammie Johnson (d. 1888) emigrated from Jamaica to Fernando Po and Cameroon. Mary Tule (1860–1923) served in South Africa and Liberia.

David George: Baptist Pioneer in Three Continents

David George was born around 1743 on a Nottaway River plantation in Essex County, Virginia.[1] He was one of nine children born in slavery to John and Judith George. According to George's autobiography, his owner, a man named Chapel, was "a very bad man to the Negroes." He whipped Patty George, David's sister, till her back was "all corruption." He treated Richard George, David's brother, so cruelly that Richard ran away twice. Sometimes, Chapel flogged David "till the blood has run down over my waistband; but the greatest grief I then had was to see them whip my mother, and to hear her on her knees begging for mercy."

Around age nineteen, George escaped and headed south towards the Savannah River. For a period, before "they came after me," he worked for a John Green. He escaped again and began working for an Indian agent named George Galphin. Around 1770, David George married Phyllis, who was possibly half-Cree Indian. After the birth of their first child, he began to frequent prayer meetings and classes, activities generally forbidden slaves but encouraged by Galphin. David George experienced liberation. As he put it, "I can now read the Bible, so what I have in my heart, I can see again in the Scriptures."[2]

Around 1774, David George was attending the black Baptist church at Silver Bluff, South Carolina where George Liele was an itinerant preacher. With encouragement from Liele, George began to preach. Subsequently, he felt "called by grace" to become pastor of the congregation. By 1776, the Silver Bluff church had thirty members. For the duration of the United States War for Independence, George found protection in Savannah, Georgia, with the British. Through the First

---

[1] A key primary source is David George's autobiography, "An Account of the Life of Mr. David George, from Sierra Leone of Africa," *Baptist Annual Register* (1793) 473-83. Secondary sources include Ingraham E. Bill, *Fifty Years with the Baptist Ministers and Churches of the Maritime Provinces of Canada* (St. John: Barnes and Company, 1880); Christopher Fyfe, *A History of Sierra Leone* (Oxford: Oxford University Press, 1962); Grant Gordon, *From Slavery to Freedom. The Life of David George* (Hantsport: Lancelot Press, 1992); Ellen Gibson Wilson, *The Loyal Blacks* (New York: G. P. Putnam's Sons, 1976).

[2] "An Account of the Life of Mr. David George," 476.

African Baptist Church, he resumed his partnership in ministry with Liele. In 1783, at the end of the war, he received a certificate stating that he was "a good subject to King George" and a "free Negro Man."

Taking this document to be a letter of emancipation, George took passage with his family and a few other blacks to Halifax, Nova Scotia. They settled in Shelburn. At once, George organized the black community. In his own words,[3]

> I began to sing the first night, in the woods, at a camp, for there were no houses then built; they were just clearing and preparing to erect a town. The Black people came far and near. . . . I kept on every night in the week, and appointed a meeting for the first Lord's-day, in a valley between two hills, close by the river; and a great number of White and Black people came, and I was so overjoyed with having an opportunity once more of preaching the word of God, that after I had given out the hymn, I could not speak for tears. In the afternoon we met again, in the same place, and I had great liberty from the Lord.

Over the next ten years George established as many as seven Baptist churches in Nova Scotia and New Brunswick. While he experienced opposition from some whites, George served both whites and blacks and frequently mediated disputes between them. In 1792, he heard an appeal from the anti-slavery advocate John Clarkson (1764–1828) to help establish a colony for free blacks in Africa.[4] Responding to the challenge, George and his family, along with several hundred blacks, moved to Sierra Leone.

As they arrived in Freetown, "there was great joy to see the land."[5] George found employment in the office of the governor. But his main contribution was with the nascent Baptist community that George served for nearly twenty years. Anticipating the rise of the modern missionary movement, he founded several congregations and served as pastor of First Baptist Church, Freetown. Between December 1792 and August 1793, David George visited Britain to establish contacts with leaders of the Baptist Missionary Society and the anti-slavery movement. He took with

---

[3] *Ibid.*, 478.

[4] Ellen Gibson Wilson, *John Clarkson and the African Adventure* (London: Macmillan, 1980); brother of the anti-slavery advocate Thomas Clarkson (1760–1846).

[5] "An Account of the Life of Mr. David George," 481.

him letters testifying that he was "a good Christian" and a "very industrious good citizen." Returning to Freetown, George helped blacks to assert their full humanity by defending their rights in several disputes. When attempts failed to locate British Baptist Missionaries in Sierra Leone, he preserved Baptist witness. As a defender of religious liberty, he was an exemplary peacemaker.

Lott Cary: Baptist Pioneer in Liberia

Another early black missionary to Africa was Lott Cary, born a slave on a tobacco plantation near Charles City, Virginia.[6] In 1804, his owner, William A. Christian, sent Cary to Richmond as a hired labourer. Cary worshiped at First Baptist Church. He was baptized in 1807 and subsequently ordained.

By 1813, Cary had saved $850, which permitted him to purchase his freedom and that of his children. He began attending a night school for blacks established by William Crane, a leader in the American Colonization Society. Encouraged by Crane, Cary resolved to settle in West Africa. Cary indicated,

> I am a African, and in [the United States], however meritorious my conduct and respectable my character, I cannot receive the credit due to either. I wish to go to a country where I shall be estimated by my merits, not by my complexion, and I feel bound to labour for my suffering race.[7]

In 1815, intending to establish a Christian mission in West Africa, Cary helped form the Richmond African Baptist Missionary Society. In 1817, Luther Rice (1793–1836), American Baptist advocate of foreign

---

[6]The standard source for Cary's life is Ralph Randolph Gurley, *Life of Jehudi Ashmun . . . with an Appendix, Sketch of the Life of the Rev. Lott Cary* (Washington, D. C.: James C. Dunn, 1835). See also, William H. Brackney, *The Baptists* (New York: Greenwood Press, 1988) 139-40; D. Elwood Dunn and Swend E. Holsoe, *Historical Dictionary of Liberia* (Metuchen: Scarecrow Press, 1985) 35; Miles Mark Fisher, "Lott Cary, The Colonizing Missionary," *Journal of Negro History* 7 (1922): 380-418; Leroy Fitts, *Lott Carey: First Black Missionary to Africa* (Valley Forge: Judson Press, 1978); William A. Poe, "Lott Cary: Man of Purchased Freedom," *Church History* 39 (1970): 49-61. Cary's legacy is enshrined in the Lott Carey Baptist Foreign Missionary Convention.

[7]Gurley, 148.

missions, visited Cary and commented on "the zeal, and intelligence and capacity, and success, discovered in the African Mission Society." Formation of the Richmond-based missionary society inspired blacks to form parallel groups in other cities. By 1821, the black missionary society had raised sufficient funds to begin a colony of former slaves in West Africa. With the encouragement of the American Colonization Society and the General Convention of the Baptist Denomination in the United States of America for Foreign Mission, based in Philadelphia, Cary sailed for Sierra Leone with the intent of founding a settlement at Monrovia, Liberia.

Leadership of the American Colonization Society envisioned the creation of Liberia as a solution to the problem of slavery. However, Cary was more concerned to organize missionary outreach. Before leaving the United States, Cary had organized a church, which was at the center of community life in Richmond. With similar vision, he started schools, churches, medical facilities, and a mission society to work in the interior once he established himself in Liberia.

Cary emerged as the most effective preacher, teacher, and leader in the colony. He dealt with such problems as hostile natives, disputes with representatives of the American Colonization Society, and personal problems such as the death of his first two wives. Initially, he declined posts in the civil service. From 1827–1828, Cary served as vice governor and, for six months, as acting governor of Liberia. He faced problems such as the need for regular shipment of supplies from the United States, improved relations with indigenous peoples, and constitutional arrangements for the colony. In 1847, many of his proposals became the basis of the constitution of the Republic of Liberia.

Cary died accidentally in an explosion at a powder magazine as he prepared to defend the colony against native raids. He was not a pacifist; however, he contributed to positive peace through his holistic understanding of mission and his effort to establish modern Liberia as a haven of independence and an outpost of good relations between settlers and natives.

Mammie Johnson: Baptist Pioneer in Cameroon

A third missionary undertaking by blacks who left bondage in the Americas to establish a Christian presence in Africa was that of free

Jamaicans in Cameroon. In 1842, Jamaican Baptists established a missionary society similar to the British Baptist Missionary Society. In collaboration with the Baptist Missionary Society, the Jamaican Baptists began work in West Africa.[8]

Initially, between 1844 and 1858, the Jamaicans pioneered Baptist witness in Fernando Po, an island near the Cameroon coast, and Cameroon. In 1858, Roman Catholic opposition led to abandonment of the work on Fernando Po. The work in Cameroon prospered.

In 1845, Mammie Johnson was among those who opened up the station at Douala, along the Cameroon River estuary. Wife of Sam Johnson, Mammie was baptized by the British Missionary Society leader Alfred Saker (1814–1880). Mammie Johnson's career was primarily that of a teacher and evangelist. As well, she cared for white and Jamaican missionaries, pioneered women's work in Cameroon, and helped bridge the Jamaican and indigenous church leadership. Among her gifts was that of encouraging. After one sermon, she shared with the preacher, "Ole Mammy Johnson do praise God for de truth you put in her heart dis morning."[9]

Mammie Johnson worked in effect as part of the Jamaican pastoral team. As a colleague of the Reverend Joseph Jackson Fuller (1825–1908), Mammie Johnson helped lay the foundations of Protestant work in Cameroon.[10] Together, they studied the native languages, undertook translation work, formed churches, and provided services in the areas of medicine, education, agriculture, and "industrial training." Missionary correspondence referred to her as an inspiring Christian.

---

[8] Paul R. Dekar, "Alfred Saker and the Baptists of Cameroon," *Foundations* 14 (1971): 325-43; Horace Orlando Russell, "The Missionary Outreach of the West Indian Church to West Africa in the Nineteenth Century with Particular Reference to the Baptists" (D.Phil thesis, Oxford University, 1972); "A Question of Indigenous Mission: The Jamaican Baptist Missionary Society," *Baptist Quarterly* 25 (1973): 86-93.

[9] Thomas Lewis, *These Seventy Years. An Autobiography* (London: Carey Press, n.d.).

[10] Robert Glennie, *Joseph Jackson Fuller. An African Christian* (London: Carey Press, n.d.). Fuller's autobiography refers frequently to Mammie Johnson.

Mary Branton Tule:
Baptist Pioneer in South Africa and Liberia

Mary Branton was born on 18 February 1860 in Chatham, Ontario.[11] As a teen, she was baptized and joined the First Baptist Church, Amherstburg, where she was an energetic member. Elizabeth Shreve inspired her to full-time Christian service. From 1890–1892, Mary Branton attended Spelman College in Atlanta, Georgia, and prepared to go to Africa as a missionary.

From 1896–1911, Mary Tule taught in southern Africa. During this period, the South African government implemented legislation that denied blacks the franchise and stripped them of their land. With her husband, the Reverend John Tule, a South African preacher, Mary vigorously denounced these policies and was forced to leave the country. On speaking tours in Europe and North America, John and Mary Tule condemned the racial injustices of the South African regime.

Barred from returning to South Africa, Mary and John Tule applied to serve in Africa under auspices of the National Baptist Convention. They ministered in Liberia, where Mary established a school.

Ontario's black Baptist congregations continued to remember Mary Tule. When she died in 1923, the Amherstburg Association adopted the following resolution in her memory:

> Her glad gospel armour she now has laid down.
> To receive from the Father a white robe and crown.
> May the light from her tomb cast its rays far and wide,
> Till Africa's sons be drawn to Christ's side.

Ontario's black Baptists established an annual commemorative Sunday in recognition of the ministries of Elizabeth Shreve and Mary Tule.

---

[11] Dorothy Shadd Shreve, *Pathfinders of Liberty and Truth* (Merlin, 1940) 66-67; Walter L. Williams, *Black Americans and the Evangelization of Africa 1877–1900* (Madison: University of Wisconsin Press, 1982) 71, 190.

Christians in South America and India

We continue with the stories of Justino Quispe (1926–1971), who ministered in Bolivia, and of three Indian Christians: L. Kijungluba Ao (1907–1981) of Nagaland; Matthew Limma of Orissa; and Mandakini JeeJatchuch of Andhra Pradesh.

Justino Quispe of Bolivia

We recall the career of Justino Quispe of Bolivia for his effort to help his people overcome economic and political problems.[12] An Aymara Indian from the Bolivian highlands, Justino Quispe grew up on an estate located at Huatajata on the shore of Lake Titicaca, sixty-five miles northwest of La Paz. The economic and spiritual conditions of the lakeshore Indians were deplorable. The peasants lived by farming and fishing. Wealthy landlords claimed at least three-fourths of their crop and catch. The ruling descendants of the Spaniards, with the Catholic church of the day as their ally, deemed the Aymara too stupid to warrant providing the Indians educational or religious development.

In 1911, thanks to the bequest of an Italian miller, a small group of Christian men organized the Peniel Hall farm, a thousand-acre hacienda dedicated to the uplift of the Aymara Indians. Canadian Baptist missionaries took over the work in the 1920s, and it was there that Justino Quispe was born, received an education, and came to affirm Jesus as his saviour. In 1937, a land distribution program began whereby missionaries would give title deeds to families after a period of time.

In 1942, forty-two families were the first to receive land. "It was a momentous day," reminisced Norman Dabbs. "One after another of the former serfs listened while the magic sentence was pronounced, 'I proclaim you the owner of this property'." One of the new landowners,

---

[12]Orville E. Daniel, *Moving with the Times* (Toronto: Canadian Baptist Overseas Mission Board, 1973); Earl C. Merrick, *Bolivia* (Toronto: Canadian Baptist Overseas Mission Board, 1959); interviews with Mary Haddow, 29 July 1988; and with Mario Rivas Perez, 5 August 1988.

Martin Chura, put his emotions into words. "Over thirty years ago, when I was forced to carry on, my back loads were far too heavy for me. I used to pray for freedom. Today, God has answered my prayer."[13]

After 1952, when nationalists came to power, the land distribution program served as a model for the new Bolivian government as it moved to implement its own land reforms. However, the success of land reform efforts contributed to growing hostility against the church. This was because, as the indigenous peoples benefitted, there were losers, and oppressors have never abandoned situations of privilege without a struggle. In Bolivia, Protestant missionaries and converts faced enormous opposition by the established Catholic church. In 1949, Norman Dabbs, a Canadian Baptist missionary; Francisco Salazar, a layperson and president of the Bolivian Baptist Union; Carlos Meneses, a dynamic pastor; and five others died as martyrs.[14]

The martyrdoms had an unintended effect of encouraging new leadership to emerge. Among those who rose to the challenge, Justino Quispe dedicated his life to serving his people. He did this primarily as a pastor and denominational leader. In 1968, he was the first Aymara elected president of the Bolivian Baptist Union. In this position, he helped reconcile factions (native and non-native Christians), classes (rich and poor), and regions (highlands and lowlands). As a role model, Quispe made it possible for other Aymara Christians to serve in positions of authority.

The following story illustrates that Justino Quispe was a Baptist peacemaker. Historic enmity between Bolivia and Peru had long rendered impossible contacts between the Aymara of the two nations. Quispe believed that God did not recognize the international boundary that divided Bolivia from Peru. In the late 1960s, after two decades of effort, he brought the two groups of Aymara together under the auspices of an international congress. As a visible symbol that love in Christ reconciles what humans rend asunder, the Bolivian and Peruvian Aymara worshiped together without interference at the Bolivia-Peru border.

---

[13]Daniel, 105. Samuel Escobar, "The Search for Freedom, Justice, and Fulfillment," in *Mission Trends 3: Third World Theologies*, ed. Gerald H. Anderson and Thomas F. Stransky (Grand Rapids: Eerdmans, 1976) 106–107, has a brief discussion of the land distribution scheme as a model for Christian mission.

[14]See chapter 14.

Justino Quispe helped his people take pride in their culture. He pioneered the use of indigenous music in the native church. One of his songs, translated into English, communicates his devotion to Jesus:

> I will journey on the way with my Saviour ever near
> Happy in His care.
> He will guide and guard my steps
> keeping by His wondrous love
> Joy to know He's there.
> Wandering, I lost the road.
> Jesus called me where I roamed,
> Led me gently home.[15]

In the early 1950s, Justino Quispe, the emerging leader of the Aymara Indians, was invited to serve as the Bolivian Minister of Indian Affairs. He declined. He had another sense of vocation, service to the people. Laboring in the name of Christ amidst difficult conditions, Justino died at an early age. Those touched by his gentle power during twenty-two years of ministry attested to his influence. A man of the people, a native, and a country person, or *campesino*, Justino Quispe exemplified a positive conception of Baptist peacemaking.

L. Kijungluba Ao

L. Kijungluba Ao was born 8 February 1907 in Lirumen, Nagaland, North India.[16] Although he did not become a Christian, his grandfather was among those who welcomed missionaries into the area. His father was among the first converts and became a pastor and school master in the village. Kijungluba Ao attended his father's school, then a boarding school under the care of an American Baptist mission.

Kijungluba Ao recalled that his mother gently directed him towards Christian service. "You will one day become a pastor." In 1926, during the mission's jubilee celebrations, Kijungluba Ao confessed Christ as savior and was baptized. Completing high school in 1932, he received an

---

[15] *Canadian Baptist Hymnal*, 227.
[16] "Life Sketch of Rev. Kijungluba Ao as Told by Himself," manuscript, Dahlberg Award Files, Board of National Ministries, American Baptist Churches, Valley Forge, Pennsylvania.

appointment as teacher in a government school but opted instead to teach at a mission school in Impur. He married a classmate, Artenjenla, who became a nurse and co-evangelist. In 1935, the Ao Baptist Association ordained Kijungluba Ao and appointed him evangelist-pastor.

For the next forty-five years, the Reverend Kijungluba Ao visited people, discussed their material and spiritual situations, identified conditions that needed to be transformed (including the custom of headhunting), baptized Christians, and helped organize new churches. He became a revered leader, advisor, and respected pastor who enabled Christians to become self-reliant. Gradually, the Christian community grew, surpassing 14,000 members in some 150 organized churches by the late 1950s. At the end of his life, he continued involvement in rural development projects such as dairy farming, preventative health care programs, and re-forestation projects.

In 1947, when India became independent from Great Britain, the Naga tribal peoples claimed that Gandhi and Nehru had promised them complete independence from India. This was not granted. Over the years, agitation against India grew in intensity. Moreover, the success of the Christian community in winning new members and providing for the material needs of the people elicited suspicion. By 1955, the Naga Hills region was in a state of insurgency. The Indian government sent in troops. Kijungluba Ao responded by helping to organize relief efforts.

In addition to seeking to alleviate the suffering caused by loss of property and life, Kijungluba Ao traveled tirelessly in quest of a mediated settlement. Underground guerilla fighters and government troops alike respected him. Several times, Prime Minister Nehru and other officials conferred with him. By December 1963, his patient efforts began to bear fruit. The government of India agreed to set up a separate Naga state. Initially, the rebels held out for complete independence, but Kijungluba Ao and other Christian leaders urged an end to war.

In January 1964, the Naga Baptist Association gathered for a key assembly. Kijungluba Ao drafted a resolution urging the government of India to appoint a peace mission "with the sole object of exploring ways and means for the speedy restoration of peace and normalcy in Nagaland."

Encountering resistance, Kijungluba Ao continued his work of mediation. As a result of these efforts, in August 1964 a cease fire went into effect. Kijungluba urged,

> The Church of Christ in Nagaland is on trial today. The nations around are watching with concern how she would behave herself in the face of such a crisis in a people's life. We certainly would place all our people under a serious moral and spiritual obligation to convert this forth-coming cease-fire into a lasting peace in our land. The Christian leaders are bound to lose their moral leadership, unless they boldly cast themselves on the side of Christ in creating a world for all people to live in as brothers and sisters. In doing this we ought to be greatly assisted by the terrible experiences of suffering and insecurity we have been enduring for the last ten years.[17]

Fighting came to an end. On 6 September 1964, the Reverend Kijungluba joined with other Naga Baptist leaders in calling their churches to a Day of Thanksgiving and the work of reconstruction. In letters dated 20 November and 4 December 1964, he reported that there had been no disturbances and prayed for a lasting peace, for mutual understanding, and resolution of the complex problems facing the people. For his role in bringing war to an end in North India, Kijungluba Ao followed Martin Luther King, Jr., as the second recipient of the Dahlberg prize. The citation read:

> For his tireless work to achieve a cease fire in Nagaland, and for his further efforts to win a lasting peace, the American Baptist Convention awards to Rev. L. Kijungluba Ao the second Edwin T. Dahlberg Peace Award, May 20, 1965.[18]

Matthew Limma

In the 1940s, a wealthy Oriya trader, Matthew Limma, prospered by cheating primitive Sora tribespeople.[19] One day, Matthew Limma rested under a tree reflecting about a business dispute that had led him to hire someone to kill his enemies. Limma heard sounds in the forest. He looked up, spotted three men coming towards him brandishing knives, and prepared to die. It was his turn to pay for prior misdeeds. The would-

---

[17]Alfred F. Merrill, "Kijungluba Ao, Christian Peacemaker," *American Baptist Missions*, June 1965, 31.

[18]Citation, Dahlberg Peace Award files, Valley Forge. In 1964, American Baptists honored the peacemaking ministry of Edwin T. Dahlberg by establishing a peace prize in his name.

[19]Personal interview, January 1988; interviews and information from Perry and Edith Allaby and Roger Cann.

be killers threatened Limma's life. A baptized Christian, he realized that he could not continue to cheat and kill. He stood up, embraced his enemies, begged for forgiveness, and offered restitution for past misdeeds. Having committed himself to Christian service, Limma served the Sora tribespeople as evangelist, translator of scripture, pastor, and friend.

Since 1970, Limma has worked primarily among his own Oriya people. He has distinguished himself as a peacemaker. When violence breaks out between the Sora and Oriya, as in situations of retribution similar to the one Matthew Limma once faced, inevitably Limma steps in to mediate. Due in large measure to his efforts, relations between the two peoples have warmed. The church has grown to over 35,000 baptized Sora and Oriya Christians, 135,000 adherents, and forty congregations.

Mandakani JeeJatchuch

Mandakani grew up in a large family supported by her widowed mother.[20] She trained as a nurse, and, when an Indian resident medical officer, Mrs. C. Coapullai, was visiting Berhampur hospital, supported by the British Baptist Missionary Society, Mandakani was invited to move to Sompeta, by the early 1950s a renowned eye hospital. Without much formality, Mandakani joined the staff at Sompeta. "I need only a living allowance. I want to serve the sick and thus serve God through your hospital."

Always loving, generous in spirit, supportive, and cooperative, Mandakani contributed to the growing fame of Sompeta as an abode of peace. When patients came for treatment, she provided pastoral care, calming fears and assisting relatives. Around 1958, Mandakani became blind. Two other members of the family also became blind, one from juvenile cataracts, the other, like Mandakani, from incurable optic atrophy. After receiving specialized training, she worked as a Bible woman, chaplain, and counsellor, especially to those with incurable eye diseases.

---

[20]C. Coapullai, "Shining Out of Darkness," *Link and Visitor* 43/8 (October 1970): 4; interview with Muriel Bent; personal interview, January 1988.

Conclusion

In this chapter we have introduced a number of Christians in the so-called two-thirds world. In Africa, David George, Lott Cary, Mammie Johnson and Mary Tule confronted divisions between North American and African blacks. In Bolivia, Justino Quispe confronted prejudice and economic injustice. In India, Christian leaders confronted similar problems of prejudice and poverty, as well as problems of caste and war. These ambassadors for Christ sought to communicate a gospel of material and spiritual life. As a result, they served as agents for peace and reconciliation. By identifying with their people, they effected transformation, renewal, and healing.

Chapter Thirteen
Howard Thurman (1900–1981)

> When the song of the angels is still,
> When the star in the sky is gone,
> When the kings and princes are home,
> When the shepherds are back with their sheep,
> The work of Christmas begins:
> > To find the lost,
> > To heal the broken,
> > To feed the hungry,
> > To release the prisoner,
> > To rebuild the nations,
> > To bring peace among people,
> > To make music in the heart.[1]

Each Advent season, many greeting cards carry afresh these words penned by Howard Thurman.[2] The meditation invites readers to explore the meaning of Christmas in the depths of the heart, to reflect on the dynamic Center the inward Presence Who enlivens the human spirit and energizes the pilgrimage to peacemaking. It encapsulates a rich legacy of forty-five major articles and twenty-two books by a Baptist who has motivated others to seek to find the lost, heal the broken, feed the hungry, release the prisoner, rebuild the nations, and bring peace among people. By personal example and through a ministry of counseling, preaching, teaching, and writing, Howard Thurman inspired Martin

---

[1] *PeaceWork*, November-December 1987, 12.
[2] Among Thurman's books in print are *Disciplines of the Spirit* (New York: Harper and Row, 1963); *For the Inward Journey. The Writings of Howard Thurman* (San Diego: Harcourt Brace Jovanovich, 1981); *Jesus and the Disinherited* (Nashville: Abingdon, 1949); *The Mood of Christmas* (New York: Harper and Row, 1973); and *With Head and Heart: An Autobiography* (New York: Harcourt Brace Jovanovich, 1979). Luther E. Smith, Jr., *Howard Thurman, The Mystic as Prophet* (Washington: University Press of America, 1981), provides a biography and theological portrait.

Luther King, Jr., who always carried a copy of Thurman's *Jesus and the Disinherited* in his briefcase, and countless others to walk the ways of peace.

An Introduction to the Life of Howard Thurman

Howard Thurman was born and raised in Daytona, Florida, in abject poverty. When he was seven, Thurman lost his father, Saul Solomon Thurman, a railroad crew worker. Because he was not a church member, the local church denied him burial. Because he was black, the local funeral house denied him a memorial service. An itinerant preacher took the service and, as Thurman recalled, "preached my father into hell."[3] The incident precipitated a severe crisis for Thurman regarding the church. A segregated Christianity had violated the spirit of his father.

Life was always on the margins for poor blacks in the southern United States. His mother, Alice Ambrose, remarried. Thurman's maternal grandmother, Nancy Ambrose, who had been born a slave and could neither read nor write nurtured him spiritually. Two or three times a week, Thurman read the Bible to her. She was very particular and loved some of the Psalms, the Prophets, the Gospels and 1 Corinthians 13—but little else from Paul because, as a youth, her master and a white minister had used such texts from Paul as "Slaves, be obedient. . . ."

When Thurman was twelve years old, he expressed a desire to join Mt. Bethel Baptist Church. According to the custom of the congregation, he presented himself to the deacons. They examined him. As they drew to a close, Moses Wright asked, "Howard, why do you come before us?" Thurman stated, "I want to be a Christian." Wright replied, "But you must come before us after you have been converted and have become a Christian. Come back when you can tell us of your conversion." Thurman recalled that he went straight home and told his grandmother what had happened. Before the deacons had time to adjourn, Nancy Ambrose was before them. "How dare you turn this boy down? He is a Christian and was one long before he came to you today. Maybe you did not understand his words, but shame on you if you do not know his heart.

---

[3]Howard Thurman, *Footprints of a Dream. The Story of The Church for the Fellowship of All Peoples* (New York: Harper and Brothers, 1959) 15.

Now you take this boy into the church right now—before you close this meeting!" They did, and Thurman was baptized in the Halifax River.[4]

Despite Thurman's general questions about the church, this particular congregation sustained Thurman through difficult years, offering him a sense of belonging to the black church with its rich heritage of communion, preaching, and spirituals. The church helped Thurman to discern his immense gifts and, when he was about eighteen, granted Thurman a license to preach.

Encountering segregation each step of the way, he went on to study at Howard University, Morehouse College, and Rochester Theological Seminary. One story gives a sense of obstacles Thurman had to hurdle. Spurning an opportunity to study economics at the University of Chicago, he hoped to study theology at Newton Theological Institute, near Boston. Barred because of race, Thurman opted for Rochester Theological Seminary, which enrolled two Negroes in any year, but he had to wait until the last minute while the school confirmed availability of one of the spaces. Thurman had to reside in one of two single rooms cordoned off for them (the theory was that they needed to be close to each other for company). He caused a stir when he accepted the invitation of two friends, Red Mathew and Dave Voss, to share a suite with them. Thurman became class president but was not allowed to participate in some responsibilities of office lest he embarrass the seminary. This was the treatment he received inside walls where Walter Rauschenbusch had taught about God's realm of justice, peace, and righteousness!

In 1922, Thurman joined the pacifist Fellowship of Reconciliation (FOR). At the time, he was not wrestling with problems of peace and war in any national or international context but trying to live in the social climate of Georgia without giving himself over to hostility and evil in that environment. Grim reality prompted Thurman to adopt pacifism to confirm his faith in the creative possibilities of nonviolence and reconciliation, a conviction strengthened by Baptist FOR members such as Walter Rauschenbusch and Shorty Collins.[5] Notwithstanding the fact that

---

[4] *With Head and Heart*, 18.
[5] Rauschenbusch is the subject of chapter 15. George L. (Shorty) Collins (1892–1991) was a Baptist pastor, chaplain, and recipient of the 1971 Dahlberg Prize. From 1923–1928 he served with the FOR as field secretary. In 1960, Collins returned to FOR service as San Francisco area representative.

they were white, they lived a gospel of peace and showed Thurman a better way than was evident about him. Thurman explained:

> The thing that attracted me to the FOR in my undergraduate days was the living witness of one of its field secretaries, Shorty Collins, to what for me at that time was a radically new spirit in the relation between the races. It was through Shorty that I received confirmation of the fact that meaningful shared experiences among people are more binding than ideology or creed. If such experiences can be multiplied over a time interval of sufficient duration, any barrier that separates one person from another can be undermined. As a secretary for the FOR, working periodically in the South where I met him, Shorty demonstrated this.
>
> During the years of my belonging, I have chosen, rather than working actively as part of the organizational structure of the FOR, to let my membership be reflected in my life and in my profession. Therefore, I have never regarded myself as a professional worker for peace, but rather have I been committed to the application of the technique and the spirit of reconciliation. . . . [T]he spirit of the FOR cannot be separated from the unity of all life and the reverence which it inspires under God.[6]

Between 1923 and 1926, while he attended seminary, Thurman became summer pastor of a Baptist church in Roanoke, Virginia. Upon graduation from seminary in 1926, the congregation ordained him. Over the next three years Thurman was pastor of Mt. Zion Baptist Church, Oberlin, Ohio. The illness of his wife Kate Keeley (she died of tuberculosis in 1930, leaving Thurman with a young daughter) prompted Thurman to take a year's sabbatical. He studied at Haverford College under Rufus Jones of the Society of Friends. Jones nurtured the development of a mystical theology that characterizes Thurman's writings. Between 1930 and 1932, Thurman taught in Atlanta at Morehouse College and Spelman College. In 1932, he became Professor of Theology and chaplain at Howard University in Washington, D.C.

In 1935, the World Student Christian Federation invited Thurman to head a delegation on a journey of friendship to Ceylon, Burma, and India. Thurman hesitated. "I did not want to go . . . as an apologist for a segregated American Christianity."[7] With the encouragement of Miriam Slade and Muriel Lester, who were in the United States on speaking

---

[6]*Why I Belong*, Fellowship of Reconciliation brochure.
[7]*With Head and Heart*, 104.

tours, Thurman accepted. He was accompanied by his second wife, Sue Bailey, whom he had married in 1932, and another couple.

The group met Rabindranath Tagore, Gandhi, and others committed to nonviolent social change. Thurman was particularly moved by Gandhi. At the close of their time together, Gandhi asked Thurman to sing "Were You There When They Crucified My Lord?" Gandhi continued, "I feel that this song gets to the root of the experience of the entire human race under the spread of the wings of suffering." Together, they prayed and they sang, "as one heartbeat." As Thurman parted, he asked Gandhi, "What do you think is the greatest handicap to Jesus Christ in India?" "Christianity itself" was Gandhi's reply.[8]

At the end of their tour, Thurman and his wife stood at the Khyber Pass, between Afghanistan and what is now Pakistan. Impressed by the nonviolent struggle of South Asia's peoples for political independence, Thurman reflected on the relevance of Gandhi's concept of *satyagraha*, or truth-force, to the struggle of blacks in United States blacks for dignity. Thurman had what he later called his "Khyber Pass experience." He realized the color bar constituted a "monumental betrayal of the Christian ethic." He resolved to return to the United States and test whether a religious community cutting across all racial barriers and carrying into the common life could be developed. At stake for Thurman would be an attempt to reconcile the ethic of Jesus with Christian practice.

Over the balance of his life, Howard Thurman achieved precisely this sort of reconciliation. He demonstrated that meaningful experiences of unity and friendship between people or nations—such as he had experienced in India—are more compelling than concepts, ideologies, fears, and prejudices that may divide them. Over an interval of sufficient duration, multiplication of these experiences can undermine any barrier that separates people.[9]

---

[8]*Ibid*, 134-35.
[9]*Footprints*, 24.

The Church for the Fellowship of All Peoples

Upon returning to Howard University, Thurman began to experiment with the visual arts, meditation, and innovative liturgies to create a worship experience that created a sense of unity among those who worshiped together. Could religion create true humanity? The answer was yes, although a predominantly black institution was not a context to work this out sufficiently.

In 1943, Thurman received a letter from FOR Secretary Abraham Johannes Muste that made possible realization of the dream. In San Francisco, a group influenced by the British pacifist Muriel Lester was looking for a pastor. The people wanted to develop an interracial fellowship and a simpler lifestyle. Moved by their sincerity, the Thurmans uprooted themselves and helped to start The Church for the Fellowship of All Peoples, one of the first congregations to resist racial conventions of the day.

In the milieu of 1944, launching The Church for the Fellowship of All Peoples in San Francisco was no easy matter. With Federal Government blessing, segregation of races prevailed in the armed forces and throughout the social system. San Francisco was a cauldron of racial antipathy and violence. Many Japanese-Americans had been removed to concentration camps. An influx of poor blacks from the South, attracted by the demands of war industries, met housing restrictions and deplorable conditions. Chinese and Mexicans fared little better. Newspapers of the day warned of the need to avert racial disorder.

Starting in rented quarters with a small nucleus of people, members engaged in intense questioning and searching. Out of this inventive period emerged a "declaration" that read in part,

> The Church for The Fellowship of All Peoples is a creative venture in interracial, intercultural, and interdenominational communion. In faith and genius it is Christian. While it derives its inspiration primarily from the source of Hebrew-Christian thought and life, it affirms the validity of spiritual insight wherever found and seeks to recognize, understand, and appreciate every aspect of truth whatever the channel through which it comes. It believes that human dignity is inherent in man as a creature of God, and it interprets the meaning of human life as essentially spiritual. It recognizes and affirms that the God of Life and the God of Religion are one and the same, and that the normal relation

of people as children of one God and Father, is one of understanding, confidence, and fellowship.[10]

Creative in its use of the arts, innovative in worship, bold in outreach, and uncondescending in service, the church encouraged members to hold dual membership. They could participate in the experiment while retaining bonds with other denominations or religions as a leaven for change.

A camp for children provides an example of the approach. Called "Adventures in Friendship," the camp brought together white, North American Indian, Mexican, Filipino, Japanese, Chinese, Jewish, Buddhist and other children. Each was encouraged to share his/her religious/cultural heritage. One child observed, "Why, they are just like us." One result of this approach was that in 1953, 60 percent of the membership of the church was white, thirty-five percent black, and five percent Mexican-American, Oriental-American, or another minority.

The war weighed heavily on the pacifist Thurman. One story typified his response. As news of the bombing of Hiroshima came over the radio on 6 August 1945, Thurman was in his office with his Japanese secretary. He shared their reaction:

> She had family there. We were both devastated by the announcement. She used my large handkerchief to absorb her tears. No words were said. There was only the sound of the broadcast, with its lurid description of the carnage. We could establish no psychological distance between ourselves and the horror of the moment. The experience flowed together as a single moment in time. This was Fellowship Church, not in action but in *being*. . . .
>
> There has not been a single day since the beginning of the church that I have not been moved by its spirit. It was not the unique essence of any particular creed or faith; it was timeless and time-bound, the idiom of all creeds and totally contained in none, the authentic accent of every gospel but limited to none, the growing edge that marks the boundaries of all that destroys and plunders and lays waste. For a breathless moment in time, a little group of diverse peoples was caught up in a dream as old as life and as new as a hope that just emerges on the horizon.[11]

---

[10]*Ibid.*, 53.
[11]Thurman, *With Head and Heart*, 162.

In part because of growing writing and speaking commitments, Thurman developed a team approach to ministry. This enabled him, in 1953, to become pastor-at-large and to accept a call as chaplain and professor of Spiritual Disciplines at Boston University. Martin Luther King, Jr., whose father was Thurman's Morehouse College classmate and lifelong friend, was a student in one of Thurman's classes and became a friend as well. After retirement in 1965, the Thurmans returned to San Francisco and The Church of the Fellowship of All Peoples and developed the Howard Thurman Educational Trust, which continues the ministry of the church.

Pastor as Peacemaker

A prolific author, Howard Thurman's writings anticipated much of the church's agenda in the 1990s: caring for earth; breaking down cultural, racial, and other barriers that separate people; developing nonviolent ways of living. In the following paragraphs we identify key elements of his teaching.

Thurman was a "nature mystic." By mysticism, he understood an inner, personal response to God. Thurman drank deep from the well of literature of classical mysticism. In a pamphlet, he cited the Psalmist, "Be still and know that I am God." He wrote on the importance of silence, of waiting on God, of readying oneself to meet the Presence of God. Thurman recalled an occasion when he was a theological student in Rochester. He was heading home late one night. As he walked along, he became aware of what seemed to be the sound of rushing water. He realized that he had been hearing this for some time but had only suddenly become aware of it. The next day, one of his professors told him the sound of water was produced by a section of the old Erie Canal. Only because other noises had stilled had he noticed it. "This is analogous to the mystic's witness of God within, whose Presence may not become manifest until the traffic of the surface is somehow stilled. This is what is meant by the experience of centering down."[12]

---

[12]Howard Thurman, *Mysticism and the Experience of Love* (Wallingford: Pendle Hill Pamphlet 115, 1961) 7-8.

Nature opened Thurman's eyes to the reality of God and gave him a sense of unity with all things. Encountering God in nature and using the natural world as the locus where one discovers God sustained him and motivated him to want to preserve the earth and all therein. As an example, in 1909 and 1910, Halley's Comet made its celebrated appearance. One night, Thurman's mother awakened him from sleep, asking if he would like to see it. Thurman expressed anxiety if it should fall out of the sky. Assured by his mother, he stood in awe of the grandeur of God. God stirred his heart to share his life with God the Creator of all Life. He wrote, "The hunger itself is God, calling to God. It is fundamental to my thought that God is the Creator of Life, the Creator of living substance, the Creator of existence, and as such expresses Himself through life."[13]

Thurman pioneered better relations among people, cutting across the barrier of religion as well as of race. While at Oberlin, Thurman recalled a Chinese student who attended the worship for a year. After a while, the young man introduced himself to Thurman as a Buddhist and explained, "I did not expect to find a Christian Service in which I could worship. This year, your church has provided that kind of experience for me and I take back to my country a genuine gratitude for what you have given me." Thurman observed, "He was the first Buddhist I had ever seen."[14]

As evidenced by his openness to Hindus, Jains, Muslims, and Sikhs in South Asia, and by the declaration of the Church for the Fellowship of All Peoples, cited earlier, Thurman was sensitive to the religious experience of people of all faiths. While proclaiming Christ's revelation as unique, he respected all traditions, as another story expresses.

A student in Boston, Zalman Schachter, a Jewish Hasid and future rabbi, found himself looking for a place to pray in the chapel. Facing Christian symbols, he was about to leave when a man came and said, "I've seen you here several times. Would you like to say your prayers in the Chapel?" Schachter explained his difficulty. Thurman replied, "If you don't mind, tomorrow morning stop by the Chapel and see if you are comfortable." The next morning, two candles burned in the candlestick, the Bible was open to the Psalms, but a big brass cross was gone.

---

[13]Thurman, *With Head and Heart*, 271-72.
[14]Thurman, *Footprints*, 22.

Moved, Schachter went on to study with Thurman. "It was one of the most exciting half year of my life studying under that man."[15]

Thurman began peacemaking with the journey inward, to the heart of God who endows each personality with significance, the capacity of love, and the possibility of experiencing wholeness, or *shalom*. Understanding his calling as a pastor, he saw his first responsibility to help people to meet God.

Thurman went on to affirm that the God of life and the God of religion are one. The normal relationship of people as children of God should be one of understanding, confidence, and celebration of community with the whole of creation. Helping people to experience God's transforming power, Thurman led them on a spiritual pilgrimage linking reconciliation with God, reconciliation with others, and reconciliation with nature. For Thurman, the religion of Jesus aimed to give the disinherited not only a new sense of dignity but also power to love in ways that transform the social order. Overcoming "rioting in the streets of the soul," Jesus empowers disciples to confront the magnitude of violence of social systems and to root out such diseases of the human spirit and body politic as demagoguery, segregation, and poverty. This is the true "discipline of reconciliation."[16]

For Howard Thurman, love was the costliest dimension of Christianity. In the Church for the Fellowship of All Peoples, he took care to enable people both to discover and to share love. He encouraged the congregation to create "a common meeting place in which there will be no Negro church and no white church, but the church of God—that is the task we all must work to finish."[17] He left this as a task to finish.

Thurman taught nonviolence as the appropriate method with which to proceed. As early as 1928, in an article entitled "Peace Tactics and a Racial Minority," Thurman outlined elements of his philosophy of nonviolence and pacifism. He placed at the heart of his philosophy two elements of Jesus' teaching: love of one's enemy and loving by example and by suffering. Thurman wrote,

---

[15]Zalman Schachter, *Anchor Chairs and Ruah Haqodesh. A Personal Story*, Thurman papers, Swarthmore College Peace Collection.
[16]Howard Thurman, "The Discipline of Reconciliation," in *Disciplines of the Spirit*.
[17]*Footprints*, 157.

[A]t the very center of the Christian faith, even the enemy must be loved. The injunction is, "But I say unto you, love your enemies that you may be children of your Father who sends His rain on the just and the unjust." It is clear and needs no underscoring that what seems to be the natural thing is to hate one's enemy. The insistence here is that the individual is enjoined to move from the natural impulse to the level of deliberate intent. One has to bring to the center of his focus a desire to love even one's enemy.[18]

Conclusion

As we conclude this chapter, it may be helpful to reflect on one of Thurman's prayers of confession:

The concern which I lay bare before God today is for the world in these troubled times. I confess my own inner confusion as I look out upon the world.
    There is food for all—many are hungry.
    There are clothes enough for all—many are in rags.
    There is room enough for all—many are crowded.
    There are none who want war—preparations for conflict abound.
I confess my own share in the ills of the times.
I have shirked my own responsibilities as a citizen.
I have been concerned about my own little job, my own little security,
    my own shelter, my own bread.
I have not really cared about jobs for others, security for others, shelter for others,
    bread for others.
I have not worked for peace; I want peace, but I have voted and worked for war.
I have silenced my own voice that it may not be heard on the side of any cause,
    however right, if it meant running risks or damaging my own little
reputation.

Thurman continues:

Having placed before God our lives, concerns and prayers of confession, we receive God's forgiveness; finding strength for these days, courage, and hope for tomorrow, in confidence we rest in God's sustaining grace.[19]

Recently, the television documentary *Eyes on the Prize* drew the attention of viewers to the persistence of racism in the United States and

---

[18]Thurman, *Mysticism and the Experience of Love*, 19.
[19]*For the Inward Journey*, 52, 26-27.

to progress that has been made to better the lot of millions of citizens. Thurman was among those who cultivated the ground for the revolution that transformed race relations in the United States for the good over the last fifty years. We give thanks for his life. We need more Baptist peacemakers like him working for reconciliation among all peoples.

Section Three
Prophetic Voices

The Letter to the Hebrews begins, "Long ago God spoke to our ancestors in many and various ways by the prophets, but in these last days he has spoken to us by a Son." God still speaks to humankind through prophets. Some, although not all, are Baptist.

Whenever and wherever they emerge, Baptists upset people. In obedience to Jesus, they baptize one another in frozen lakes, muddy rivers, or other available water. As followers of the Prince of Peace, many refuse war. As followers of Jesus' way of the cross, many risk death.

In the seventeenth century, English foes branded Baptists as anabaptists, antinomians, heretics, rattlesnakes, or schismatics. In the Americas, opponents hurled similar epithets at them. In 1713, when a German Baptist congregation took hold, believers appeared in Brobdingnagian proportions. Their leader, Alexander Mack, gave assurance that the community threatened no one: "No Baptist will be found in war, and few in prison or on the gallows because of their crimes. The majority of them are inclined to peacefulness. It would be desirable that the whole world were full of these 'deteriorated' Baptists."[1]

Only a few of these disturbing Baptists can be called prophets. This section profiles several. Their witness to the God of peace may make contemporaries feel uncomfortable. We need to hear their uncompromising voices for peace with justice.

Chapter fourteen honors the witness of Baptist martyrs from the English seventh-day observer Dorothy Traske (d. 1645) to the El Salvador teacher Maria Gomez (d. 1989). Chapters fifteen, sixteen, and seventeen recall figures who significantly shaped twentieth-century thought and action for peace, Walter Rauschenbusch (1861–1918), Muriel Lester (1883–1968), and Martin Luther King, Jr. (1929–1968). Chapters eighteen and nineteen explore the founders of the first Baptist pacifist groups. British and North American conscientious objectors formed these bodies in response to the approach of the Second World War. Many

---

[1] *PeaceWork*, November 1989–February 1990, 25.

combined work for positive peace with witness against war. For example, Howard Ingli James (1889–1956), pastor at Queen's Road, Coventry, condemned war without reservation from the pulpit while organizing a social ministry that helped members of the congregation cope with the lingering depression. In southeast Georgia, Clarence Jordan (1912–1969) and Florence Jordan (1912–1987) expressed their pacifism by establishing Koinonia Farm in an effort to promote racial harmony and eliminate rural poverty.

These prophetic voices testify that Jesus cares for the poor and the oppressed; that Jesus is our Peace, in whom God is reconciling the world and through whom God calls us to a ministry of peacemaking; that his disciples must root their lives deeply in the love of God; and that the harvest of the Spirit in the lives of those who dare to work for peace is justice and love, for the foundation of peace is justice, and the force of peace is love. Having put on sandals of peace, these figures inspire us as much by what they did as by what they wrote. They constrain us to dream creation of an inclusive social order based on goodness, justice, love, and reconciliation. Having seen the promised land, they beckon all to act upon our dreams and to dwell therein.

Chapter Fourteen

Martyrs

Martyrdom means witness. Martyrdom is not the only form of Christian witness. Martyrdom is not exclusively a Christian, or religious, phenomenon. Nonetheless, for two thousand years, martyrdom in the face of persecution and suffering has been, for many Christians, the ultimate test of discipleship.

To suffer and die for one's faith is an extreme manifestation of commitment. It is not surprising, therefore, that martyrdom has had pre-eminence in Christian hagiographical and devotional literature. This harsh expression of love has served as a compelling form of witness to Jesus' way of the cross.

Christianity arose amidst persecution, exile, and death. So did specific movements within Christian history, including the Baptist movement. Since the seventeenth century, real and spiritual persecution, suffering and death, have dominated the ordeals of thousands of Baptists. This has enabled them to identify with early Christian experience and to understand suffering for Christ's sake as a true test of what Christian commitment requires.

During the nineteenth century, a popular movement among Baptists in the southern United States nurtured awareness of the "trail of blood" in Christian history. Known as Landmarkism, this movement traced history through key episodes, or landmark events. According to Landmarkists, one may discern the true church (characterized by recovery of the practice of believer's baptism and by renewal of persecution and martyrdom) only at certain times. Christianity began with Jesus and a group of apostles, all of whom were baptized and martyred. For three centuries, their successors experienced periods of intense persecution, prompting the apologist Tertullian to observe that the blood of the martyrs was the seed of the church. After the conversion of Constantine, Christianity came to be entangled with empire. Repeatedly, but without success, the official church sought to suppress the true church. The true church re-emerged, notably in the fifteenth century with the Czech Brethren, in the sixteenth century with the Anabaptists, and in the seventeenth century with the Baptists.

This simple, albeit simplistic, version of history has merit in that it recalls that the way of Jesus is the way of the cross. Throughout Christian history, martyrs have born witness to the love and salvific power of God as revealed through Jesus Christ. The experience of suffering, death, and martyrdom may seem something of the past, but it is not. This century has produced hundreds of thousands of martyrs, a figure that will continue to increase.[1] While the names of Martin Luther King, Jr. (d. 4 April 1968), Oscar Romero (d. 21 March 1980), and Janani Luwum (d. 17 February 1977) spring to mind among prominent contemporary Christian martyrs, *the names* of most Christian martyrs have been known only to family members and to God. However, *the significance* of their witness has not been lost.

In this chapter, we recall the prophetic witness of several Baptist martyrs. In three sections we note early Baptist martyrs; missionary martyrs; and the witness of Baptists in El Salvador, the nation which bears the name of the Holy One of God whose way of the cross subsequently shaped the willingness of Christians to suffer and die as a positive form of witness.

Sixteenth- and Seventeenth-Century Martyrs

During the sixteenth century in Europe, Anabaptism arose as hundreds of Anabaptists experienced persecution and martyrdom. Through their trials, Anabaptists came to understand suffering for Christ's sake as a true sign of Christian discipleship and the most direct way to gain entrance into eternal life. A "martyr's theology" became an important characteristic of Anabaptist faith. As expressed by a widow named Weynken, burnt to death on 20 November 1527, "care not [if they put me to death]; as the Lord has ordained it, so it must be, and not otherwise; I will adhere to the Lord."[2]

---

[1]David B. Barrett, "Annual Statistical Table on Global Mission: 1986," *International Bulletin of Missionary Research* 12 (1986): 22-23, and successor tables.

[2]Thieleman Jan van Braght, *The Bloody Theatre or Martyrs Mirror of the Defenseless Christians* (Scottdale: Mennonite Publishing House, 1951) 423. *Martyr's Mirror*, a collection of Anabaptist martyrology, is an important source for understanding Anabaptist faith. A. Orley Swartzentruber, "The Piety and Theology of the Anabaptist Martyrs in van Braght's *Martyrs' Mirror*," *Mennonite Quarterly Review* 28 (1954): 5–16, 128-42; Walter

From the numerous accounts of persecution and martyrdom, the following account of Elizabeth Dirks presented characteristic themes: arrest; defiance of authorities; refusal to retract her witness to the gospel of Jesus Christ; hope derived from God's sustaining presence and death.

Apprehended on 15 January 1549, Elizabeth Dirks went to prison. Arraigned before town council, she was asked about her beliefs concerning baptism. She affirmed her baptism as a believer and explained, "All the water in the sea could not save me; but salvation is in Christ (Acts 4:10), and He has commanded me to love God my Lord above all things, and my neighbor as myself." Her accusers tortured her, so that blood squirted out at the nails. She cried out, "Oh! I cannot endure it any longer." She was told to confess, but she cried out to God, "Help me, O Lord, Thy poor handmaiden! for Thou art a helper in time of need." According to the narrative, God took away her pain. She gave no evidence detrimental to her or her brothers and sisters in Christ. On 27 March, 1549, her accusers sentenced her to death by drowning.[3]

In the seventeenth century, British Baptists identified strongly with Anabaptist martyrology. As Baptists experienced persecution, many fled, took refuge among Dutch Anabaptists, and imbibed the narratives of Anabaptist martyrs. Some returned to Britain to face imprisonment, torture, and death. Two women were among early Baptist martyrs.

Dorothy Traske (née Coome) was a radical seventh-day sabbatarian. While no one preserved records of her birth, parentage, and upbringing, one narrator described her as a woman "endowed with many and particular virtues." Traske must have been a person of considerable learning. She conducted a private preparatory class. She must have been a person of compassion, for she returned part of the tuition collected to poor parents "out of conscience and as believing that she must one day be judged for all the things done in the flesh."[4]

Klaassen, ed., *Anabaptism in Outline. Selected Primary Sources* (Scottdale: Herald Press, 1981) ch. 4.

[3]*Martyrs Mirror*, 481-83.

[4]*Seventh Day Baptists in Europe and America* (Plainfield: Seventh Day Baptist General Conference, 1910) 109–11; R. L. Greaves entry under John Traske (1585–1636) in Richard L. Greaves and Robert Zaller, eds., *Biographical Dictionary of British Radicals in the Seventeenth Century* (Brighton: Harvester Press, 1982). For general works, see James T. Dennison, Jr., *The Market Day of the Soul* (Latham: University Press of America, 1983); John H. Primus, *Holy Time. Moderate Puritanism and the Sabbath*

In February 1617, Dorothy married John Traske. As part of a small group of Christians who formed the nucleus of the Mill Yard Seventh Day Baptist Church, Dorothy and John Traske imbibed the conviction that the fourth commandment prescribed to the letter observance of the Jewish sabbath. As a result of their advocacy of the Saturday-Sabbath, the Traskes were arrested. Because of her views on vegetarianism, domestic life, and scripture, Dorothy Traske remained in prison from 1628 to 1645. She died in her cell.

Sequestered in the same prison with Dorothy Traske was Richard Lovelace, who wrote the following lines in memory of her:

> Stone walls do not a prison make,
> Nor iron bars a cage;
> Minds innocent and quiet take
> That for a heritage.

Dorothy Traske left no such literary legacy herself. It is not possible to know how she interpreted her experience. Through most Christian history, martyrs found the great love of God hidden in their suffering. This gave them hope and courage. What we can say about Dorothy Traske is that, by dying for her beliefs, she helped launch the Seventh Day Baptist movement with her martyrdom. Similarly, another Seventh Day Baptist leader, John James, pastor of the congregation in Bulstake Alley, Whitechapel, suffered for his convictions and was executed on 26 November 1660 despite a petition by his wife to the king for mercy.[5]

After restoration of the monarchy in 1660, Baptists encountered a wave of persecution. In response, General and Free Will Baptists articulated a position of nonresistance. They utterly condemned taking up arms and participation in the military. "Marvel not O King at my single hearted conclusion, in that I said, I shall neither swear nor fight for thee."[6] Such protestations of nonviolence did not prevent many from

---

(Macon: Mercer University Press, 1989).

[5]B. R. White, *The English Baptists of the Seventeenth Century* (London: Baptist Historical Society, 1983) 99.

[6]*Original Records of Early Nonconformity under Persecution and Indulgence*, transcribed and edited by G. Lyon Turner (3 vols., London: T. Fisher, Unwin, 1911–1914): 3:36; *General Baptist Magazine* 1 (April 1798): 139; Louise Fargo Brown, *The Political Activities of the Baptists and Fifth Monarchy Men in England during the Interregnum* (Washington: American Historical Association and London: Henry Frowde, 1912) 9, 53.

suffering. Some found themselves expelled from pastoral charges. At least one Baptist woman, Elizabeth Gaunt, died for her convictions.

Elizabeth Gaunt was a devout Baptist layperson known for acts of charity such as visiting prisons and looking after the poor, whatever their persuasion. In 1683, many non-conformists supported a muddled affair known as the Rye House Plot. When the military uprising failed, the government named a number of Baptists as conspirators, including Elizabeth Gaunt. Gaunt was jailed at Newgate, London, and charged (falsely) with treason for hiding James Burton, a man imputed in the plot. At her trial on 23 October 1685 she gave the following testimony:

> I desire to offer up my all to him [God], it being my reasonable service that he who will be Christ's disciple must forsake all and follow him. Therefore let none think hard, or be discouraged at what hath happened unto me.... it is but my lot in common with poor desolate Zion at this day. Neither do I find in my heart the least regret for anything I have done in the service of my Lord and Master Jesus Christ, in securing and succoring any of his poor sufferers that have shewed favour . . . to his righteous cause . . . therefore, let all that love and fear him not omit the least duty that comes to hand or lies before them, knowing that now Christ hath need of them, and expects they should serve him.

As she faced death, Gaunt explained, "I did but relieve an unworthy, poor, distressed family and lo, I must die for it." She was burned at the stake. Her zeal inspired others to imitate her piety, courage, and commitment to liberty.[7]

Missionary Martyrs

Traske and Gaunt died within the context of a wider struggle for religious liberty. The struggle continued in many places, including mission fields where Baptists have died through self-denial or persecution. Baptist outreach to China illustrates these two forms of martyrdom.

Eastern rite and Catholic churches have a long history of involvement in China. Protestant witness dates from the early nineteenth century.

---

[7]Joseph Ivemey, *A History of the English Baptists* (4 vols., London, 1811–1830), I: 456-57; Joy Worstead, "Elizabeth Gaunt," in A. S. Clement, ed., *Great Baptist Women by Baptist Women* (London: Carey Kingsgate, 1955) 17-28; William Henry Brackney, *The Baptists* (New York: Greenwood Press, 1988) 174-75.

Through efforts of Joshua Marshman (1768–1837) of Serempore, India to secure publication in 1823 of the Bible in Chinese, Baptists helped initiate new work. In 1833, American Baptists commissioned missionaries to work among the Chinese, followed by the British General Baptists in 1845, British Seventh Day Baptists in 1850, and the British Baptist Missionary Society in 1859. In 1858 and 1860, conventions and treaties with western powers opened China to further missionary penetration. English Baptist pioneers included Timothy Richard (1845–1919), who spent forty years in China. When famine devastated Shansi [Shanxi] Province from 1877–1879, Timothy Richards responded by organizing food distribution. Subsequently, he sought to break down resistance to the application of western science to addressing China's economic condition.[8]

Charlotte Digges [Lottie] Moon (1840–1912), a Baptist from the southern United States, confronted the same famine early during her forty-year career in China. Born amidst privilege at the Viewmont Plantation on the road between Charlottesville and Scottsville in Albemarle County, Virginia, overlooking the Blue Ridge Mountains, Lottie Moon descended from Quakers on her mother's side and from Presbyterians on her father's side. She received a good education, including the Master of Arts degree from the University of Virginia. She was among the first women in the southern states to achieve this level of academic distinction.[9] At the time, the role of women was largely that of presiding in the parlor and keeping silence in the church. For Lottie Moon, one of the few avenues of employment outside the home was to teach. Accordingly, she taught at the Caldwell Institute in Danville, Kentucky (1866–1871) and became principal of a school for young ladies in Cartersville, Georgia (1871–1873).

On 22 December 1858, John A. Broadus, pastor of Charlottesville Baptist Church and missionary advocate, baptized Moon. For the balance

---

[8]Kenneth Scott Latourette, *A History of Christian Missions in China* (London: Society for Promoting Christian Knowledge, 1929) 379-80. For romanization of Chinese place names, I follow conventions of the period used in published sources.

[9]Catharine B. Allen, *The New Lottie Moon Story* (Nashville: Broadman Press, 1980), 39; also, see R. Pierce Beaver, *All Loves Excelling. American Protestant Women in World Mission* (Grand Rapids: Eerdmans, 1968) 99–101; Edith Deen, *Great Women of the Christian Faith* (New York: Harper and Brothers, 1959) 259-65; Una Roberts Lawrence, *Lottie Moon* (Nashville: Sunday School Board of the Southern Baptist Convention, 1927); Leon McBeth, *Women in Baptist Life* (Nashville: Broadman Press, 1979) 90-92.

of her life, she expressed her Christian commitment through her life rather than through doctrinal writing. One early concern had to do with restrictions limiting women as they tried to serve God through the church. At university, she wrote a paper supporting the work of deaconesses among the poor and degraded. She encouraged the appointment of single women as missionaries. Despite considerable opposition, in 1872, the Foreign Mission Board of the Southern Baptist Convention commissioned her sister Edmonia to serve at Tengchow, Shantung. The next year, Lottie Moon followed Edmonia to China, where she served (apart from three brief furloughs) until her death.

Lottie Moon pressed for full recognition of the gifts of women in mission and ministry. She declared women missionaries could care for themselves and should have a full voice in deciding mission business as well as have the right to their own homes and work. When male missionaries and board executives questioned giving single women missionaries equal status, Moon threatened to resign. Her protest carried the day.

Lottie Moon conducted the school at Tengchow. For ten years, she pioneered work among "cloistered women." Because married missionary women had limited time for this work and because the Chinese culture demanded separation of the sexes, she was free to develop this side of the work. Subsequently, she directed her energies to work in interior villages and towns by pioneering a new field around P'ingtu, itinerating widely, establishing new churches, and undertaking translation work. Referring to Moon's enormous impact, a mission executive declared "I estimate a single woman in China is worth two married men."[10]

Lottie Moon became one of the best scholars of Chinese literature and history of any missionary and mastered the language. During an imperialist age, Lottie Moon encouraged Chinese Christians to be self-supporting, self-propagating, and self-governing—ideas that later characterized the three-self movement. During an era of racism, she related to Chinese Christians as equals. She adopted Chinese dress and renounced use of the word heathen. Moon insisted that Chinese be treated with respect and noted that China had been civilized when Anglo-Saxons were stalking the forests of Europe. "It is time that followers of Jesus revise

---

[10] Allen, 136, quoting Henry Allen Tupper, who was responsible in 1872 for the Foreign Mission Board policy which allowed single women to serve in China.

their language and learn to speak respectfully of non-Christian people."[11] During the tumultuous events 1911–1912, when China became a republic, she protested when some Christians joined the revolutionaries who plundered the temple of the pagan deity of the city. "This is religious persecution—the very thing Christians have objected to and have been subjected to. Such behavior is not Christian!"[12]

Lottie Moon became one of the most celebrated missionaries of the period. She developed a vast support network among correspondents. Friends and family contributed to the expanding women's work of foreign mission. As early as 1881, Moon launched a Christmas appeal among Southern Baptist women. In 1887, she appealed that the week before Christmas be observed as a time of prayer and self-denial for missions.

> Need it be said why the week before Christmas is chosen? Is not the festive season, when families and friends exchange gifts in memory of The Gift laid on the altar of the world for the redemption of the human race, the most appropriate time to consecrate a portion from abounding riches and scant poverty to send forth the good tidings of great joy into all the earth?

Dismissing the charge of "impracticable idealism," Lottie Moon's appeal for more resources in the form of financial help and volunteers to serve in P'ingtu resulted in funding three new missionaries.[13] Generally, Southern Baptists ignored Moon's plea for increased support.

Towards the end of the century, tensions between the Chinese and Westerners increased. Moon continued self-sacrificially, but in July 1900, the Boxer rising made it impossible for her to continue. After receiving repeated demands by the United States consul that she leave China, and following the death of some of the Christian martyrs, Moon briefly taught in Japan.

During the revolution of 1911–1912, famine wreaked havoc throughout the country. Moon renewed her Christmas appeal to support the cause. She met indifference. Destitution overwhelmed her. She gave all the possessions and funds that she had to the Famine Relief Fund. A friend summarized, "She [Lottie Moon] sank into a state of melancholy,

---

[11] *Ibid.*, 201-202.
[12] *Ibid.*, 271.
[13] *Ibid.*, 170.

refusing to eat, lest she might further impoverish her people or the Board." Too late, the Tengchow missionaries realized the seriousness of her condition. Despite her frailty and age, 72, they arranged to send her to Virginia to recover. She died on board ship. Her ashes were buried in Virginia. Her gravestone bears the inscription, "Faithful unto death." In China, a marker recalled her witness with these words, "The Tengchow church remembers forever."[14]

Through her impressive career, Lottie Moon witnessed revolutionary strife (1900; 1911–1912); divisions among mission personnel; and four wars: Civil War in the United States (1861–1865); the French-Chinese wars (1880s); Japan against China over Korea (1894–1895); and the Russo-Japanese War (1904–1905). While she was not a pacifist, she acted as a peacemaker through providing relief to the victims of war and seeking reconciliation whenever possible. A witness to abject need and revolutionary turmoil, Lottie Moon developed a self-sacrificing lifestyle that eventually led to her death. After her death, Southern Baptists instituted an annual Christmas appeal for foreign mission in her memory. Since then, they have contributed over US $500,000,000 towards the annual Lottie Moon Christmas mission appeal.[15]

Like accounts of other Christian martyr's, the story of Moon's sacrificial service and death has a heroic quality. Moon responded to human suffering by self-sacrifice. If we accept that martyrdom entails suffering and death, we may include her witness among that of the great company of Christian martyrs over the past two thousand years. Martyrdom characterized the deaths of missionaries and native Chinese Christians who died as well during the Boxer rising in 1900.

There were many causes of the revolt.[16] Essentially, the Boxer rising

---

[14]*Ibid.*, 270, 288-89; Lawrence, 312–15.

[15]Allen, 3; Rachel Gill, "Lottie Moon: A Nineteenth-Century Christian Paradigm for Today's Woman," paper, 1985, 11.

[16]Latourette, 501-26. For memorial notices of English Baptist missionaries, E. H. Edwards, *Fire and Sword in Shansi. The Story of the Martyrdom of Foreigners and Chinese Christians* (New York: Fleming H. Revell Company, n.d.) and Robert Coventry Forsyth, *The China Martyrs of 1900. A Complete Roll of the Christian Heroes Martyred in China in 1900 with Narratives of Survivors* (London: Religious Tract Society, 1904). Also, see Luella Miner, *China's Book of Martyrs* (Philadelphia: Westminster Press, 1903); Joseph W. Esherick, *The Origins of the Boxer Uprising* (Berkeley: University of California Press, 1987); George Nye Steiger, *China and the Occident. The Origin and*

came after a century of reaction by many Chinese to the western economic, military, political, and religious invasion. By the end of the nineteenth century, the Boxers included anti-foreign Chinese organized in groups that practised secret rites or bands that engaged in attacks on western imperial interests. Persecution of indigenous Christians and foreign missionaries became more and more common. On 9 July 1900, the first English Baptist missionaries and many of their converts died at T'ai Yuan Fu. Among the dead were missionaries including the Reverend George Bryant Farthing (b. 19 December 1859), Catharine Pope Farthing (née Wright; b. 16 February 1864), their three children (Ruth, aged ten; Guy, aged eight; and Elizabeth, aged three), their governess Ellen Mary Stewart (b. 11 May 1871), the Reverend Silvester Frank Whitehouse (b. 14 August 1867), and Mrs. Whitehouse (née Legerton). Three days later, Boxers attacked the Baptist mission at Hsin Chou, forty-five miles away. Among the martyrs were the Reverend Herbert Dixon, Mrs. Dixon *(née* Williams; b. 14 June 1855), the Reverend William Adam McCurrach (b. 30 March 1869), Clara Vovello McCurrach (*née* Scholey; b. 30 January 1869); the Reverend Thomas John Underwood (b. 6 December 1867), Mrs. Underwood (*née* White), the Reverend Sydney W. Ennals (b. 1 November 1872), and Bessie Campbell Renault (b. 1871).

In all, 50 Roman Catholic and 200 Protestant missionaries died along with an estimated 30,000 native Roman Catholics and 2,000 native Protestants. The martyrdom of the Chinese Christians and missionaries coincided with the outbreak of the Anglo-Boer War. In an article entitled "A Dark Week," the English Baptist pastor Charles Williams commented on the cruelties, infamies, and chaos of the times. "What has come over the closing year of the nineteenth century? Will the sun of this boastful century set in blood? Are its fair promises to issue in shame, and loss, and failures? Is militarism to take the place of predicted peace?" He urged reliance on God and God's peace.[17]

Initially, Christians viewed events as a disaster. However, the martyrdom of so many Chinese Christians and missionaries had the longterm effect of strengthening commitment and devotion. Memory of the valor

---

Development of the Boxer Movement (New York: Russell and Russell, 1966); Edmund S. Wehrle, *Britain, China, and the Antimissionary Riots 1891–1900* (Minneapolis: University of Minnesota Press, 1966).

[17]*Baptist Times*, 13 July 1900.

of martyrs and the testimony of survivors encouraged recruits to volunteer to serve in China and led to maturation of the indigenous church. As for a response by the colonial powers, Britain, France, and United States violently suppressed the Boxers. Compelled to pay for damage to foreign-owned property, many Chinese harbored anti-western and anti-Christian sentiment.

The witness of Canadian and native Christians in Bolivia offers a third example of martyrdom in a Baptist mission context. Baptist work in Bolivia may be traced to the arrival in 1898 of Canadian Baptist missionary Archibald B. Reekie. He encountered a number of barriers to developing a Protestant mission, notably the geography (mountain/lowland), demography (a minority of Spanish extraction vs. those of native extraction), and religions of the country (Roman Catholic and native), as well as limitations of resources. At times, Baptist workers met violence. In 1927, for example, a mob stoned a missionary and a native Christian, leaving both men unconscious. During the same period, Baptist involvement in land reform, discussed in chapter twelve, also engendered opposition.[18]

In 1949, amidst growing Catholic anti-Protestant agitation, believers at Melcamaya, a small Indian pueblo or community prepared for a regular Monday night church meeting by inviting Canadian Baptist missionary Norman Dabbs (1912–1949) and Francisco Salazar, president of the Bolivia Baptist Union, to share in their worship. Carlos Meneses, pastor of the Llallagua church, and other members of the congregation accompanied Dabbs and Salazar to Melcamaya. On 8 August, a small congregation of Indian Christians gathered. As Dabbs was showing pictures of the life of Christ with a projector and Meneses translated in Quechua, a local Catholic priest incited a crowd to attack the party. The meeting could not continue. The visitors attempted to retreat to Llallagua, but the mob attacked them and killed eight Christians: Dabbs, Salazar, Meneses, Antanasio Coronel, sixteen-year old Aniceto Flores, thirteen-year old Vincente Choque ,and twelve-year old Emilio Llanos.

As in the case of earlier martyrdoms, news of the deaths challenged Canadian and Bolivian Baptists to deepen their lives of prayer, to dedicate their lives afresh to the furtherance of God's mission, and to

---

[18]Orville E. Daniel, *Moving with the Times* (Toronto: CBOMB, 1973) chaps. 7-8.

strengthen determination to carry on. Proclaiming a gospel of forgiveness, the church in Bolivia experienced a revival.[19]

Maria Christina Gomez

Over seventy thousand have died in one of this century's most violent civil wars, in El Salvador. Victims have included many Baptists. Another of the great company of Christian martyrs is Maria Christina Gomez (1942–1989). Mother of four and member of Emmanuel Baptist Church from 1964, Gomez served as a Sunday School teacher, as a representative to the Latin America Evangelical Commission for Christian Education, as a member of the National Ecumenical Committee for Peace, and as a teacher.

On Wednesday morning, 5 April 1989, as Maria Christina Gomez was leaving the John F. Kennedy School in the Santa Lucia neighbourhood of Ilopango accompanied by young students, two men in civilian clothes jumped out of a Cherokee jeep, called out "Christina?" and forced her into the vehicle.[20] Witnesses immediately alerted appropriate church and human rights groups. An hour later, the body of Gomez was found in a cemetery outside San Salvador, El Salvador.

The victim and the modality of this particular killing stand out among recent murders. While Maria Christina Gomez knew many people and played an active role in her church and other groups, she was not a prominent leader. Her brutal death seemed to have been designed to send a message of terror to all people active in popular organizations, including the church: "No matter who you are, you are a target. We can kill you in public in broad daylight." In response, members of Emmanuel Baptist Church have sent a clear message to the murderers of Maria Gomez:

---

[19]Lorna Dabbs [widow] to Dr. Bingham [Secretary, CBOMB], 19 September 1949, Canadian Baptist Archives; Norman Harold Dabbs, *Dawn over the Bolivian Hills* (Toronto: CBOMB, 1952) ch. 12, "The Tragedy and Triumph of Melcamaya;" Orville E. Daniel, *Moving with the Times* (Toronto: CBOMB, 1973) 191-92; Jaime Goytia, "25 Years after Melcamaya," *Enterprise* (June 1974): 9–11.

[20]Since 1979, Cherokee jeeps have characteristically served as El Salvador's death squad vehicles.

We, her brothers and sisters are suffering for our Saviour in the land which bears His name. Our days are filled with anguish and with joy. We know that, by our suffering, we are making a way for the establishment of a society founded on peace and justice.[21]

Maria Christina Gomez and other Salvadoran Baptists have long dreamed that they might participate in establishing a society founded on peace with justice. They have taken responsibility for acting upon this dream and shown that individuals and congregations can make a difference in a world of sin. Standing against forces of death, they are part of a great stream of witnesses to the God whose will is peace. Pursued, harried, hunted down, called by name, and murdered, they stand with Baptist non-conformists who, since the seventeenth century, have articulated a faith that sustained them amidst the unjust social order of the day.

Conclusion

Elizabeth Dirks, Dorothy Traske, Elizabeth Gaunt, Lottie Moon, the Chinese martyrs, the Bolivian martyrs, Maria Christina Gomez, and other El Salvador martyrs are witnesses to a God of peace. Through their courage and testimony, God speaks as God spoke through the prophet Isaiah, "How beautiful upon the mountains are the feet of the messenger who announces peace, who brings good news, who announces salvation, who says to Zion, 'Your God reigns!' " (52:7). Dreamers of God's dream of the peaceable kingdom, these Baptist peacemakers are, in Zechariah's arresting phrase, "prisoners of hope" for whom a humble messiah, riding on an ass, banishes weapons, and brings freedom. We do well to follow in the pathways of peace they have first trod.

---

[21]Marta Benavides, "The Death of Maria Gomez," *Christianity and Crisis*, 10 July 1989; "Pastoral Letter from a Salvadoran Congregation," *Peace Work*, March–April 1989; "Killing of Maria Christina Gomez," Instituto de Derechos Humanos de la Universidad Centroamericano.

Chapter Fifteen
Walter Rauschenbusch (1861–1918)

An Introduction to Rauschenbusch's Life

Walter Rauschenbusch was born in Rochester, New York on 4 October 1861.[1] His father, August Rauschenbusch (1816–1889), was a sixth-generation Lutheran pastor who went to North America to work with unchurched German immigrants. In 1850, he adopted Baptist convictions and, in 1858, helped found a German department at Rochester Theological Seminary. Marital disharmony marred the Rauschenbusch household, but Walter recalled "a very religious family, and I thank God for it." In a 1913 talk he said,

> We had household religious service every day, and from childhood I was taught to pray, read the Bible, go to Sunday school, to be in church often. . . . I ran with a gang; for a time I tried very hard to become their leader in swearing, but I never could. I think, however, that other people who observed me thought I was on the road to the devil. And then . . . I came to my Father, and I began to pray for help and got it. And I got my own religious experience. . . . It turned me permanently, and I thank God with all my heart for it. It was a tender, mysterious experience. It influenced my soul down to its depths. Yet, there was a great deal in it that was not really true.[2]

---

[1] Primary sources for study of Walter Rauschenbusch's life and teachings are in 180 boxes housed in the American Baptist-Samuel Colgate Library, which, along with three scrapbooks in the Ambrose Swasey library may be consulted in Rochester, New York. In 1988, Norman J. Kansfield compiled a 28-page preliminary survey of literature by and about Rauschenbusch. The best biography is Paul M. Minus, *Walter Rauschenbusch: American Reformer* (New York: Macmillan, 1988).

[2] "The Kingdom of God," *Cleveland's Young Men* 27 (January 9, 1913), from Robert T. Handy, ed. *The Social Gospel in America* (New York: Oxford, 1966) 264-65.

In these autobiographical excerpts, Rauschenbusch expressed gratitude for a religious milieu that nurtured a deep, mystical relationship with God. Rauschenbusch could criticize personal religion for its excessive piety and individualism, but he always taught that social Christianity begins with conversion, salvation, and personal commitment to social transformation.

Rauschenbusch received a classical education. In 1879, his father sent him to Westphalia, Germany, to study at the Gutersloh Gymnasium, a conservative school that resisted the liberalism dominating much of German theology. After four years, he studied at the University of Rochester and Rochester Theological Seminary. Rauschenbusch wanted to follow his sister Emma to India as a missionary. Questions about his orthodoxy resulted in a determination of the mission board to reject his application. He then decided upon a career in ministry. In 1886, he settled into the pastorate at the Second German Baptist Church in a slum area known as Hell's Kitchen on New York City's west side. For eleven years, Rauschenbusch and his wife Pauline, *née* Rothens, served a small German immigrant congregation there. At times, they lived in poverty themselves.

Rauschenbusch went to New York City "to be a preacher and to help save souls." He never ceased to be an evangelist. Once, he asked Dores Robinson Sharpe (1885–1981), a former student and Rauschenbusch's first biographer, "How do you think of me and my work?" Sharpe replied, "I think of you as an evangelist and of your work as evangelism of the truest sort." Rauschenbusch threw his arms around Sharpe and said, "I have always wanted to be thought of in that way. Your testimony gives me new fighting power."[3]

Even when his theological views became more progressive, Rauschenbusch emphasized the need to follow Jesus Christ in one's personal life. "The main thing is to have God, to live in Him; to have Him live in us . . . to realize His presence; to feel His holiness and to be holy."[4] Publication of *Prayers of the Social Awakening*, Rauschenbusch's favorite book, attested to his warm evangelical faith. Rauschenbusch had been to

---

[3]Dores R. Sharpe, *Walter Rauschenbusch* (New York: Macmillan, 1942) 43; Winthrop S. Hudson, ed., *Walter Rauschenbusch: Selected Writings* (New York: Paulist Press, 1984) 46.

[4]Hudson, 98.

Europe. Upon his return, a customs inspector noticed his name and said, "I've seen your name somewhere." Rauschenbusch asked where. "A book." "The prayers?" queried Rauschenbusch. "That's it. Damn fine prayers too." Rauschenbusch considered that a fine compliment.[5]

In New York City, Rauschenbusch sought out contact with the people and increasingly identified with their needs. Calling on parishioners, visiting the poor or riding his bike through Hell's Kitchen, Rauschenbusch gave attention to minute particulars. Once, for example, he recalled noticing a mother who lived in a tenement building. "One, two, three . . . twelve. . . ." he counted, as the woman lifted her baby carriage up and down curbs to find a playground. "She only wants some grass for the child to play on, and there is no playground in Hell's Kitchen."

Increasingly, Rauschenbusch found his preaching had nothing to do with the lives of his parishioners. People toiled all their lives with almost nothing to show for their labours. Children died needlessly. All these things troubled him. Rauschenbusch found that his inherited religion of personal pietism proved inadequate to address such problems.

In response to the urgent needs of people, Rauschenbusch gradually changed the fundamental focus of his ministry. It took on a new, social note. Rauschenbusch found authority for his new views in the Bible. He sought to apply the teachings of the Hebrew prophets and Jesus to contemporary social issues by modeling his ministry on that of Jesus and Jesus' prayer "your kingdom come, your will be done on earth."

Rauschenbusch formulated a program for Christian revolution in two parts: regeneration of individuals and establishing God's realm on earth. He believed that the Spirit of Christ would overcome over the spirit of the world by transforming both persons and institutions. Because his growing radicalism arose chiefly from the Bible, Rauschenbusch's Bible studies became a sensation. He found himself increasingly in demand as a speaker, writer, and organizer.

---

[5]"Edwin Dahlberg in Conversation: Memories of Walter Rauschenbusch," *Foundations* 18 (1975): 213. Rauschenbusch published his prayers under two titles: *Prayers of the Social Awakening* (Boston: Pilgrim Press, 1910) and *For God and the People: Prayers of the Social Awakening* (Boston: Pilgrim Press, 1910). The spirituality expressed in these prayers is characteristic of Rauschenbusch's deep faith, which led Dahlberg to call him, "the most Christ-like man I ever knew."

In 1891, after a bout of Spanish flu left him nearly deaf, Rauschenbusch took a year's leave from pastoral duties to recuperate, read, and write. He visited Germany and England, where he explored various models for mission. In England, he appreciated Salvation Army workers who combined revivalism and social ministry, but he believed they failed to touch the root causes of poverty. In Germany, he imbibed liberal theological trends but expressed alarm by nationalism and the narrow dogmatism of some socialists. Around this time, he drafted a book on the righteousness of the kingdom but never completed the project.[6]

With sadness, Rauschenbusch acknowledged that the Christian church was a bulwark against change. Although major elements of the church railed against social Christianity, nonetheless, he found some support within the institution. Indeed, during his years in New York City, intimate friendship with two young Baptist ministers, Leighton Williams, pastor of the Amity Baptist Church, and Nathaniel Schmidt (1862–1939), a Swedish Baptist pastor, sustained Rauschenbusch. Regularly they met for prayer and encouragement. In 1889, they began to publish a journal *For the Right,* which sought to address the needs and concerns of the working class from the perspective of Christian socialism. In 1892, they formed a Brotherhood of the Kingdom, an informal association that had as its aim, "realization of the ethical and spiritual principles of Jesus, both in their individual and social aspects." For over thirty years, the Brotherhood met in retreat at Leighton Williams' family farm overlooking the Hudson River. These gatherings provided Rauschenbusch a forum for his radical ideas and a vision of God's coming realm of justice, peace, and righteousness.

Rauschenbusch embarked upon a whirlwind of activity, advocating a wide variety of reforms such as public ownership of railroads, city transit lines, and utilities. He sought better working conditions for women, an eight-hour working day, an end of child labor, safer working conditions in factories, institution of social security insurance, and the development of public parks and libraries. Largely because of his growing deafness, in 1897 Rauschenbusch reconsidered an earlier offer to teach

---

[6]Handy, 256; Minus, 71-82; Klaus Juergen Jaehn, "The Formation of Walter Rauschenbusch's Social Consciousness as Reflected in His Early Life and Writings, Part II," *Foundations* 17 (1974): 73-76. The manuscript was discovered and edited by Max L. Stackhouse, *The Righteousness of the Kingdom* (Nashville: Abingdon, 1968).

and left Hell's Kitchen for the German department at Rochester Theological Seminary. Five years later he joined the English-language seminary as church historian. During a period of twenty-one years of teaching and writing, Rauschenbusch regarded himself as a professional church historian. Though he never wrote a book on church history, he left his mark on the craft.[7]

Withdrawal from the pastorate did not remove Rauschenbusch to an ivory tower. Members of Andrew Street Baptist Church (now a community Bible church) regarded Rauschenbusch highly for his piety if not his progressive political and theological views.[8] In capacities such as author of reports for the local Young Men's Christian Association or school board, speaker at the Labour Lyceum, political activist, and reform advocate, Rauschenbusch helped the community. His impact over a period of twenty-one years was such that a historian called it Walter Rauschenbusch's Rochester.[9]

Rauschenbusch did not simply become a social worker. He remained, at heart, an evangelist. Two stories told by Edwin Dahlberg accented Rauschenbusch's concern for evangelism. On one occasion, Rauschenbusch invited a man named Spike Williams to speak in a class. The man had gone to Syracuse to rob a bank but somehow dropped into a Billy Sunday revival. When Sunday gave the invitation, Williams became a Christian and hit the sawdust trail as a revivalist.

On another occasion, silverware had been taken from the Rauschenbusch home. Police apprehended the thief. Rauschenbusch went to the police station. The man looked so downhearted and poorly dressed that Rauschenbusch had the charges dropped and the man discharged to his custody. Rauschenbusch then invited the thief into his home for supper and to share the gospel of Jesus Christ.[10]

---

[7] Walter Rauschenbusch, "The Value and Use of History," *Record* 9 (1914) reprinted in *Foundations* 12 (1969): 263-72; Henry W. Bowden, "Walter Rauschenbusch and American Church History," *Foundations* 9 (1966): 234-50.

[8] A memorial window in the church has the inscription "In memory of Walter Rauschenbusch, who delighted to worship here."

[9] Blake McKelvey, *Rochester: The Quest for Quality 1890–1925* (Cambridge: Harvard University Press, 1956); *Walter Rauschenbusch's Rochester* (Rochester: Rochester Public Library, 1952).

[10] "Edwin Dahlberg in Conversation: Memories of Walter Rauschenbusch," 211.

Rauschenbusch drew strength from the Brotherhood of the Kingdom and co-workers in Rochester such as Helen Barrett Montgomery (1861–1934), civic reformer, educator, supporter of foreign missions, and translator from the Greek New Testament. A list of some of her accomplishments attested to the wide impact of the social gospel movement: forty-four years as teacher of a Bible class at Rochester's Lake Avenue Baptist Church; ten years as president of the Women's Educational and Industrial Union, which opened a legal aid centre, the first public playground in the city, and milk stations; ten years as member of the Rochester school board; chair of a fund at the University of Rochester to open the university to women; ten years as head of the Women's American Baptist Foreign Mission Society; from 1921–1922, president of the Northern Baptist Convention; co-founder of the Women's World Day of Prayer.

However pressing were the social circumstances in Rochester, in his desire to awaken the church to its responsibility to address the needs of the poor, Rauschenbusch turned to writing. During his early career, he published primarily in German. His later literary output—seven books and countless articles—was in English. His first major work, *Christianity and the Social Crisis* (1907), catapulted him into prominence as the leading teacher of social Christianity in North America.

Despite satisfaction Rauschenbusch derived from the response to his call for a social gospel, the First World War cast a shadow over the last years of Rauschenbusch's life. As a sign of mourning, he wore a piece of black crepe in his lapel. For years he had traveled regularly to Canada to preach and vacation. Now, Canada denied him entry. Unknown Canadians burnt his cottage outside Algonquin Park. Melancholy and despair characterized his last years. "Since 1914 the world is so full of hate that I cannot expect to be happy again in my lifetime," he wrote near the end of his life.[11] He died of cancer on 25 July 1918.

Prophet of God's Realm

The theme of God's coming realm of justice, peace, and righteousness dominated Rauschenbusch's teaching and writing.

---

[11]Sharpe, 448.

> The Kingdom of God is divine in its origin, progress, and consummation. It was initiated by Jesus Christ. . . . [I]t is sustained by the Holy Spirit, and it will be brought to its fulfilment by the power of God. . . . The Kingdom of God is miraculous all the way and is the continuous revelation of the power, the righteousness and the love of God.[12]

Rauschenbusch's first great plea for the kingdom of God was *Christianity and the Social Crisis*. He stated, "the essential purpose of Christianity was to transform human society into the kingdom of God by regenerating all human relations and reconstituting them in accordance with the will of God."[13] He believed the Hebrew prophets and Jesus sympathized fundamentally with the poor and the oppressed. "[Jesus'] healing power was for social help, for the alleviation of human suffering. It was at the service of any wretched leper, but not of doubting scribes."[14]

Rauschenbusch explored the failure of Christianity as a social religion, the nature of the present crisis and the stake of the church in responding to it. In his final chapter, he outlined his manifesto for change. What was required was repentance for social sin, social renewal (beginning with personal salvation), to turn against the materialism and mammonism of the industrial and social order, to find a *via media* between capitalism and communism, to identify with the working class, and to promote social justice. He proposed that nineteen centuries of Christian history had laid foundations of a new, beloved community:

> If at this juncture we can rally sufficient religious faith and moral strength to snap the bonds of evil and turn the present . . . resources of humanity to the harmonious development of a true social life, the generations yet unborn will mark this as that great day of the Lord for which the ages waited, and count us blessed for sharing in the apostolate that proclaimed it.[15]

Rauschenbusch realized that his book was "dangerous" and might create a backlash, even dismissal from the seminary. He went ahead with its publication to discharge a debt to the working people among whom he had labored for twenty years. Understandably, he was surprised by its

---

[12]Walter Rauschenbusch, *A Theology for the Social Gospel* (1917; Nashville: Abingdon Press, 1987) 139.
[13]*Christianity and the Social Crisis* (New York: Macmillan Company, 1907) xiii.
[14]*Ibid.*, 83.
[15]*Ibid.*, 422.

success. Readers as varied as Augustus Hopkins Strong, his seminary president, and Harry Emerson Fosdick praised the book. Perhaps the most striking testimony came years later. Martin Luther King, Jr. identified reading the book as prompting his "pilgrimage to nonviolence."[16]

Rauschenbusch believed his was not novel teaching. "The Social Gospel is the old marriage of salvation, but enlarged and intensified." What was needed was to put the old into action. "We [Christians] already have a social gospel. We need a systematic theology large enough to match it and vital enough to back it."[17]

Rauschenbusch drew insights from Henry George, reform mayoral candidate in New York City, and Christian reformers such as Washington Gladden, Frederick Dennison Maurice, John Ruskin, Leo Tolstoy and the Fabian socialists. Rauschenbusch severely criticized capitalism and focused on the coming realm of God.

> The great sin of men is to resist the reformation of predatory society. We do not want God to be charged with that attitude. A conception of God which describes him as sanctioning the present social order and utilizing it in order to sanctify its victims through their suffering, without striving for its overthrow, is repugnant to our moral sense. Both the Old Testament and the New Testament characterization of God's righteousness assure us that he hates with steadfast hatred just such practices as modern communities tolerate and promote. If we can trust the Bible, God is against capitalism, its methods, spirit and results. The bourgeois theologians have misrepresented our revolutionary God. God is for the Kingdom of God, and his Kingdom does not mean injustice and the perpetuation of innocent suffering.[18]

Rauschenbusch was not against possessions, but he regarded capitalism as competitive, covetous, indifferent to human life, and a denial of justice and love among all God's people. He envisioned a form of economic democracy that would give people control of their lives. "No outward economic readjustments will answer our needs," he wrote. He added:

---

[16]Sharpe, 233; Handy, 258; Martin Luther King, Jr., "Pilgrimage to Nonviolence," *Christian Century*, 27 April 1960, reprinted in *A Testament of Hope. The Essential Writings of Martin Luther King, Jr.*, ed. James Melvin Washington (San Francisco: Harper and Row, 1986) 37-38

[17]*Theology for the Social Gospel*, 1, 5.

[18]*Ibid.*, 184.

It is not this thing or that thing our nation needs, but a new mind and heart, a new conception of the way we all ought to live together, a new conviction about the worth of a human life and the use God wants us to make of our own lives. We want a revolution both inside and outside.[19]

Prophet of God's Peaceable Reign

Among the *Prayers of the Social Awakening*, Rauschenbusch offered a prayer "Against War." It read in part,

> Lord . . . break thou the spell of the enchantments that make the nations drunk with the lust of battle and draw them on as willing tools of death. Grant us a quiet and steadfast mind when our own nation clamors for vengeance or aggression. Strengthen our sense of justice and our regard for the equal worth of other peoples and races. Grant to the rulers of nations faith in the possibility of peace through justice, and grant to the common people a new and stern enthusiasm for the cause of peace. Bless our soldiers and sailors for their swift obedience and their willingness to answer to the call of duty, but inspire them none the less with a hatred of war, and may they never for love of private glory or advancement provoke its coming. . . . O thou strong Father of all nations, draw all thy great family together with an increasing sense of our common blood and destiny, that peace may come on earth at last, and thy sun may shed its light rejoicing on a holy brotherhood of peoples.[20]

Rauschenbusch first published the prayer in 1909 before he embraced pacifism and nonviolence. The language seemed scarcely that of a prophet of the coming peaceful reign of God. His was to be a long pilgrimage to peacemaking.[21]

In 1898, Rauschenbusch supported war against Spain to end Spanish atrocities and give people the right of self-determination. On Thanksgiving Day, he said he hated war and wished for the peaceful settlement of disputes. "But I do not rule God out of war." He prayed for a victory

---

[19]*Christianizing the Social Order* (New York: Macmillan, 1912) 323, 363, 376, 458-59.

[20]Rauschenbusch, *Prayers of the Social Awakening* 97-98.

[21]Harry Baker Robins, *The Contribution of Walter Rauschenbusch to World Peace* (pamphlet, reprinted from the Colgate Rochester Divinity School *Bulletin*, 1940).

that would enshrine personal conscience and a sense of duty in American life.[22]

Three months later, Rauschenbusch made a definite advance in his journey to pacifism and nonviolence. In February 1899, after the Czar of Russia proposed a peace conference, Rauschenbusch spoke on behalf of the proposal. He called for disarmament and a treaty of arbitration.[23] To pressure the White House, he organized a post-card campaign with the words, "We greet with thankfulness to God the appeal of the Czar to the nations, and trust that the hearts of the peoples and their rulers will . . . hasten the reign of peace and goodwill on the earth."

Over the next few years, Rauschenbusch commented occasionally on the problem of peace. He published his own translation of the letter by Grebel and his friends to Thomas Müntzer.[24] In *Christianity and the Social Crisis*, he mentioned peace in a paragraph in which he equated preparation for war with capitalist oppression.[25] Two years later, he gave a commencement address on the fiftieth anniversary of the German department at Rochester Theological Seminary. He spoke on "The Contributions of Germany to the National Life of America" and defended Germans at a time when feeling in the United States was growing against Germany and immigrants in general. He praised the humanity of all and urged "honest effort" to defend human equality.[26] In *Christianizing the Social Order*, he named war as an evil and praised Jesus for restraint in use of force to bring about his realm.[27] In other articles and unpublished sermons, he highlighted themes such as the beloved community, love of enemy, non-resistance, and the interdependence and equality of all people.

As the First World War approached, he launched a campaign against military preparations with the Reverend Charles F. Aked, a British Baptist opponent of the Anglo-Boer War who had moved from Liverpool

---

[22] "The Present and Future. Remarkably Able Sermon by Professor Rauschenbusch," *Post Express*, 25 November 1898.

[23] "Opening Gun for the Czar. Movement in Favour of the Peace Conference," *Democrat and Chronicle* 13 February 1899.

[24] *American Journal of Theology* 8 (1905): 91-99.

[25] *Christianity and the Social Crisis*, 350.

[26] The text is in Box 20, American Baptist-Samuel Colgate Library.

[27] *Christianizing the Social Order*, ix, 408.

to the United States in 1907. In 1914, Rauschenbusch inaugurated a "Peace Group" at Rochester Theological Seminary. In 1915, he criticized the war effort on grounds that the conflict was fueled primarily by the profit motive rather than fundamental issues of justice. In April 1916, he discovered the newly-formed pacifist organization, the Fellowship of Reconciliation. Excited by its religiously based opposition to war and social injustice, he wrote Dores Sharpe that it was "an electric shock to get together with people more radical than I am, that take the Sermon on the Mount seriously." By the end of the year, he became an active member and actively embraced the organization's pacifist stance. In published letters and in *A Theology for the Social Gospel* he stressed his opposition to war and his commitment to Jesus' ethic of nonviolent love. His journey into peacemaking was now complete.[28]

The vision of Rauschenbusch continued to find expression after his death, through his writings, family, and former students. In recognition of his advocacy of the FOR, the organization granted Pauline Rauschenbusch life membership. In a letter published in 1918, Rauschenbusch recalled Jesus weeping over Jerusalem. He closed, "We best realize some things through our children."[29] This proved prophetic. His son Stephen became a noted peace activist. Around 1938, Rauschenbusch was still regarded a dangerous figure, as suggested by the following song sung by future generations of Baptist peacemakers:

That Rauschenbusch of title unpronounceable
Is poisoning the student mind.
His theories are great but irresponsible,
They are poisoning the student mind.

Pious folk are sure that we will go to frost our toes in
    furnaces below
If we give heed to preachers and other people that we know
Who are poisoning the student mind.

---

[28]"Private Profit and the Nation's Honour. A Protest and a Plea," broadside, 1913; *Theology of the Social Gospel*, 4, 162; "If We Enter Into War," *Rochester Evening Times*, 21 February 1917; Minus, ch. 11, 182 for the reference to Rauschenbusch's letter to Sharpe.

[29]"Where Dr. Rauschenbusch Stands," *The Congregationalist and Advance*, 11 July 1918.

Chorus: Poisoning the student mind,
Poisoning the student mind,
Poisoning the student mind.

Young folk, old folk, villains double dyed
Are poisoning the student mind.
'Neath their smiling countenances hide spiritual arsenic, moral cyanide,
They are poisoning the student mind. (repeat chorus).[30]

Conclusion

How are we to assess Rauschenbusch as prophet and Baptist peacemaker? His importance rests in at least four areas. First, his theology of the social gospel gave fresh attention to such themes as the beloved community, social sin, and love. He was not an armchair theologian. He actively sought to realize God's realm by caring for people and alleviating their suffering. "We together have to work it [God's realm] out. It is a matter of community life. The perfect community . . . would be the kingdom of God!"[31]

Secondly, Rauschenbusch demonstrated that one does not have to choose between evangelism and social action. Throughout this century, Baptist critics of social ministry have warned against any ministry that departs from the great mission of saving sinners and making souls. Rauschenbusch taught that justified sinners must live godly lives in the world.

Thirdly, Rauschenbusch taught nonviolence. He taught that Jesus' law of love must control our thinking and action. For Rauschenbusch, the essence of Christianity revolved less around certain orthodox ideas as it did in living out a Christ-like life in the world. Although he never drew up a systematic plan for nonviolent action, he did develop a strategy for non-violent resistance: identify evil, organize for change, spread the message, critique your plans, take direct action. Walking in Jesus' footpaths of peace, he discovered that peace is not only a goal but also a means.

---

[30]As recalled by Al and Dorothy Hassler, interview, 7 March 1990.
[31]"The Kingdom of God," in Handy, 267.

Finally, although Rauschenbusch was a Baptist by conviction, his was no sectarian faith. One of his major achievements was the establishment in 1908 of the Federal Council of Churches, an organization that championed many of his causes. He wrote,

> I do not want to make Baptists shut themselves up in their little clamshells and be indifferent to the ocean outside of them. I am a Baptist, but I am more than a Baptist. All things are mine; mine because I am Christ's. The old Adam is a strict denominationalist; the new Adam is just a Christian.[32]

Circumstances and a remarkable stream of writings propelled Walter Rauschenbusch to international prominence during the first decades of this century. As a prophet of the kingdom of God, he did more than any other figure of the day to make North Americans aware of the misery arising from the industrial revolution, of the relevance of the Gospel to doing something about the situation, and of concrete strategies to alleviate human suffering. As a prophet of Christ's peaceable realm, he challenged contemporaries to claim the power of Jesus for the healing of the nations.

One becomes a prophet only by a personal experience of God, who motivates the individual to stand with Jesus in solidarity with the poor amidst the conflict between the realm of God and the realm of evil.[33] In the life, teaching, and witness of Walter Rauschenbusch, we discern a prophetic voice speaking the language of the biblical prophets and calling Christians, yet today, to radical discipleship in pursuit of the common good.

---

[32]"Why I am a Baptist," in Sydnor L. Stealey, *A Baptist Treasury* (New York: Thomas Y. Crowell, 1958).

[33]*Theology of the Social Gospel*, 277-79.

Chapter Sixteen
Muriel Lester (1883–1968)

An Introduction to the Life of Muriel Lester

Born in Leytonstone, Essex, in December 1883, Muriel Lester came to maturity in idyllic circumstances that made her journey into peacemaking quite remarkable. In *It Occurred to Me*, the first volume of her autobiography, Lester described growing up in a large household characterized by relative prosperity.[1] Her paternal grandfather, Henry Edward Lester, Sr. (1806–1894) and father, Henry Edward Lester, Jr. (1834–1927), were successful in the ship construction business. Her father was a Justice of the Peace. Her mother was Rachel Lester, *née* Goodwin (ca. 1853–1918).[2]

The Lester family, prominent in Baptist circles, helped form several congregations. From 1887 to 1888 and from 1903 to 1904, Henry Lester,

---

[1] Muriel Lester, *It Occurred To Me* (New York: Harper and Brothers, 1937) ch. 1, "A Child's Mind." She wrote a second volume, *It So Happened* (New York: Harper and Brothers, 1947). Richard Deats provides ample excerpts in a recent anthology entitled *Ambassador of Reconciliation. A Muriel Lester Reader* (Philadelphia: New Society Publishers, 1991).

[2] Jill Wallis, author of *Valiant for Peace. A History of the Fellowship of Reconciliation 1914 to 1989* (London: Fellowship of Reconciliation, 1991), is writing a biography of Muriel Lester. In addition to Lester's publications, documents for the project include Lester's papers at Kingsley Hall, Bow; Kingsley Hall, Dagenham; Local History Library, London; Swarthmore College Peace Collection, Document Group 13 (FOR), Box 9 (correspondence for the years 1940–1947); Document Group 50 (A. J. Muste papers; correspondence for the years 1958–1963). Secondary sources include Vera Brittain, *The Rebel Passion* (Nyack: Fellowship Publications, 1964); Caroline Moorehead, *Troublesome People. The Warriors of Pacifism* (Bethesda: Adler and Adler, 1987); Lilian Stevenson, *Towards a Christian International. The Story of the International Fellowship of Reconciliation* (London: International Fellowship of Reconciliation, 1941).

Jr. was president of the Essex Baptist Union. In his presidential address for 1904, he stressed helping others and bringing reconciliation to a broken world, themes characteristic of Muriel Lester's future career.

In 1898, Muriel Lester was baptized and joined Fillebrook Baptist Church.³ A few years later, she transferred to Loughton Union Church. In 1908, Lester and her youngest sister Verona Doris Lester (1886–1965) reorganized the approach to Sunday school. By dividing classes according to age and gender, they pioneered graded Sunday School programs. This enabled them to form strong bonds of friendship with young girls and boys.⁴

Muriel Lester imbibed the religious radicalism of the non-conformist conscience. Her father was "a passionate iconoclast of the old legalisms." She heard arguments against the Anglo-Boer War, but she was then in a pro-military phase of her life. Later, she discovered the writings of the Russian novelist Leo Tolstoy, whose *The Kingdom of God Is Within You* "changed the very quality of life for me."⁵

After a good education with ample opportunities to travel, Muriel Lester contemplated attending Cambridge University. Already committed to social service and issues of justice, however, she left school at age eighteen. On one occasion during these formative years, as she traveled through the slums of London, Lester observed poverty from the train window and thought,

> I was utterly terrified at first, because we ordinarily only rushed through it on a fast train up from Leytonstone, where we lived, to the West End, shopping, or to go to a Pantomime . . . [N]ow and then the train would stop dead quiet in the middle of the East End. There was a ghastly smell. . . . I couldn't imagine that it was a human habitation. "Do people live down there?" I enquired. The answer came—I can hear it almost in my ears still—"Oh yes, plenty of people live down there, but you needn't worry about them, they don't mind it, they're not like you, they don't mind any of these smells. Besides,

---

³Personal correspondence, Raymond L. Vincent, pastor Leytonstone United Free Church, 5 March 1991.
⁴Vivian Lewis, *"Come with Us and We Will Surely Do You Good!" The Story of the Loughton Union Church 1813–1973* (Loughton: Loughton Baptist Church, 1974) 22-23.
⁵*It Occurred To Me*, 6, 10–12.

even if they did, they only have themselves to blame. They get drunk. That's why they're poor."[6]

In 1902, a visit with her father to a party at a factory girls' club in Bow, a extremely poor part of East London, marked a turning point in Lester's life. She began to go to Bow regularly as a social worker. In 1912, Muriel and her sister Doris rented rooms in a Victorian working class cottage for a base and, as they spent more time there, a residence. Their brother Kingsley, who received his Christian name in recognition of an older generation of Christian socialists, lived with them until his death in 1914.

Gradually, Muriel Lester became sceptical about institutional Christianity. For all its idealism, the church failed to be transformative. The campaign against abuses by the government in the Congo when the King of Belgian held it privately provided a grim example. While the church leaders joined in mounting pressure that led the government of Belgium to assume control of the Congo, they did nothing concrete to ameliorate conditions of the people there or in Britain. Lester concluded that it was not enough to denounce government in sermons, books, or meetings. The revolutionary dimensions of Christianity had to make an impact personally and in the structures of society.

Becoming more radical in her thinking, Lester deepened her study of Tolstoy's teachings of non-resistance. She taught these ideas to her students at Loughton Union Church. Together they came to the conviction that they had to do "Jesus Christ the honour of taking Him seriously, of thinking out His teaching in terms of daily life, and then acting on it even if ordered by police, prelates, and princes to do the opposite."[7]

In 1914, the Lester sisters purchased Zion Chapel, previously used by a Strict and Particular Baptist congregation on Botolph Road, which was little more than a blind alley. Earlier, Muriel Lester had questioned whether she could love Jesus or love God, "unless the hymns were untrue when they talked about punishment and justice and mercy and blood."[8] Zion Chapel reminded her of this past. She said that the congregation

---

[6]Typescript, interview with Mr. A. H. French, 17 January 1968, Local History Library.
[7]*It Occurred to Me*, 42.
[8]*Ibid.*, 6.

left behind some of their dreadful beliefs. They left behind a notice saying "We deny that salvation is free. We deny that Christ died for all men," so we had no objection at all of getting rid of the pews and turning it into this very happy teetotal pub; but . . . because we were keen Christians . . . we kept quiet prayers and so on.⁹

She helped transform Zion Chapel into Kingsley Hall, named after Kingsley Lester. For eighteen years, the community center served as a base for her work. In 1921, Muriel Lester was elected as a socialist for a term on the city council of Poplar. Bow constituted roughly a third of the borough. In 1923, she co-founded with her sister Doris the Children's House, Bow. In 1927, she used a legacy to construct a new Kingsley Hall and to expand to Dagenham, another poor district of East London.

Muriel Lester identified with residents of Bow. She became a "parson." Sharing intimately in the troubles and joys of the people, she performed "priestly functions" for the "little company of the believers of Christ." She led Sunday worship, re-wrote hymns, led prayers, officiated at communion and marriage services, blessed babies, provided pastoral care, organized a nursery school, initiated a men's adult school, and started other programs. She invited people to follow Christ and become part of his fellowship of believers.¹⁰

Early in the First World War, when politicians were promising a swift triumph, Muriel Lester resisted the patriotic ground-swell and, by December 1914, had become a pacifist. As a committed Christian believing that a victor's peace would sow seeds of future wars, she experienced the condemnation of other Christians for her refusal to pray for victory. She joined the Fellowship of Reconciliation (FOR) and later recalled its launch:

> In December, 1914, a hundred or so Christians of all sects met in Cambridge, drawn together by the immovable conviction that a nation cannot wage war to the glory of God. The doctrine of the Cross, self-giving, self-suffering, forgiveness, is the exact opposite of the doctrine of armies and navies. One must choose between the sword and the Cross. Thus the Fellowship of Reconciliation was formed, providing us with anchorage as well as with a chart for all adventuring.¹¹

---

⁹*Ibid.*, 56-57; typescript, interview with Mr. A. H. French, 17 January 1968.
¹⁰*It Occurred to Me*, ch. 12, "On Trying to Be a Parson."
¹¹*Ibid.*, 61-62.

Four years later, in 1919, she joined the International Fellowship of Reconciliation (IFOR) shortly after its founding meeting at Bilthoven, Holland.

After the war, reports of Gandhi and India's nonviolent struggle for independence gave Lester's pacifism fresh impetus. In 1926, Professor Gangulee, son-in-law of Rabindranath Tagore, spoke at Kingsley Hall. Impressed by her work, Gangulee invited Lester to India. Her subsequent visit, accompanied by her nephew, Daniel Hogg, led to lifetime friendships, notably with Gandhi.[12] When Gandhi came to Britain in 1931 for the Round Table Conference, he made Kingsley Hall his home for three months. In 1933, she turned over leadership of Kingsley Hall to her sister and became IFOR traveling secretary. In this role she made nine world tours.

Throughout her career, Muriel Lester depended upon God's Spirit for spiritual nurture. In the words of a biographer, she combined "a practical mysticism and deeply grounded activism."[13] Disciplines of the spiritual life sustained her through personal crises and led her to publish books and pamphlets on prayer and worship.[14] An aspect of Lester's spirituality was her love of God's creation. During her career, she retreated regularly to the country to walk through the forest glades or listen to nightingales. Still, she wrote,

> I can't forget the pain of the world. One mustn't forget. It's as necessary to keep aware and sensitive to it all, as it was for the narcotic drink offered on Calvary to be refused.
> So the rhythm emerges: the tension between the beauty God put into the world for the human race to enjoy, and the torments we invent for one another.

---

[12]Lester wrote an account of the trip *My Host the Hindu* (London: Williams and Norgate, 1931). She returned in 1934, 1935, 1938, 1946 and 1949 when she helped form an FOR chapter. See Acharya K. K. Chandy, *The Fellowship of Reconciliation (India)* (Manganam: Ashram Press, 1980).

[13]Richard Deats, "Muriel Lester Made a Difference," *Fellowship* 54 (July/August 1990): 5.

[14]*Let Your Soul Catch Up with Your Body* (London: Independent Press, 1942); *The Prayer School* (Nashville: Upper Room, 1942); *Training* (Nashville: Abingdon-Cokesbury, 1940); *Ways of Praying* (London: Independent Press, 1932); *Why Worship?* (Nashville: Abingdon-Cokesbury, 1937).

One *can* keep one's balance, but vertigo is always waiting to engulf the unwary.[15]

Retiring in 1954, Muriel Lester moved from Bow to a cottage in Loughton. She continued to campaign for peace with justice. On 29 February 1964, in recognition for her efforts to improve social conditions in East London, Muriel Lester received the Freedom of the Borough of Poplar award. At her death, tributes from around the world acknowledged her selfless service in the cause of humanity.

Prophet of Social Justice

For twenty years, Muriel Lester lived and worked in Bow. Recalling interdenominational conferences at which a stock subject for discussion was "How to reach the masses," she expressed astonishment that no one suggested the simple expedient of going to live with them.[16] She chose to do this, although ultimately she found that going to the people was not sufficient to reach the masses with the gospel of reconciling love. Many people felt dispossessed by the church as one of the organizations that contributed to their oppression. Lester observed that many left the church because of the failure of Christians to practice the teachings of Jesus.

Attempting to put Jesus's teachings into action, Muriel Lester faced particular obstacles. As a woman tenant in a poor area of East London, she encountered barriers of sex, station, and custom. Inherited wealth made her a chief beneficiary of the existing social order and created barriers between herself and others.

These circumstances threatened to stifle the energizing Spirit of God and prevent Lester from helping people to do something about their condition. As a result, she took four additional steps along her road to radical discipleship: she adopted voluntary poverty, a particular approach towards social change, socialism, and feminism.

A crucial aspect of Lester's pilgrimage had to do with life-style. As we have noted, Lester grew up in relative affluence. Because of her inherited wealth, she gradually became uneasy with Jesus' words about

---

[15]*It So Happened*, xii.
[16]*Ibid.*, 46.

the "eye of the needle." She became convinced that, in order to achieve justice, Christians could not simply talk, do an occasional good deed, and placate conscience by giving to worthy causes. Rather, she concluded she could not possess wealth while most of her neighbours lacked essentials of life. Since in principle, as a pacifist, she had given up any claim to armed protection, repudiation of the right to any possessions meant that she would be free to put her money to some communal use.

Stephen Hobhouse and his wife, Rosa Waugh Hobhouse, two of Muriel Lester's closest friends, had a major role in shaping her thought about voluntary poverty.[17] Believing that Christians should be concerned about those dispossessed by war or the church itself, the Hobhouses had diverted the whole of their income to an endowment called a "restitution fund" through which they channeled their work among the poor.

In 1921, Muriel Lester, Rosa Hobhouse, and another friend, Mary Hughes, undertook to simplify their life-style. Lester donated most of her personal resources to the restitution fund or Kingsley Hall. With her friends, she formulated a notice in the press:

> We know those who cannot obtain adequate clothing, sheets and warm covering, or necessary food for their children and themselves. The poverty which we refer to is commonly known as a state of privation or destitution. But we prefer to call this condition of theirs compulsory want, being brought upon them by force of hard circumstances. Our invitation to you is not into this enforced poverty, but into a very glorious alternative, involving a drastic readjustment in your affairs, called voluntary poverty.
>
> We invite you into this condition, that the needs of others, whether in our country or abroad, may generously be supplied by the overflowing of your treasure. We do not here wish to encourage the charity of patronage, but rather the large charity of God, which rejoices in richly providing.
>
> Nor do we desire to indicate the exact consequences of the step into voluntary poverty, into which we invite you. It will suffice to say we have many visions of possible blessing, derived from intimate contact with the sorrows of the oppressed.[18]

---

[17] Imprisoned during the First World War as a conscientious objector, Stephen Hobhouse wrote an autobiography published under the title *Forty Years and an Epilogue* (London: J. Clarke, 1951). The father of Rosa Hobhouse was Benjamin Waugh, founder of the National Society for the Prevention of Cruelty to Children.

[18] *It Occurred To Me*, 88-89.

The announcement attracted publicity, visitors, and recruits. A dozen East Enders agreed to share a common life. While they took no formal vows, they based their life together on *The Brethren of the Common Life* of Thomas à Kempis. Calling themselves "The Brethren of the Common Table," they ate and prayed together. They adopted forms of mutual accountability. They shared their goods and sought to give themselves as freely as Christ gave and shared.

Lester found it difficult but ultimately liberating to abandon the capacity to live as she had been raised. Knowing that this was the only means by which she could attain intimacy with the majority of those limited and inhibited by penury, she gained a sense serenity and freedom from the burden of wealth. She genuinely loved the masses and was loved by them. This led her to contrast the "rough and ready sanity of the working people" with the "too meticulous . . . finicky particularism" of middle-class folk.[19]

Kingsley Hall used the restitution fund for basic needs such as food for the hungry and decent housing for people crowded into rat-infested facilities. The center purchased a country place for family holidays, camps, conferences, and other needs. The center cared for growing numbers of children, in whose plight Lester took a special interest. The services outstripped the physical capacity of the hall. After complaints from the local education board about crowded conditions, Muriel and Doris Lester realised that the rooms were inadequate for what had become a children's home and school.

Muriel Lester's response typified another dimension of her radical discipleship, empowerment of the people. At Kingsley Hall, she encouraged people to determine issues together. People in the community developed their own strategies for dealing with problems such as alcoholism, unemployment, poor health care, crowded housing, or legal difficulties. Two illustrations of her approach to decision-making indicate how Lester empowered people.

In 1923, when it was necessary to build facilities for the growing children's work of Kingsley Hall, Lester identified an architect who consulted with the people. Drawing inspiration from Tolstoy, the community planned every detail, raised funds for the project, helped with

---

[19]*Ibid.*, 86, 92-93.

construction, and undertook other menial tasks.[20] The newly named Children's House opened in September 1923. Accommodating a broad range of activities, Children's House had as its goal to "build up the Kingdom of Heaven upon earth and to Him who went about doing good with all His heart, and loved His neighbour as Himself."[21] For five years, Muriel Lester lived at Children's House, although a expanding locus of her work was the increasing number of unemployed workers in Bow.

This dimension swelled, especially after she took part in the 1926 General Strike. Facilities became inadequate until she inherited 400 pounds from the estate of her father in 1927. Claiming that the legacy was not hers in the sight of God, Lester organized community meetings to discuss the best way to spend the money for the benefit of people in the neighborhood.[22] In 1928, the new Kingsley Hall opened at its present site on Powis Road. In 1929, another Kingsley Hall opened in Dagenham for former residents of Bow moved out through slum clearance.

A third area of Lester's pilgrimage into peacemaking was Christian socialism. Believing that capitalism was inherently selfish, causing much wretchedness, Lester adopted the political party of George Lansbury.[23] Standing as a socialist, she was elected in 1921 to the Poplar Council, on which she served nearly five years. Bow constituted roughly one-third of the borough. As an Alderman, Lester chaired the Maternity and Child Welfare Committee of an area that had the highest child mortality rate in London. Under her leadership, Poplar became the first local authority in Britain to establish dental clinics for mothers, distribute milk to poor children, and provide other health benefits.

A fourth area of Lester's road to radical discipleship was her concern for the rights of women. One aspect was the fact that she assumed pastoral functions at Kingsley Hall. Many objected that there was no place for woman in ministry. She responded in an essay entitled *Why Forbid*

---

[20]*Ibid.*, 109–10; *Daily Chronicle*, 14 October 1927.

[21]*East London Advertiser* 14 April 1923.

[22]*Reynold's Illustrated News* 16 October 1927.

[23]As Member of Parliament representing Bow and Bromley from 1910–1912 and 1922–1935, Lansbury (1857–1940) championed social reform. As a defender of the rights of workers and women, he became, in the words of a biographer Raymond Postgate, "one of the best loved men in the world." *The Life of George Lansbury* (London: Longmans, Green and Co., 1951) 134.

Us?. "It seems a trifle ludicrous to write a pamphlet to prove that women should be accepted as ministers of the Church. Rather the onus of proof is on the other side." She showed how God's creative spirit had pushed, urged, and thrust her into situations where she had to do all the work of a minister—prophetic, pastor, and priestly. With other women, she opened ministry to innovative approaches and recognized the unique role of women in solving practical problems.[24]

Lester believed that women had a particular role in peacemaking. Throughout human history, the relationship of women to war has differed from that of men. It has been a method used ostensibly to defend the interests of women, but war has engendered suffering through death, rape, starvation, and loss of loved ones. Reflecting on the movement for women's suffrage, of which she had been a part, Lester called on women to look at war, strip it of its glamor and condemn it, "as a maelstrom of conflicting passions—greed, pride, lust, hate, lies, spying, ignorance, misunderstanding, fear, fortune-hunting, profiteering, prejudice, and ambition."[25] Consistently, Lester called on women to take the lead in ending particular wars and the institution of war.

Summarizing this section, we see in Lester an example of ancient Chinese teaching:

> Go to the people
> learn from them,
> live with them,
> love them,
> start with what they know
> build with what they have.
> But of the best leaders,
> when the job is done,
> when the task is accomplished,
> the people will all say:
> "We have done it ourselves."[26]

---

[24] *Why Forbid Us?* (Shanghai: Christian Literature Society, 1935) excerpted by Deats, *Ambassador of Reconciliation*, 57-63.

[25] *Kill or Cure?* (Nashville: Cokesbury, 1937) *ibid.*, 64.

[26] Lao Tsu cited by Joseph G. Donders, *Non-Bourgeois Theology* (Maryknoll: Orbis, 1985) 164-65.

Living among the poor and loving them, Lester created enduring bonds of helpfulness. During the First World War, the destitution of East End "dregs of war" deepened with rationing and the bombing raids. Amidst war, Lester threw herself into efforts to help the needy. She learned that the struggle against poverty could not be uncoupled from the struggle for world peace, as Martin Luther King, Jr. would realize in the 1960s. Gradually, her stage of peacemaking shifted from Bow to the world at large.

Prophet of International Reconciliation

We have already identified Muriel Lester's pacifist commitment. During the First World War, Lester protested in several ways. She spoke at Speakers Corner in Hyde Park. She attended tribunals of conscientious objectors and visited them in prison. When Kingsley Hall and the surrounding environs were bombed in 1916 during Graf Zefflin raids, she shared in the reconstruction work. She took to the streets.

In April 1917, during one anti-war demonstration organized in part by the FOR, she headed a contingent carrying a large black cross. Counter-protesters disrupted the procession before it could complete the march from Kingsley Hall to Victoria Park. Frank Hancock recalled, "The March enabled us pacifists to demonstrate for peace. It also enabled East London to show that they would have none of it."[27]

After the war, in January 1919, Muriel Lester again took to the streets to support famine relief. Frustrated by government inaction and apathy in other quarters, Lester brought together a soldier and a conscientious objector to make a rough wooden cross. The two men with the cross headed a procession from Bow to the House of Commons. Ordinary people carried hand-made clothing to send to the continent. Other bore carried placards stating, "We do not want any children anywhere to go hungry." Humanitarian aid began to flow, the "Save the Children Fund" becoming a testament to Lester's approach to peacemaking.

During her thirteen-week visit to India in 1926, Gandhi challenged her to share with the British public what she had seen in India. "Speak

---

[27]Wallis, 28.

the truth, without fear and without exaggeration, and see everyone whose work is relative to your purpose. You are on God's work, so you need not fear men's scorn."[28] Lester invited Gandhi to visit Kingsley Hall to "learn from us." When Gandhi came to Britain for the Round Table Conference, Kingsley Hall hosted his three-month stay. Mildred Fahrni, a Canadian working then at Kingsley Hall, recalled that Gandhi broke free from his busy schedule to maintain disciplines of ashram life in India. He spent an hour each morning in meditation, followed by an hour to walk, meet people, teach and learn from the poor in the Bow.[29]

After 1933, in her capacity as traveling secretary for the IFOR, Muriel Lester helped organize chapters around the world. She conducted prayer schools and reached out to adherents of all religions—Muslims, Jews, Hindus—without manifesting any prejudice. Lester investigated injustices such as the drug trade in India under British rule and the effects of Japanese colonization upon China. She collected documentation about various issues, which became part of her speaking and writing. In 1934, during her second visit to India, she traveled about the country with Gandhi to campaign against untouchability. In 1938, after her visit to China, she spent two weeks in Japan courageously telling people the terrible things done to the Chinese by their country.

During the 1920s, 1930s, and 1940s, a period when air travel was uncommon, maintaining an arduous schedule such as Lester's was not easy. Invariably, Lester encountered risks. In August 1941, she was returning to Britain after a speaking tour through Latin America. When her liner docked in Trinidad, British authorities seized her and detained her for ten weeks. During her time of confinement, she attempted to lift up the spirits of others imprisoned with her whilst struggling with her own growing depression and sense of isolation. Public outcry helped secure her release, but back in Britain, she was detained several days in Holloway Gaol, and her passport was confiscated for the duration of the war.[30] She continued to travel throughout the United Kingdom,

---

[28]Muriel Lester, *Entertaining Gandhi* (London: Ivor Nicholson and Watson, 1932), 157-58. In other publications, such as *Gandhi. World Citizen* (Allahabad: Kitab Mahal, 1945), Lester became a leading advocate for Gandhi's cause.

[29]Personal interview, 25 May 1990.

[30]*East End News* 31 October 1941. For an account, *It So Happened*, ch. 11, "Behind Barbed Wire."

campaigning against the war. In Bow, she organizing anti-war activity and resumed her work at Kingsley Hall. With other peace activists, she raised funds that the community center used for food, clothing, and the Children's House.[31] She also helped break a blockade that made it hard to send humanitarian relief to the continent. She stated:

> Seeing that it is the common instinct to feed the hungry, no political or military situation is likely to be able to hold back for long the great stream of generosity once it has burst its way through the obstructions that have so long impeded its life-bringing flow.[32]

After the Second World War, Lester resumed her international activity. Her first trip was to Europe, where she warned that the atom bomb threatened the newly-won peace. During visits to areas devastated by war, Lester ministered to former resistance leaders and Germans taken as prisoners of war alike and organized humanitarian relief efforts.

Conclusion

East London is a bustling area of varied neighbourhoods. Now, among signs of prosperity, some areas appear to house wealthier people. Some homes have become gentrified. Nevertheless, if one explores the side streets or climbs to the rooftop terrace of Kingsley Hall, Bow, one gains another perspective. Looking about the neighborhood, one sees tenement houses, gutted buildings, Victorian row houses that survived the bombings of two world wars, benches where street people sleep, and garbage heaps. These provide a haunting reminders of the poverty that catapulted Muriel Lester from a life of comfort to one of service.

Kingsley Hall remains as a busy community center, offering a range of educational and recreational programs, opportunities for counseling and advocacy services. Elderly people, youth, and members of immigrant communities still gather there. Volunteers working for various groups, including the Gandhi Foundation, organize in the community. The room where Gandhi slept in 1931 serves as a Meditation Centre. A memorial garden allows people to pray or meet friends.

---

[31] *Vera Brittain's Letter to Peace-Lovers* broadside.
[32] *It So Happened*, 235.

Only a few aging folk actually remember Muriel Lester, or the visit of Gandhi in 1931, but millions have caught a glimpse of the modern Kingsley Hall when viewing the film *Gandhi*, directed by Richard Attenborough. Along with several recent publications, the film has rekindled interest in Kingsley Hall and in the life of its co-founder Muriel Lester. Gandhi stated that Muriel Lester manifested the gospel of reconciliation to people in daily life as did few others.[33]

It is a testimony to Lester's commitment to serve the people that she is remembered most by ordinary people. Principally, she derived strength from the residents of Bow. In an interview given at the end of her life, Muriel Lester reflected on what had most helped her in life. She responded,

> It was just the ordinary people. We were completely happy, being one of a crowd, and finding them utterly natural and accepting me with my awfully luxurious upbringing . . . not having the slightest bitterness towards me or any sort of feeling, and always telling each other what we thought and being quite honest and happy. No it was just like being treated as relations . . . it was just glorious wide friendships.[34]

At the same time, Muriel Lester won the friendship and support of people in high standing. The work of Kingsley Hall was widely known, and Muriel Lester challenged her family and friends to engage with her in its ministry. Many renowned friends helped. For example, the author H. G. Wells joined in opening Children's House. The actress Sybil Thorndike wrote of Lester as one whose exploring of the Spirit helped her and others to share a living experience of how God works.[35]

Lester had a gift of friendship. Her home in retirement was a pilgrimage site, where she spent time with friends old—for example, members of Loughton Union Church—and new, such as Dorothy Day

---

[33]In *Harijan*, Gandhi printed an article by Lester, "Wanted: A Manifestation of Christ in Daily Life." In a preface, Gandhi observed, "Many persons have written like Muriel Lester before now . . . she endeavors every moment of her life to practice what she professes and preaches in her writings." See Deats, "Muriel Lester Made a Difference," 8.

[34]Typescript, interview with Mr. A. H. French, 17 January 1968, Local History Library.

[35]Foreword, *It So Happened*.

(1897–1980), a leader in the Catholic worker movement who attended a peace conference in London in 1963 and visited Lester.[36]

Combating injustice and working for peace never led Muriel Lester to despair or cynicism. She had a lively wit and could laugh at herself or the most difficult of circumstances. Lester was a powerful speaker and exhorted others against the temptation of evading responsibility. A remarkable woman in her own right, she believed that women were guardians of life with a particular destiny to combat imperialism and share in the responsibility of building God's realm of peace with justice. Throughout her life, she sought to release spiritual and moral forces that she believed are present within every human being. This releasing, she wrote, "is something we can learn, explore and practice and train ourselves to perfect—all of us, boy, girl, brown skin, white skin, slum-dweller and woodsman, diplomat and navvy, bishop and atheist."[37]

Muriel Lester was a seeker of truth, justice, and peace. The rediscovery of her life story may help us to recover her vision. As a prophet of social justice and international reconciliation, Lester challenged those who followed along her path to contribute in building up God's peaceable realm and healing among the nations. As a Christian shaped by the ethos of evangelicalism, Lester owed to her Baptist inheritance a passion to live fully in the light of Resurrection power. Describing an Easter service at Kingsley Hall, she sought to share with all, "the vision of God as Love and Beauty, and the sense of comradeship which brings strength and vigour to the weakest."[38]

---

[36]Personal correspondence, Kathleen Whittle, 26 February 1991; Eileen Egan, "Foreword," *Ambassador of Reconciliation*, vii; Jim Forest, *Love Is the Measure. A Biography of Dorothy Day* (Mahwah: Paulist Press, 1986) 153.

[37]*It So Happened*, xiv. For Lester's contribution to the struggle for the rights of women, see Deats' anthology, 57ff.

[38]"Easter at Kingsley Hall," *Reconciliation* 1 (May 1924): 72.

The words of a contemporary hymn, appropriately entitled "Muriel Lester," expresses the spirit she exhibited in her life.

Chorus: Muriel Lester, with a loving heart
God had blessed her
She lived in peace each day.
No matter what came her way.

Stanza: She once had lots of money
and though it sounds rather funny
she gave up everything she had
to help the poor, the sick, and the sad.

Chorus: (Repeat above)

Stanza: In England during World War One
everyone was called upon
to help fight the enemy
but Muriel didn't agree.
She said war is wrong
'cause God loves everyone
so let us help the poor along,
instead of making guns and bombs.

Chorus: (Repeat above)

Stanza: Her house was hit by an enemy bomb
but Muriel just kept right on,
loving everyone the same,
remembering why Jesus came.

Chorus: (Repeat above)

Chapter Seventeen
Martin Luther King, Jr. (1929–1968)

An Introduction to the Life of Martin Luther King, Jr.

Martin Luther King, Jr. was born in Atlanta, Georgia on 15 January 1929.[1] His parents were the Reverend Martin Luther King, Sr. and Mrs. Alberta Williams King. After primary school, King passed a special examination to enter Morehouse College without finishing high school. He attended Morehouse from 1944–1948, Crozer Theological Seminary in Chester, Pennsylvania, from 1948–1951, and Boston University from 1951–1955. At age twenty-five, King completed his doctoral thesis and accepted a call to serve as pastor of Dexter Avenue Baptist Church in Montgomery, Alabama.

King's subsequent rise to prominence was meteoric. A few months after moving to Montgomery, a 382-day bus boycott from 1 December 1955 to 21 December 1956 took place. His leadership in the Montgomery bus boycott catapulted King to a position of authority in the broader movement for the moral, economic, and political transformation of the United States.

During the Montgomery campaign, King developed the practice of nonviolence as the best way to achieve the goals of racial equality and economic justice. This led to formation of the Southern Christian

---

[1] Boston University and the Martin Luther King, Jr., Center for Nonviolent Social Change, Atlanta, house the most important primary sources. A twelve-volume collection of King's writings and sermons has begun to appear. Presently, the best collection is James M. Washington, ed., *A Testament of Hope. The Essential Writings of Martin Luther King, Jr.* (San Francisco: Harper and Row, 1986). Two volumes of study materials for church, home, and school and for the family, *Dreaming God's Dream. Celebrating the Life and Legacy of Dr. Martin Luther King, Jr.* (1989) are available from The Baptist Peace Fellowship of North America, 499 Patterson Street, Memphis TN 38111, USA.

Leadership Conference (SCLC); the freedom rides (1960–1961); mass direct action in Albany, Georgia, and Birmingham, Alabama (1961–1963); the March on Washington and passage of the Civil Rights Act (1963, 1964); attempts to bring about desegregation of schools and other public facilities in several cities culminating in the Voting Rights Act (1965); active opposition to United States involvement in Vietnam; and the "war on slums" in Chicago, Washington, and Memphis (1965–1968). King was assassinated 4 April 1968 in Memphis, Tennessee, where he had come in solidarity with sanitation workers on strike.

For a brief period of twelve years, King was at the center of a maelstrom. Claiming the right to protest for right, he led campaigns to eliminate social evil in such forms as segregation, poverty, and war. He contributed to legislative advances in areas of racial equality, such as access to public facilities and to the ballot box. He demonstrated the relationship between poverty at home and poverty abroad. His criticism of United States military involvement in Vietnam helped to hasten America's withdrawal. While he did not singlehandedly produce these advances, he led the revolution that brought them to reality. Perhaps his greatest gift was to teach blacks to believe that they could overcome obstacles they confronted as they struggled nonviolently for economic justice, racial equality, and peace.[2]

Since January 1986, the United States has set aside a day annually to celebrate the memory of King. Amidst mountains of words and myriad voices singing his praises (or damnation), we have witnessed the rapid metamorphosis of mortal being to mythic hero. In this process, we have risked loss of perspective. King died at age thirty-nine while serving apparently a fragmented movement. He was coming under increasing attack by more radical advocates of black power. He was in a modest position as associate to his father as pastor at Ebenezer Baptist Church in Atlanta, Georgia. We may ask why he has gained such prominence? What remains of his legacy? To what extent has King inherited, transformed, and passed on the legacy of Baptist peacemakers? In the following sections we attempt to behold the dreamer and to see what became of his dream (cf. Gen 37:20).

---

[2]Stephen B. Oates, *Let the Trumpet Sound: The Life of Martin Luther King, Jr.* (New York: Harper and Row, 1982) 372.

Some Sources of the Dream

It is suggested in this section that Martin Luther King, Jr. initiated a new era in Christian thought and practice by reformulating and holding together classical Christian categories such as sin and grace, God and human experience, the cross and the resurrection, bondage and freedom, suffering and redemption. He made this contribution by re-conceptualizing the church in a non-racial form and by developing a strategy to bring it about.

Like his namesake Martin Luther, King represented a rare convergence of thought and action. Like Luther, King insisted that there is a great difference between writing about God, knowing who God is, and experiencing God. King exemplified an observation of Luther: "One becomes a theologian through life, and even through death and through the experience of damnation, and not through understanding, reading, or speculation."[3]

King's doctoral thesis was an analysis of conceptions of God in the thought of Paul Tillich and Henry Nelson Wieman. In it, he anticipated two themes that mark his particular contribution to Christian theology. First, he asserted that one cannot posit a "too sharp dualism" between the theoretical and the practical. Second, he insisted on maintaining the tension between the transcendence and immanence of God. God must be both "beyond" and "in" the world.[4] For King, it was not enough to think about God. God must be encountered in the world.

King did not develop these ideas abstractly but out of life experience. From his youth, he carried vivid memories of his discovery of the twin evils of segregation and economic injustice. First-hand he knew that racism worsened the plight of blacks, generating the bread lines and inadequate housing of the Depression years. He wrote,

---

[3]Gerhard Ebeling, *Luther. An Introduction to His Thought*, trans. R. A. Wilson (Philadelphia: Fortress Press, 1972) 200.

[4]Martin Luther King, Jr., "A Comparison of the Conceptions of God in the Thinking of Paul Tillich and Henry Nelson Wieman," (Ph.D. thesis, Boston University, 1955) 64, 281.

> I . . . learned that the inseparable twin of racial injustice was economic injustice. Although I came from a home of economic security and relative comfort, I could never get out of my mind the economic insecurity of those living around me. During my late teens I worked two summers . . . in a plant that hired both Negroes and whites. Here I saw economic injustice firsthand, and realized that the poor white was exploited just as much as the Negro. Through these early experiences I grew up deeply conscious of the varieties of injustice in our society.[5]

Specific incidents shaped King's perception of racism. As a preschooler, he had a white playmate, the son of a grocer whose store was across the street from the King family home. King recalled how their friendship began to break down as soon as they entered school and, finally, how the climax came one day when his friend told King that they could no longer play together.[6]

Another time, his father took the younger King into a store to buy a pair of shoes he had spotted. The clerk greeted them coldly by announcing they should go to the back of the store. Daddy King protested and was told, "You take it like everybody else, and stop being so high and mighty." King Sr. took Martin's hand, and they left the store. King told his son, "I don't care how long I have to live with this system, I am never going to accept it." He never did, and he encouraged his son to fight the system in thoughtful and determined ways.[7]

According to Martin Luther King, Jr., such incidents nourished anti-white feelings that he harbored until he went to university and came into contact with white students through working in interracial organizations. King considered a legal career but opted to enter the ministry. A number of spiritual mentors, including Howard Thurman and Daddy King, influenced King in the direction of ministry as a springboard from which to confront the racial problems in the United States.

Even before he attended Crozer Theological Seminary and Boston University, King had begun to formulate the basic truths, worldview, and

---

[5]*Stride Toward Freedom. The Montgomery Story* (San Francisco: Harper and Row, 1958) 90.

[6]"An Autobiography of Religious Development," manuscript, King papers, Martin Luther King, Jr., Center for Nonviolent Social Change, Atlanta. King wrote this in 1951 for a class while a student at Boston University.

[7]*Stride Toward Freedom*, 19; Martin Luther King, Sr., with Clayton Riley, *Daddy King. An Autobiography* (New York: William Morrow and Company, 1980) 108–109.

tools by which he would endeavour to live the Christian faith. Building on this foundation, he undertook higher education as part of a "serious intellectual quest for a method to eliminate social evil."[8]

In 1954, King made a conscious choice as to how he could work for his people and where he could *do* theology. He received offers to teach but left a situation of probable academic security for a pastorate. Making this decision, he reflected his specific religious tradition. Blacks in the United States have *done* theology in sermon, song, prayer, testimony, and stories of slavery and subjugation.[9] The black church has empowered blacks to survive against odds, readying them to seek justice and generating action, including protest and resistance, to counteract their oppressed status.

What, specifically, did King derive from his religious roots? In his "An Autobiography of Religious Development," King recalled a closely knit family where love was central and in which it was quite easy for him to think of a God of love. King came from a long line of Georgia Baptist preachers from whom he learned about central biblical themes of freedom, justice, and hope. He frequently acknowledged this debt. He stated to Alex Haley, who interviewed King for *Playboy* magazine, "As one whose Christian roots go back through three generations of ministers—my father, grandfather and great grandfather—I will remain true to the church as long as I live." In *Ebony* magazine, he wrote

> I am many things to many people; Civil Rights leader, agitator, trouble-maker and orator, but in the quiet resources of my heart, I am fundamentally a clergyman, a Baptist preacher. This is my being and my heritage for I am also the son of a Baptist preacher, the grandson of a Baptist preacher and the great-grandson of a Baptist preacher. The Church is my life and I have given my life to the Church.[10]

---

[8]*Stride Toward Freedom*, 91.

[9]Coretta Scott King, *My Life with Martin Luther King, Jr.* (New York: Holt, Rinehart and Winston, 1969) 94. James H. Cone, "Martin Luther King, Jr., Black Theology—Black Church," *Theology Today* 40 (1984): 409-20.

[10]*Playboy* interview cited in *Testament of Hope*, 345; Martin Luther King, Jr., "The Un-Christian Christian," *Ebony* August 1965, 7, cited by James H. Cone, "The Theology of Martin Luther King, Jr.," *Union Seminary Quarterly Review* 40 (1986): 26.

In King, we find a rare convergence of *charisma* and *kairos*. King had enormous personal gifts. He was raised in a racist society and sheltered by the church. He went to Alabama prepared, like black church leaders before him, to use his position as pastor to challenge contemporary Christians to live in conformity with the mind of Christ and to challenge contemporary Americans to live in conformity with the ideals of the republic.

King's coming of age coincided with a larger cultural, religious and social crisis. Amidst a generalized period of unrest, King responded to circumstances that drew him into a key role of the Montgomery bus boycott, a role he initially was reluctant and hesitant to accept. In the days immediately after the seamstress Rosa Parks refused to give up her seat on a Montgomery bus and sparked the bus boycott, King had to undergo his own "dark night of the soul."

King felt overwhelmed with feelings of inadequacy and anxiety. Amidst threats of violence to himself, his family, and others, King endured an agonizing religious crisis. Later, he wrote and spoke about a key moment in which uncertainty, doubt, and fear overwhelmed him. Then, on 27 January 1956, King received a call from an angry citizen. "Listen, nigger, we've taken all we want from you. Before next week you'll be sorry you ever came to Montgomery." King prayed, felt the presence of the Divine as he had never before experienced God, and heard the quiet assurance of an inner voice saying, "Stand up for righteousness, stand up for truth; and God will be at your side forever." His fears began to go and uncertainty disappeared. Thus readied to face anything, King knew he had a mandate to make a better world, to make of this old world a new world. Three nights later, the King home was bombed. The bombing did not have the desired effect of deterring him. Rather, it served to strengthen him to move forward to the "city of freedom."[11]

King was moving to a new paradigm for Christian thought and action. Called to arouse his generation to the dream, King now found methods to bring about a revolution. Remarkably, this revolution originated in some measure in pulpits and basements of hundreds of Baptist churches throughout the United States.

---

[11]*Stride Toward Freedom*, 134-38. *Strength to Love* (1963; Philadelphia: Fortress, 1981) 112–14.

Prophet of the Beloved Community

On 22 January 1989, at a commemorative service in Hamilton, Ontario, Rosa Parks stated, "King made us believe in ourselves. He dreamed a beloved community, and we are now part of it. There is no pretending that we don't have problems. We have work to do. But King made it possible. We honor his legacy by seeking to live the Christian life, as he taught it."[12]

A key phrase in this quotation was "beloved community." While King never attempted to systemize the content of this phrase, it expressed his vision for the church and society reformed in non-racist, inclusive ways. King probably owed the phrase to two intellectual mentors, Josiah Royce and Walter Rauschenbusch, yet he gave the words fresh significance.

How did King conceive the beloved community? From the start of his ministry in Montgomery, he spoke of a "restored community," a community of justice and harmony, a community of love, understanding, goodwill, and nonviolence, a world without slavery and segregation, inferior schools, slums, and second-class citizenship, a world without war and destruction.[13] In a sermon preached in the Dexter Avenue Baptist Church on 4 November 1956. King called upon the church in the United States not to be conformed to worldly standards, standards that are racist, economically unjust, and spiritually arrogant, but to be transformed into a true "fellowship" exemplifying unity, racial integration, a better distribution of wealth:

> Let me . . . say something about the church. . . . The church is the Body of Christ. So when the church is true to its nature it knows neither divisions nor disunity. But I am disturbed about what you are doing to the Body of Christ. They tell me that in America you have within Protestantism more than two hundred and fifty six denominations. The tragedy is not so much that you have such a multiplicity of denominations, but that most of them are warring against each other with a claim to absolute truth. This narrow sectarianism is destroying the unity of the Body of Christ. You must come to see that God is neither a

---

[12]For a profile of Rosa Parks, see *Reconciliation International* 1 (June 1968): 4-5.
[13]*Stride Toward Freedom*, 105–106, 224.

Baptist nor a Methodist; He is neither a Presbyterian nor an Episcopalian. God is bigger than all of our denominations.[14]

Envisioning a world without slavery, segregation, inferior schools, slums, second-class citizenship, war, or destruction, King frequently targeted the church for its failure to realize its ideals. In his book *Stride Toward Freedom. The Montgomery Story*, King criticized the church for perpetuating the yoke of segregation. "It is appalling that the most segregated hour of Christian America is eleven o'clock on Sunday morning, the same hour when many are standing to sing, 'In Christ there is no East nor West'." To American Baptists he affirmed that the church of Jesus Christ, when it is true to its nature, knows neither division nor disunity. King warned that narrow sectarianism destroys the unity of the Body of Christ and undermines the ability of Christians to be true witnesses for Christ.[15] In his "Letter from Birmingham Jail," King expressed disappointment with the failure of the white church to lead in the struggle for justice:

> I must honestly reiterate that I have been disappointed with the church. I do not say that as one of the negative critics who can always find something wrong with the church. I say this as a minister of the gospel, who loves the church; who was nurtured in its bosom; who has been sustained by its spiritual blessings and who will remain true to it as long as the cord of life shall lengthen.[16]

In other contexts, King envisioned a role for the church in bringing the beloved community to reality. However, he believed that this would be through new forms of expressing the Christian life together. For example, he described the newly founded Southern Christian Leadership Conference as a model for Christians because it stressed human solidarity.

---

[14]"Paul's Letter to American Christians," in *Strength to Love*.

[15]*Stride Toward Freedom*, 207. At the fiftieth meeting of the American Baptist Convention held at Philadelphia, Pennsylvania 29 May–4 June 1957, King addressed delegates on the theme, "Paul's Letter to the American Churches." An edited version appeared in *Strength to Love*.

[16]Originally a pamphlet, the text appeared in *Why We Can't Wait* (Toronto: New American Library, 1964) 89-90 and Washington, 298.

> The ultimate aim of SCLC is to foster and create the "beloved community" in America where brotherhood is a reality. . . . SCLC works for integration. Our ultimate goal is genuine intergroup and interpersonal living.[17]

A theologian informed by biblical realism, King knew that sin operates individually *and* collectively. He understood that the reign of God would not come easily. But as soon as the Montgomery campaign began, he knew that the time had come to make the dream of the beloved community a reality. "We can no longer lend our cooperation to an evil system." He continued:

> [A] religion true to its nature must be concerned about man's social conditions. Religion deals with both earth and heaven, both time and eternity. Religion operates not only on the vertical plane but also on the horizontal. It seeks not only to integrate men with God but to integrate men with men and each man with himself.[18]

Confronting collective sin as a stark, grim, and colossal reality, King transformed Montgomery and charted a new course for the church in the world. His mission was to make known Christ's work of love and reconciliation, thereby making possible the creation of the beloved community. But this could only come about through conversion to the gospel of peace. In a sermon preached during the early weeks of the Montgomery campaign, King contrasted "true" or positive peace with negative peace:

> Peace is not merely absence of some negative force—war, tension, confusion, but it is the presence of some positive force—justice, goodwill and the power of the kingdom of God. . . . Peace is not merely the absence of tension in race relations, but it is the presence of justice. . . . If the Negro accepts his place, accepts exploitation, accepts injustice, there will be peace. But it would be a peace boiled down to stagnant complacency, deadening passivity, and if peace means this, I don't want peace. If peace means accepting second-class citizenship, I don't want it. If peace means keeping my mouth shut in the midst of injustice and evil, I don't want it.[19]

---

[17]Cited by Kenneth L. Smith and Ira G. Zepp, Jr., *Search for the Beloved Community. The Thinking of Martin Luther King, Jr.* (Lanham: University Press of America, 1988) 120.

[18]*Stride Toward Freedom*, 36, 51, 97-99.

[19]"When Peace Becomes Obnoxious," sermon preached on March 29, 1956, King Papers, Atlanta, Series III.

King found in nonviolent struggle the means to actualize his dream of the beloved community and became probably the most important practitioner of nonviolence in the history of the United States. He developed a simple approach to the application of nonviolence: study the problem, strategize, negotiate, act. Action required applying Jesus' teaching about love of enemy to oppressors able and willing to use force. Amidst the Montgomery campaign, he announced a willingness to suffer and sacrifice. "We will match your capacity to inflict suffering with our capacity to endure suffering. We will meet your physical force with soul force. We will not hate you, but we cannot in all good conscience obey your unjust laws. Do to us what you will and we will still love you." During the Montgomery campaign, as well as subsequent campaigns, King developed "ten commandments" that fused his vision of the beloved community with use of nonviolent means.

1. Meditate daily on the teachings and life of Jesus.
2. Remember always that the nonviolent movement . . . seeks justice and reconciliation—not victory.
3. Walk and talk in the manner of love, for God is love.
4. Pray daily to be used by God in order that all men might be free.
5. Sacrifice personal wishes in order that all might men be free.
6. Observe with friend and foe ordinary rules of courtesy.
7. Seek to perform regular service for others and for the world.
8. Refrain from the violence of fist, tongue, or heart.
9. Strive to be in good spiritual and bodily health.
10. Follow the directions of the movement and of the captain on a demonstration.[20]

As a result of his Montgomery experience, King had come to recognize that racism was not confined to the southern United States but had its roots in a cruelly unjust society as a whole. He realized that fulfilment of his dream of the beloved community entailed struggle not only against racism but also against war and for economic justice. This led to comprehensive efforts to create a different kind of society and, tragically, to realism about the obstacles ahead, in the South, in the North where King failed to make any significant impact on institutional racism and

---

[20]*Stride toward Freedom*, 179, 216–17; *Why We Can't Wait*, 63-4; Washington, 537.

economic injustice, or in the world. In the end, for King, the way of nonviolence became the way of the cross. Engagement in direct action and civil disobedience would result in beatings, jail sentences, and martyrdom.

Preaching at Ebenezer Baptist Church on 4 February 1968, King concluded by describing the funeral that soon would be his:

> I'd like somebody to mention that day, that Martin Luther King, Jr., tried to give his life serving others. I'd like for somebody to say that day, that Martin Luther King, Jr., tried to love somebody. I want you to say that day, that I tried to be right on the war question. I want you to be able to say that day, that I did try to feed the hungry. And I want you to be able to say that day, that I did try, in my life, to clothe those who were naked. I want you to say, on that day, that I did try, in my life, to visit those who were in prison. I want you to say that I tried to love and serve humanity.
>
> Yes, if you want to say that I was a drum major, say that I was a drum major for justice . . . peace . . . righteousness, and all the other shallow things will not matter. I won't have the fine and luxurious things of life to leave behind. But I just want to leave a committed life behind. If I can do my duty as a Christian ought, if I can bring salvation to a world once wrought, if I can spread the message as the master taught, then my living will not be in vain.
>
> Yes, Jesus, I want to be on your right side . . . not for any selfish reason, not in terms of some political kingdom or ambition, but I just want to be there in love and in justice and in truth and in commitment to others, so that we can make of this old world a new world.[21]

Two months later an assassin ended his quest for this new world.

Conclusion

In a recent study, Taylor Branch observed that King probably influenced the pace, substance, and progress of social change more than any other individual of his day. He did this by making blacks conscious of their ability to change the world.[22] These observations have been underscored by the television series, *Eyes on the Prize*.

---

[21]"The Drum Major Instinct," in Washington, 267.
[22]*Parting the Waters: America in the King Years 1954–1963* (New York: Simon and Schuster, 1988).

King was inspired by a dream of a coming new age when the governments of this world become the realm of God and of his Christ. This will be a time when love, justice, truth, and commitment to others prevail. This dream inspired him King to work for the beloved community.

Over twenty years after King's death, systemic evil persists. What remains of the dreamer's dream? I believe that it continues to inspire those who struggle for justice in Berlin, Nitassinan, San Salvador, Soweto, and elsewhere. I believe that it continues to motivate people to walk the road of peace. I believe that it continues to lead people to use nonviolence: to love, not hate; to sacrifice, not hoard; to affirm the dignity of all, not deny it.

A few months before his death, King delivered the annual Canadian Broadcast Corporation Massey Lectures. He called for a "revolution of values" and a "revolution of love and creativity." He said,

> Our freedom was not won a century ago. It is not won today; but some small part of it is in our hands, and we are marching no longer by ones and twos but in legions of thousands, convinced now it cannot be denied by any human force. Today the question is not whether we shall be free but by what course we will win. . . . In a world facing the revolt of ragged and hungry masses of God's children; in a world torn between the tensions of East and West, white and colored, individualists and collectivist; in a world whose cultural and spiritual power lags so far behind her technological capabilities that we live each day on the verge of nuclear co-annihilation; in this world, nonviolence is no longer an option for intellectual analysis, it is an imperative for action.[23]

Recalling dreams of prophets and Jesus, he concluded:

> I still have a dream that one day every valley shall be exalted and every mountain and hill will be made low . . . and the glory of the Lord shall be revealed, and all flesh shall see it together. I still have a dream that with this faith we will be able to adjourn the councils of despair and bring new light into the dark chambers of pessimism. With this faith we will be able to speed up the day when there will be peace on earth and good will toward men. It will be a

---

[23]*The Trumpet of Conscience* (New York: Harper and Row, 1967) excerpted in Washington, 653.

glorious day. The morning stars will sing together, and the sons of God will shout for joy.[24]

The Martin Luther King, Jr. Center in Atlanta expresses the dream in *Living the Dream Pledge*:

> In honor of Martin Luther King, Jr.'s life and work, I pledge to do everything that I can to make America and the world a place where equality and justice, freedom and peace will grow and flourish. I commit myself to living the dream by loving, not hating; showing understanding, not anger; making peace, not war.

For the sake of our children, let us dedicate ourselves to realizing the dream. It is deeply rooted in the Bible. It is an imperative if there are to be future generations. King's dream may become a reality; his remains a prophetic voice for Baptists, the people of God, and all humanity. The beloved community is not yet reality.

---

[24]"A Christmas Sermon on Peace," first broadcast as part of the annual Massey lectures on the Canadian Broadcasting Corporation, Christmas eve, 1967, Washington, 258.

Chapter Eighteen
British Conscientious Objectors

British Baptists Confront Conscription

With the exception of a few figures, including Muriel Lester, introduced in chapter sixteen, pacifism has scarcely figured in this study. In this chapter and the next, pacifism and related concepts such as conscientious objection, civil disobedience, and nonviolence dominate our inquiry.

Decades after other European nations had introduced mandatory military service, the British armed forces remained voluntary. Memory of the press gangs and coercive Militia Acts of the Napoleonic wars served until this century as a deterrent to introduction of conscription. After the Anglo-Boer War, a powerful aristocratic-military lobby began to campaign for conscription. In 1902, a National Service League formed. In 1904 the Norfolk Royal Commission advocated a year's conscription for home defence. The Territorial and Reserve Forces Act (1907) extended the scope of voluntary training and enabled some patriotic employers to "encourage" employees to offer their services for defence training. Subsequently, the government introduced virtually every year a bill intending to expand the scope of the act. Each failed until 1916 when conscription came into force.[1]

Throughout history, war has challenged Christians to examine conscience and loyalty. On 4 August 1914, the outbreak of the First

---

[1] Devi Prasad and Tony Smythe, ed., *Conscription. A World Survey* (London: War Resisters' International, 1968) 54; R. J. Q. Adams and Philip P. Poirie, *The Conscription Controversy in Great Britain 1900–1918* (London: Macmillan, 1987); Denis Hayes, *Conscription Conflict. The Conflict of Ideas in the Struggle for and against Military Conscription in Britain between 1901 and 1939* (London: Sheppard Press, 1949); Caroline Moorehead, *Troublesome People. The Warriors of Pacifism* (London: Hamish Hamilton, 1986).

World War shattered the hopes and illusions of leading Baptists such as John Clifford and James Henry Rushbrooke. They had opposed the Anglo-Boer War and the military build-up that preceded the First World War. They had worked for international understanding through such bodies as the Associated Councils of Churches in the British and German Empires for fostering Friendly Relations between the Two Peoples, the World Alliance for Promoting International Friendship through the Churches, and the Baptist World Alliance. They were not pacifists, however, and, when conflict erupted, they were swept along by a wave of patriotic fever.

Generally, most Baptists reconciled their consciences to the necessity of war. In some measure, they responded within the framework of traditional just war thinking. Germany's invasion of Belgium warranted a response of self-defence. "War is anti-Christian," John Clifford told his congregation, but this was a fight between "the forces of freedom and those of slavery. . . . The progress of humanity in my judgement hinges upon this war. . . . We were forced into it." From every part of the chapel there were murmurs of "Hear, hear."[2] Baptists also portrayed the war as part of the march of progress. Charles Brown, another prominent pastor, intoned to the annual Baptist assembly,

> My hope . . . is that out of this unparalleled slaughter and destruction, this good will come, that every nation will be made so sick of war as to determine that war shall be no more, and that those who incite to it shall be regarded as the greatest enemies of their kind.[3]

Many Baptist churches opened their facilities as recruitment centers. Pastors who served as chaplains occupied a place of honor at Baptist assemblies. Support for conscription grew.

Initially, the military secured sufficient voluntary resources. The threat of conscription increased as the response diminished. Two organizations formed to meet this threat. The Fellowship of Reconciliation (FOR) and the No Conscription Fellowship (NCF) mobilized opposition to conscription. They were unsuccessful. On 27 January 1916 the Military

---

[2]*British Weekly*, 20 August 1914 quoted by Alan Wilkinson, *Dissent or Conform? War, Peace and the English Churches 1900–1945* (London: SCM, 1986) 23.
[3]*Baptist Times and Freeman*, 30 April 1915, supplement.

Service Act received royal assent. FOR and NCF members continued to defend the rights of conscientious objectors (COs).

The FOR emerged from the tentative beginnings of the ecumenical movement and from friendships engendered by contacts between British and European Christians. Despite the deteriorating international situation, important relationships existed. For example, on the eve of the First World War, Henry Theodore Hodgkin (1877–1933), a member of the Society of Friends and a missionary doctor, and Friedrich Siegmund-Schultze, pastor at Potsdam and chaplain to the kaiser, attended the conference at Constance establishing the World Alliance for Promoting International Friendship through the Churches. As Hodgkin departed for England, Siegmund-Schultze declared, "Whatever happens, nothing is changed between us. We are one in Christ and can never be at war."[4]

In Germany, Siegmund-Schultze soon faced the death penalty for his pronouncements on the war. For his part, Hodgkin returned to England and drafted a "Message to Men and Women of Goodwill." A Meeting for Sufferings of the Society of Friends accepted this statement with a few modifications and issued it on 7 August 1914. Nine newspapers carried the announcement as a paid advertisement, and copies circulated in Britain and Germany as a pamphlet. The document urged Christians to examine the basis on which to construct a better order of society.

In late December 1914, 130 persons gathered to discuss how to respond to war. The conference concluded,

> 1. That Love, as revealed and interpreted in the life and death of Jesus Christ, involves more than we have yet seen, that it is the only power by which evil can be overcome, and the only sufficient basis of human society.
>
> 2. That, in order to establish a world-order based on love, it is incumbent upon those who believe in this principle to accept it fully, both for themselves and in their relation to others, and to take the risks involved in doing so in a world which does not as yet accept it.

---

[4] Jill Wallis, *Valiant for Peace. A History of the Fellowship of Reconciliation 1914 to 1989* (London: Fellowship of Reconciliation, 1991) 4. For biographical information, see H. G. Wood, *Henry T. Hodgkin, A Memoir* (London: Student Christian Movement Press, 1937), and John S. Conway, "Friedrich Wilhelm Siegmund-Schultze," in Harold Josephson, ed., *Biographical Dictionary of Modern Peace Leaders* (Westport: Greenwood Press, 1985).

3. That, therefore, as Christians, we are forbidden to wage war, and that our loyalty to our country, to humanity, to the Church Universal, and to Jesus Christ, our Lord and Master, calls us instead to a life service for the enthronement of love in personal, social, commercial and national life.

4. That the Power, Wisdom and Love of God stretch far beyond the limits of our present experience, and that He is ever waiting to break forth into human life in new and larger ways.

5. That since God manifests Himself in the world through men and women, we offer ourselves to His redemptive purpose, to be used by Him in whatever way He may reveal to us.[5]

This declaration became the basis of FOR witness to peace in Britain. As an explicitly Christian statement, it could not serve as the only vehicle of pacifism. In 1914, a second organization parallel to the FOR formed. The No Conscription Fellowship drew support from the socialist Independent Labour Party and various traditionally libertarian, pacifist, and political groups.[6]

The bill authorizing conscription included provision for COs to do alternative military service or work of national importance under civilian authority. Overall, there were 16,500 COs. The largest number of religious objectors were Christadelphians, Jehovah's Witnesses, Plymouth Brethren, and members of the Society of Friends. The total number of Baptist COs was small. According to one study, tribunals that assessed cases involving civilian service reviewed the cases of seventy-three

---

[5] Wallis, 7-8. Among those who attended were Luch Gardner, later a key figure in the Conference of Politics, Economics and Citizenship movement; W. E. Orchard, minister of the Congregational King's Weigh House; Richard Roberts, Minister of the Presbyterian Church at Crouch Hill, North London; Maude Royden, who in 1917 became the first English woman to have a permanent pulpit; and Leyton Richards. Recently returned from Australia, Richards turned down an invitation to become pastor of a Baptist congregation to serve as FOR General Secretary from 1916–1918. See Edith Richards, *Private View of a Public Man. The Life of Leyton Richards* (London: George Allen and Unwin, 1950) 71.

[6] Thomas C. Kennedy, *The Hound of Conscience. A History of the No Conscription Fellowship 1914–1919* (Fayetteville: University of Arkansas Press, 1981); Jo Vellacott, *Bertrand Russell and the Pacifists in the First World War* (Brighton: Harvester Press, 1980).

Baptists.⁷ At least fifteen Baptists served prison terms. In other categories there probably were several hundred Baptist COs and a larger number of pacifists.

One was Edwin Foley (1877–1972).⁸ Foley trained at Midland College and entered first pastorate in Lincolnshire. Over the next twenty-five years, he served five churches. When the First World War broke out, he was minister at Shepshed, a small town near Loughborough. Preaching against the war, he lost the support of his congregation and had to change pastoral charge. Undaunted, he joined the FOR and sought unsuccessfully to organize a Baptist pacifist chapter of the FOR. For the rest of his life, Foley was a determined campaigner for peace. Called in 1937 to Spurgeon Memorial Church on Guernsey, Foley helped secure demilitarization of the Channel Islands during the Second World War.

Another leading Baptist pacifist during the First World War was Herbert Dunnico (1876–1953). Between 1902–1916, Dunnico served pastorates at Golborne Street, Warrington, and Kensington Chapel, Liverpool. From 1916–1953, Dunnico was secretary of the century-year old Peace Society. He used the position to fight conscription and, after the war, to speak on behalf of the cause of peace. Between 1922–1931, Dunnico represented Consett as Labour Member of Parliament. While the Peace Society abandoned pacifism, other groups such as the FOR and, in the 1930s, the Peace Pledge Union (PPU), became the main voice for Christian pacifists.⁹

Even if there were relatively few Baptist COs, nonetheless, stories of ill-treatment of COs elicited memories of persecution by the state. A few eminent Baptists courageously supported COs even though they did not share their position. For example, on 25 May 1916, the Leader published a letter defending the rights of COs. Signatories included John Clifford and F. B. Meyer.¹⁰ In 1916 F. B. Meyer put forward a proposal designed

---

⁷John Rae, *Conscience and Politics. The British Government and the Conscientious Objector to Military Service, 1916–1919* (London: Oxford University Press, 1970) 178.

⁸Edwin Foley, "An Octogenarian Looks Back," *Reconciliation* 35 (1958): 193-94. For an obituary, see *Baptist Handbook* (1973) 288.

⁹Foley, "Octogenarian," mentions Dunnico's pacifism. For a sketch, *Baptist Handbook* (1955) 323; *Who Was Who 1951–1960* (London, 1961); interview, Clive R. Dunnico, 24 May 1991. In a book entitled *The Church and Social Problems* Dunnico took up issues other than war and peace.

¹⁰Wilkinson, 37.

to improve the position of absolutists (those who refused to co-operate in any way with the military) by providing for revision of possible exemptions given objectors, many of whom served harsh prison terms. In 1917, Meyer published a 19-page pamphlet *The Majesty of Conscience.* Meyer eloquently summarized traditional Baptist principles of soul-liberty and separation of church and state.

> Conscience is the supreme authority on Right and Wrong. It is the vice-gerent of the Eternal Throne. It is a replica, in miniature, of the great white throne. . . . It demands from all the court of faculties that stand around its throne, the homage due to a king. Even when it is dethroned, disgraced, mocked, silenced, and consigned to the dungeon, it never abdicates—it never withdraws its claims. Men instinctively recognise them, and do them homage. Joseph's brethren spluttered, but his dreams came true.[11]

Meyer went on to appeal to the government to modify the procedures of tribunals and to free those in prison. According to statistics cited by Meyer from NCF sources, there were 337 men of religious standing in prison. He affirmed their right to hold their views and expressed agreement with their long-term objective, to abolish war by universal accord.

During the war, such arguments had limited appeal. The government and general public reacted strongly against pacifists. To a nation which lost 745,000 servicemen, the plight of the pacifist engendered little pity. Pacifists suffered, notably absolutists who went to prison. At least nine died due in part to prison conditions. While conscientious objectors could claim few successes, their cause was not without achievement. They stood firm against the hysteria of war. They held to a vision of a different world. Their treatment engendered a reaction that led to more favorable treatment of COs during the Second World War.

British Baptist Pacifist Fellowship

While an attempt to organize a Baptist pacifist group failed during the First World War, the idea did not disappear. In 1929, the Reverend William Henry Haden inquired about forming a "Baptist Ministers' Peace

---

[11]*The Majesty of Conscience* (London: C. W. Daniel, 1917).

Movement."[12] Receiving more than three hundred encouraging letters, Haden asked to speak to the pastoral sessions of the Baptist Union at its 1930 annual meetings. He received a place on the agenda the following year, and in 1932, the pastoral session resolved to form a Baptist ministers' peace group. A steering committee, including Haden and at least one future Baptist Union president, Frank Colin Bryan,[13] took responsibility to circulate peace literature to pastors. In 1934, a Baptist Ministers' Pacifist Fellowship was formally constituted with 580 members paying an annual subscription of one shilling.

The British Baptist Pacifist Fellowship (BBPF) emerged from these first steps. In 1935, the pastoral group opened its membership to all Baptists and adopted the present covenant,

> We, members and adherents of Baptist Churches, covenant together to renounce war in all its works and ways; and to do all in our power, God helping us, to make the teaching of Jesus Christ effective in all human relations.[14]

During the 1930s, the BBPF regularly met during the annual meetings of the Baptist Union. General assemblies of the Baptist Union adopted anti-war resolutions. For example, in 1936, the assembly agreed to a motion that, "modern war means the organised killing of men and women and children on a wide scale, and is manifestly contrary to the will of God." In 1937, another motion called for international friendship.[15] Baptist congregations adopted similar resolutions. For example, at meetings held in March and April 1935, members of Queen's Road Baptist Church, Coventry approved motions calling on the government to pursue a vigorous policy of disarmament and collective security, and

---

[12]Minute Book, Baptist Pacifist Fellowship. Haden (1875–1952) trained at Midland College and Oxford and held pastorates at Market Harborough (1906–1914), Union Church, Luton (1914–1924), West Bridgford (1924–1932) and Salem, Burton-on-Trent (1933–1939). *Baptist Handbook* (1953) 322.

[13]1891–1972. *Baptist Handbook* (1973) 283-84.

[14]Minute Book; *Reconciliation* 12 (August 1934): 220; successive issues of the *Newsletter* of the Baptist Peace Fellowship.

[15]Alan Betteridge, "Baptist Peace Fellowship of Britain," *Peace Work* 9 (January-February 1987): 4; Minute Book.

affirming that "reliance on Armed Force can neither be reconciled with our Master's Law of Love, nor give the world peace."[16]

BBPF membership increased to 700 members by the eve of war. This did not mean that Baptist pacifists were members of the BBPF. By formal agreement, all members of the BBPF were members of the FOR. But one could be a member of the FOR without joining one of the denominational peace groups. Others joined the PPU, League of Nations Union, or worked through political parties.

Pacifism in general and Christian pacifism in particular have never been a unitary phenomenon. Reading minutes, resolutions, sermons, and general literature from the period prior the Second World War, one discerns five features of Baptist pacifism and peace activity at the time.

First, Baptist peace activists held an optimistic view of the goodness of human beings. This shaped their principal approach to peacemaking and education. By appealing to the teachings of Jesus and to reason, they sought to win co-religionists to the cause.

Second, Baptist peace activists focused on issues of individual conscience. As the world situation worsened, Baptist peacemakers directed attention more to issues such as conscientious objection and military chaplaincy, than to the question of how to prevent the war that loomed on the horizon.

Third, the BBPF had no uniform political program or set of political objectives. The BBPF gave some attention to the broad political context in its response to a committee's report examining the denomination's attitude to war.[17] The BBPF warned about the danger of government military spending and advocated a strengthened League of Nations through creation of peacekeeping forces.

Fourth, successive BBPF chairpersons stressed the need for a practical pacifism. For example, in 1937, Howard Ingli James, pastor of Queen's Road Baptist Church, Coventry, from 1931–1943, gave an address entitled "Christian Pacifism, the Only Way Out." He stressed that Christian pacifism offered the world real salvation and the church a door

---

[16]Clyde Binfield, *Parsons and Persons. The Biography of a Baptist Church* (Coventry: Queen's Road Baptist Church, 1984) 217.

[17]*Attitude of the Baptist Denomination to War* pamphlet, 1937; *The Baptist Pacifist Fellowship in Relation to the Report of the Special Committee of the Baptist Union on War* pamphlet, 1937.

of hope. He encouraged members of Queen's Road Baptist Church to illustrate the dimension of positive peace through compassionate, progressive service. Congregation members from this period recalled this aspect of his ministry. With encouragement from James, Rene Beasely (1912–1990) and John and Themla Humphrey helped form a group, Pathfinders of Peace. They studied issues of peace and international relations. They assisted labourers, the poor, and young people affected by the depression. During the Second World War, they went before the tribunals as conscientious objectors.[18]

Finally, Baptist peacemakers stressed a spiritual basis of their witness. They emphasized Bible study, prayer, and repentance. Through the International Fellowship of Reconciliation they forged a world network of peaceful people. Many supported Gandhi's method of nonviolent struggle developed in Britain by figures such as Muriel Lester and Dick Sheppard (1880–1937), who as vicar of St. Martin-in-the-Field, London, was associated with two developments among pacifists, the peace army and PPU.

The Second World War did not confront members of the BBPF and other Christian pacifist organizations with the question whether the war was right or wrong. Rather, pacificists generally had to make a grim choice between two evils, identify with a nation whose fate hung in the balance and live with the wrenching consequences of their deeds. Some pacifists modified their beliefs or defected from the pacifist position altogether. Nonetheless, many leading pacifists including Vera Brittain, Muriel Lester, Charles Raven, and Donald Soper remained steadfast. Specifically religious groups such as the BBPF grew during the war. Pacifists bore individual witness but characteristically took care not to appear subversive. When they expressed their faith in public, pacifists appealed for a negotiated peace, attacked Allied bombing practices, or urged humanitarian measures such as controlled food relief for women and children suffering from starvation in Europe.

In all during the Second World War, 60,000 persons, including some women, went before tribunals as conscientious objectors. In contrast with

---

[18]Interviews with Rene Beasely and John Humphrey 23 August 1989; and with John and Thelma Humphrey 17 November 1990. For an obituary of James (1889–1956), *Baptist Handbook* (1957). Binfield, 202-64, discusses extensively the remarkable ministry of James.

the First World War, those who objected on religious and ethical grounds received relatively more lenient treatment. When supported by a letter attesting to the honesty of the applicant's beliefs, an objector declaring, "I conscientiously object to taking up arms because it is contrary to the laws of God. Christ teaches us to love our enemies and I must not disobey his word, cannot take that which I cannot give, namely life," was likely to convince a tribunal of his or her sincerity. Pacifists still had to face the possibility of imprisonment or, as indicated by the experience of Gladys Portis and her husband-to-be Arthur Portis, abuse in the community.

> I registered as a C. O. but was never called, which mystified me, as it was against Government Regulations for any Civil Servant to be reserved. I can only think that as so many Clerical Assistants had been replaced by local temporary staff . . . Clerical Officers were needed to oversee them, and these were scarce. When my registration became known in the office I was shunned for about a month, until they all cooled down.
>   My fiance—from my own church—went before a Tribunal and was given land work. He served for five years. . . . although we had a conscience clause in this country, there was no provision for a medical examination. Many fit men helped out their weaker brothers who couldn't possibly cope alone. Arthur's brother, an involved & working pacifist, supported by his non-pacifist vicar, was struck off and imprisoned. My husband-to-be was disliked by my parents because of his views. . . . After marriage we were disliked by neighbours, most of them knew about Arthur and his brother John. . . . Many lost their jobs or any chance of advancement. Ours was the latter case.[19]

Baptist COs generally opted to do non-combatant military service or alternative service of national importance in coal mining, agriculture, forestry, or hospital service. In one report, the South-West tribunal revealed that of 4,056 cases heard in 1942, seventy-one percent objected on religious grounds; 187 were Baptist. Another survey recorded eleven Baptists serving with the Christian Pacifist Forestry and Land Units.[20]

---

[19]Personal correspondence from Gladys Portis, 15 March 1991; other correspondents mention having encountered abusive reactions, but most found, and still find, that people respect views that are held sincerely. The minutes of the BBPF for 15 February 1943 mentioned Walter Abbotts, minister of Carrington Baptist Church, Nottingham, received a sentence of three months imprisonment and a fine of 100 pounds.

[20]Wilkinson, 291; Lewis Maclachlan, *C.P.F.L.U. A Short History of the Christian Pacifist Forestry and Land Units 1940–1946* (London: Fellowship of Reconciliation,

Three examples of service rendered by long-time BBPF members must suffice. Cyril Rusbridge, a retired Baptist pastor, worked the land and helped to build a sea wall at Lymington in Hampshire. Tom Slade, a retired civil servant, worked on an ambulance unit. Derek Deavin, a retired transit station attendant and lay preacher, served as a hospital porter. Each felt strongly that they could take no part in armed conflict. Each has continued to uphold Christian pacifism through the BBPF, FOR and local congregations.[21]

As during the First World War, the precise number of Baptist pacifists was difficult to ascertain. Conscription exempted many categories such as ministers of religion, women, and those in reserved occupations, with the result that conscientious objectors accounted for only some members of the BBPF.[22]

The war engulfed everyone. Because of its location in Coventry, a city of strategic importance, Queen's Road Baptist Church served the nation irrespective of the specific beliefs of members. One psychological effect of German bombing raids on the city was to make everybody feel more vehemently exactly what they had felt before. Some members supported military means, while others did not. As a result, part of the building was used for the war cause, yet more members served by doing alternative service or working in reserved occupations than those who actually fought overseas. Due to the leadership of Ingli James, a vengeful or divisive spirit did not prevail.[23]

During the war, the BBPF attempted to assist COs in several ways. Through meetings and correspondence, members provided a support network. On 12 December 1944, the tenth anniversary of the BBPF, members called upon Baptists to set aside a Sunday to pray for peace and to remember the peace witness of the BBPF. At Baptist assemblies and congregational meetings, resolutions kept pacifist issues before the

---

1952) 75.

[21]Personal correspondence, Cyril Rusbridge, 27 February 1991; Tom Slade, 2 May 1991; interview, Derek Deavin, 13 May 1991.

[22]Rachel Barker, *Conscience, Government and War. Conscientious Objection in Great Britain 1939–1945* (London: Routledge and Kegan Paul, 1982) 38, mentions that 187 Baptists appeared before the South-Western Tribunal in 1942.

[23]Vera Brittain, *Testament of Experience* (London: Fontana, 1981) 277.

denomination. As the Second World War came to an end, BBPF members faced the terrifying costs of the war and new moral challenges.

Towards a Wider Vision.
The Baptist Peace Fellowship

After the war, the BBPF shared in the post-war marches and debates over such issues as Britain's nuclear weapons program, post-war conscription, and arms sales. The Cold War confronted members with a different sort of conflict. Conscientious objection was much less an issue than the threat of ever increasing nuclear arsenals. In 1957 and 1958, motions put to the annual Baptist Union assembly calling for Britain to abandon nuclear tests unilaterally were defeated. In 1961, a resolution based on the BBPF covenant was defeated by a substantial vote.[24]

Despite these discouraging defeats, the BBPF sought to strengthen its witness in three broad areas. One was education. The BBPF produced literature, including a newsletter, and organized information tables and meetings at annual Baptist assemblies. In 1969, Peter Lorkin, a pastor and secretary of the BBPF at the time, published a pamphlet *Baptist Views on War and Peace* in a "Living Issues" series of the denomination. He urged all Baptists, whatever their specific views on the personal issue of pacifism, not to ignore the issue of war. He called on Baptists to "speak and act, pray and give with far greater urgency, sacrifice and awareness" to build a more peaceful world by adopting methods of non-violent resistance and by bridging the gulf between haves and have-nots.[25]

As an organization, and as individuals, the BBPF undertook initiatives in a number of areas, including international arms sales, disarmament, Welsh nationalism, and British presence in Northern Ireland. In 1984, after the Falklands-Malvina Conflict, it helped organize a delegation that went to Argentina on a mission of reconciliation.[26]

---

[24]Betteridge, 5.
[25]H. F. Lorkin, *Baptist Views on War and Peace* (London: Baptist Union of Great Britain and Ireland, 1969) 16; personal interview 27 October 1990.
[26]*Baptist Quarterly* 31 (April 1985): 66-73.

Finally, the organization sought to broaden its membership base. Conscription, conscientious objection, and military chaplaincy remained issues, especially during the Korean conflict, but it sought to recruit more laity, more women, and more youth. New, contentious issues emerged. For example, some older members have insisted that the BBPF remain a Christian pacifist organization. One consequence has been a loosening of ties with the British FOR, which has begun to follow the lead of the IFOR by reaching out to non-Christian members. In 1989, the BBPF modified its constitution by creating an associate membership for non-pacifist Baptists having broad sympathy with the Covenant and sharing the concern of the BBPF for issues of peace and justice.[27] In 1991, BBPF membership stood at around eight hundred. The generation that struggled against conscription has largely died, but a younger generation, buoyed by the rise of an international Baptist peace movement is continuing to struggle for peace without resort to weapon or war.

In respects, the prospects for realizing this dream are not bright. War continues to be a reality. Citing a recent example, as the Persian Gulf crisis unfolded in late 1990, BBPF members attending an annual meeting declared, "Our prayer is that in the name of God there should be no war in the Gulf." Many Baptists prayed for peace. Before and after 16 January 1991, when the conflict expanded, some joined in forms of non-violent resistance. Michael Cheong, a member of Eden Baptist Church, Cambridge, a Strict Baptist church not in the Baptist Union of Great Britain, became a CO during the war and has become a member of the BBPF administrative committee.[28]

Conclusion

During the 1930s, the journal *Reconciliation*, organ of the British FOR, characterized its mandate as "looking towards a Christian world." In 1930, an article by the Congregationalist minister Cecil Cadoux elaborated on what this meant as working for the healing among the nations. He characterized FOR members, including Baptists, as having embarked

---

[27]*Newsletter*, 1989.
[28]Correspondence, Alan Betteridge, 12 February 1992. Also, *Baptist Times*, 22 November 1990.

upon realization of Christ's healing impulse, removing all obstacles that exist between people and that separate people from the love of God. He recalled the witness of early Christians who sought to follow Jesus by seeking to cure the manifold diseases of the day. He cited the early Christian visionary who pictured a splendid city and a river running through it, with trees on both its banks, the leaves of which were for the healing of the nations. He concluded by stating that it rests for us to make that dream a reality.[29]

Since its inception, the BBPF has been an instrument of healing among the nations. Members have protested against war, taking part in vigils, candlelight processions, worship, meetings, and myriad other undertakings. As recently as the Persian Gulf War, British Baptist peacemakers have exercised a prophetic witness. As the war ended, in the words of one long-time member, "Now we pray that the more difficult task of winning the Peace might be achieved."[30] Consistently, they have affirmed that no war is ever acceptable to God, that war is never an option, and that war has never brought peace. In a century of war, British Baptist peacemakers have been a small minority able to claim few victories. Hoping against hopes, they have stood for a better way.

---

[29]*Reconciliation* 7, 12 (December 1930): 221-22.
[30]Muriel Ennals, personal correspondence, 15 March 1991.

Chapter Nineteen
The Baptist Peace Fellowship of North America

Background to the Baptist Pacifist Fellowship

Like the British Baptist Pacifist Fellowship, the story of the Baptist Pacifist Fellowship (BPF) goes back to the First World War. In 1917, the United States entered the war to make the world safe for democracy. Generally, Christians supported the war but yearned for a peace without victory. Most ministers backed the war effort, as did the recently formed Federal Council of Churches of Christ. Most denominations adopted resolutions embracing the war cause.[1]

Nevertheless, there were Christians who witnessed against the war by adhering to biblical pacifism or refusing combatant service in the military. Officially, the three historic peace churches opposed the war. Smaller denominations including the Christadelphians, the Pentecostals, and some fundamentalist groups opposed the war. In other denominations, there was a discernable minority of Christian pacifists. However much Christian pacifists differed in terms of denominational affiliation or theological background, generally they agreed that the teachings of Jesus rejected war.

While older peace societies went into decline, new organizations resisted the war. The Fellowship of Reconciliation (FOR) became the most important group for Christian pacifists. As we have seen in the

---

[1] Ray H. Abrams, *Preachers Present Arms* (New York: Round Table Press, 1933). H. C. Peterson and Gilbert C. Fite, *Opponents of War 1916–1918* (Madison: University of Wisconsin Press, 1957) ch. 11; John F. Piper, Jr., "The American Churches in World War I," *Journal of the American Academy of Religion* 38 (1970): 147-55.

preceding chapter, the FOR began in Britain. In the United States, the FOR emerged during a conference in Garden City, New York.² On 11 November 1915, sixty-eight founding members, including thirty-five women, rejected war unconditionally. They proclaimed their reliance on God and determination to live according to God's revolutionary principle of love.

For many Christians in the United States, the First World War raised questions about how to bridge the nineteenth-century vision of a "Christian America" and twentieth-century realities. During the war, the FOR served three roles: helping scattered members resist patriotic war fever, assisting conscientious objectors, and protesting the militaristic attitude of the Christian church. After the war, FOR members dedicated themselves to applying the precepts of social Christianity and Christian pacifism. Disillusionment with the Versailles Treaty and memory of the unfulfilled promise of the nineteenth-century peace crusade led contributed to growth of the movement, as Christians undertook a sober reappraisal of the gospel of peace and sought to raise a voice of faith that was more than an echo of culture.

Baptists mirrored these developments. A few refused wartime service. Several leading Baptists, including Walter Rauschenbusch, Edwin T. Dahlberg, Harry Emerson Fosdick (1878–1969), and Dores Sharpe (1885– 1981) joined the FOR during the war or immediately after the war. In earlier chapters, we have profiled Rauschenbusch and Dahlberg. Fosdick was the greatest preacher of his generation, and some, including Martin Luther King, Jr., regarded him a prophet. Although he had supported United States' involvement in the war, Fosdick toured the trenches at the end of the war and turned to pacifism. He resolved, "I must never again put my Christian ministry at the nation's disposal for

---

²Vera Brittain, *The Rebel Passion: A Short History of Some Pioneer Peace-Makers* (Nyack: Fellowship Publications, 1964); Christie Jungwirth, "History of the Fellowship of Reconciliation in the United States," (M.A. thesis, University of Munich, 1989); Lilian Stevenson, *Towards a Christian International. The Story of the International Fellowship of Reconciliation* (new and enlarged ed; London: International Fellowship of Reconciliation, 1941). The International Fellowship of Reconciliation began in 1919. A Canadian chapter began in 1929.

the sanction and backing of war."[3] He joined the FOR in its early days, explaining,

> Having seen at first hand what war means in the first world conflict, my conscience could no longer dodge the issue: that war, in its cases, processes and results, is the complete denial of everything that Jesus Christ stands for. I welcomed then, as I do still, a fellowship which takes Christ's ways of life seriously—not simply as an ideal dream for tomorrow but as a practical program today.[4]

Dores Robinson Sharpe, Rauschenbusch's student and first biographer, grew up on a farm near the St. John's River in New Brunswick, Canada. He ministered with distinction in Canada and the United States. Bernard Loomer described him thusly.

> The range and depth of his passion for justice in the economic, political, and social dimensions of our common life, and the degree of his contributions to the advance of the concerns of the kingdom constitute surely one of the finest exemplifications of the social gospel in American Protestantism during the present century. Walter Rauschenbusch sired a worthy disciple indeed.[5]

Baptist pacifists undertook a variety of transforming initiatives. Some recovered earlier emphases of nineteenth-century peace workers, including opposing the war system and supporting internationalism. Some left jobs in defense industries. Others focused on the need for treaties of arbitration and efforts to limit the production and international trade in armaments. As well, Baptist pacifists engaged in such issues as labor-management relations, poverty, and racism. Adapting Gandhian methods of nonviolence, some challenged segregation, while others organized labour unions. By this activity, they sought to contribute to positive peace.

In part, Baptist pacifists exercised through local initiatives. As an example, Kenneth L. Cober was pastor of the Baptist church in

---

[3]*The Living of These Days* (London: SCM Press, 1957) 293. See also, Harry Emerson Fosdick, "The Trenches and the Church at Home," *Atlantic Monthly* 123 (January 1919): 22-33.
[4]FOR-USA brochure, 1958.
[5]Bernard M. Loomer, "Dores R. Sharpe, Portrait of a Christian Rebel," *Foundations* 24 (1981): 104.

Canandaigua, New York. An FOR member because of Howard Thurman's influence, in November 1932 he organized a "peace week" as an experiment in educating the entire community in world peace and friendship. Drawing together pastors from several churches, educationalists, librarians, and other civic leaders, Cober created public forums, a poster contest, school programs, and other activities.[6]

Baptist pacifists sought to influence the Northern Baptist Convention (reorganized, 1950, as American Baptist Convention, and 1972 as American Baptist Churches) at its annual assembly through resolutions. These consistently condemned war as evil. In 1939, the assembly resolved:

> Whereas war is utterly contradictory to the spirit and ideals of Christianity, carries with it destruction of spiritual and moral values and is always accompanied by propaganda, unbridled lust and other forms of evil; therefore, be it resolved, that we declare our emphatic opposition to the whole war system and all things related to it; furthermore be it resolved that we give our support to pacific means for settling international disputes, and that, as fundamental to this, we work for the establishment of the Kingdom of God on earth.[7]

Such resolutions addressed in very general terms concerns of war and preparation for war. How to apply pacifist sentiments to concrete issues, such as war in Ethiopia or Spain, was left to individual believers. During the inter-war period, Christian pacifism thrived. According to several interviewees, "We were all pacifist in the 30s." As war clouds menaced on the horizon, some estimated three and a half million would declare themselves conscientious objectors (COs) to war. This did not happen. At most, 100,000 took this stance.[8]

---

[6]Kenneth L. Cober, "Peace Week. A Community Project," *International Journal of Religious Education* November 1932. Personal communication.

[7]From the first BPF brochure.

[8]Statistics are based on the *Directory of Civilian Public Service, May 1941 to March, 1947* (Washington, D.C.: National Service Board for Religious Objectors, 1947). The best account is Mulford Q. Sibley and Philip E. Jacob, *Conscription of Conscience. The American State and the Conscientious Objector 1940–1947* (Ithaca: Cornell University Press, 1952). Accounts of Baptists include *The Story of 50 Southern Baptist Civilian Public Servicemen* (pamphlet, 1945); Paul A. Wilhelm, *Civilian Public Servants. A Report on 210 World War II Conscientious Objectors* (Washington, D. C.: National Interreligious Service Board for Conscientious Objectors, 1990). For the Debate on conscientious

The Baptist Pacifist Fellowship

Christians confronted stark choices. The Northern Baptist Convention formed a committee on "Exemption from Military Service of Baptist Conscientious Objectors," which stressed the principle of supremacy of conscience and called for treatment of Baptists equal to that accorded Quakers or Mennonites. As other denominations spawned pacifist groups, the idea of forming a Baptist pacifist group took root. First proposed at gatherings of the Roger Williams Fellowship, a Baptist Pacifist Fellowship was seen as a mechanism to bring together like-minded Baptists in fellowship and to strengthen support for COs. The FOR took the lead in organizing a meeting on 18 November 1939, held at the home of Baptist pastor and FOR staff member, Laurence Hosie. Afterwards, prominent Baptists, including Hosie, Shorty Collins, Edwin T. Dahlberg, Harry Emerson Fosdick, and E. McNeil Poteat, Jr., who was at that time caring for a congregation in Cleveland, sent a letter to every Northern Baptist Convention congregation. They invited individuals to meet during the annual convention at Atlantic City, New Jersey, "to consider the formation of a Baptist Pacifist Fellowship." The invitation stressed that this would be an unofficial body.[9]

The breakfast was held 24 May 1940. Over one hundred fifty attended and agreed to an executive, with Edward C. Kunkle, president of the denomination, as first president, and Ruth E. Murphy, a religious educator, as secretary-treasurer of the BPF. The meeting established seven regional groups, $2 dues (with permission, $1 went to the FOR) and a statement of commitment that read: "As I view my loyalty to the Person, Spirit, and Teachings of Jesus Christ, my conscience commits me to His way of redemptive love and compels me to refuse to participate in or give moral support to any war." The BPF called people to repentance, faith in Jesus Christ, and constructive work for a truly Christian commonwealth, in short, realization of God's realm of peace.

---

objection within the Northern Baptist Convention, see J. Douglas Archer, "Conscientious Objectors and the Northern Baptist Convention of 1940," *Foundations* 15/4 (October-December 1972): 342-54.
[9]*PeaceWork*, May–June 1989, 4.

The statement of purpose of the BPF expressed lofty ideals. The BPF sought to unite members in a positive stand for Christ's way of redemptive love in all individual and social relationships of life. It identified several roles: to work to eradicate the many social ills out of which war springs, to endeavor to work out nonviolent alternatives for solving conflicts, to engage in all possible healing processes, to offer spiritual guidance to all who want such help, and to make available to its members strength and comfort to be derived from knowing that there were other Christian pacifists and of their readiness to support each other in the time of testing and crisis that lay ahead.

According to legislation of the day, COs had three choices: noncombatant military service, alternative service in church-run Civilian Public Service (CPS) camps, or prison. Neither the government nor any other agency provided financial help. This placed an incredible burden on COs, their families, and those committed to ensure their livelihood. After vigorous debate, the 1940 assembly of the Northern Baptist Convention adopted a resolution that expressed approval of maintaining a registry of Baptist COs. The Convention explicitly stated that this action was not to be construed as approval of any effort to recruit either COs or military conscripts. In consenting to have the convention keep their names in permanent records, COs signed a pledge, "My Purpose Concerning War" by which they agreed to an understanding of pacifism as a positive stance for peace and daily duty.

The Northern Baptist Convention agreed to maintain a registry. Implementation of this obligation fell to the American Baptist Home Mission Society, which seconded Professor John W. Thomas of Crozer Divinity School to the American Friends Service Committee. He provided counseling and a mechanism permitting those who so desired to designate gifts through the World Emergency Forward Fund.[10] The Southern Baptist Convention established a similar procedure to assist Southern Baptist pacifists.

It is impossible to know how many Baptist COs there were since the Selective Service Act exempted ministers of religion and seminarians from the draft, although some clergy pacifists were forced from their

---

[10] In 1942 individuals and local groups sent $35 per CO per month for eighty Baptists in CPS camps, a total of nearly $34,000. In solidarity, the executive urged members to spend a day a week in fasting and prayer.

congregations. Women did not register. Just as Baptists generally differ among themselves, Baptist pacifists disagreed both theologically and in terms of the degree to which they were willing to cooperate with the system of conscription. Some Baptists did non-combatant military jobs. At least thirty-three persons served jail terms. Four hundred and three persons from several Baptist denominations worked at CPS camps in a variety of roles. Some fought forest fires. Some did land or farm reclamation. Some became attendants in mental hospitals. Some served as human guinea pigs in starvation projects, drifting in life rafts or experimenting with new drugs for malaria or pneumonia.[11]

Towards the end of the war, Baptist pacifists debated the merits of withdrawing from the system. One issue concerned the treatment of COs. Obliged to do menial or meaningless work without pay, CPSers found themselves enmeshed in what Harry Emerson Fosdick described as "a system of internment camps at which forced labor without pay is exacted as the price for being allowed to hold a religious belief."[12] Another concern related to the fact that, in effect, by agreeing to manage part of the selective service system, the churches appeared to nullify the witness of COs and to cross the boundary separating church and state. Alluding to the BPF role, however minimal, in administering the camp at Skillman, New Jersey, Palmer Bryant, one of many who walked out of CPS camps, argued: "No religious or pacifist group should continue to administer this evil business for our present government."[13]

Accepting the will of CPSers and the lead of the FOR-USA, Friends, and other religious pacifist bodies, the BPF executive advised the American Baptist Home Mission Society to withdraw from the system. It emphasized that,

> if the churches continue in CPS they will be administering peace-time conscription. Instead . . . we believe churches should put their energy into opposing it. We believe Baptists, with their heritage of separation of church and

---

[11]This was one of the most criticized aspects of treatment of COs. At least one Baptist, Warren Dugan, contracted infantile paralysis and died of the disease he was working to control. See his "Faith of a C.O.," *Baptist C.O.*, no. 3 (November 1945): 5.

[12]*Baptist C.O.*, no. 1 (June 1945): 3.

[13]*Baptist C.O.*, no. 2 (September 1945): 5.

state, should be especially wary of an arrangement with the government to put men to forced labor.[14]

By resolving the debate in this manner, the BPF accentuated positive and negative aspects of peacemaking. On the one hand, Baptist pacifists sought a way of service and sacrifice. They drew strength and encouragement from the example of Jesus. They believed Jesus lived and taught love for all, returned good for evil, and overcame evil with good. On the other hand, they made a powerful critique of war and all that contributes to war. Through this dual witness, Baptist pacifists were able to influence denominational positions on the war. As an example, in 1942, a debate developed over a resolution commending the YMCA, YWCA, and AFSC for their work in feeding the starving peoples of the world as a means of creating the mutual trust and fellowship necessary for a just and durable peace. An attempt was made to emasculate the resolution and turn it to a blessing of war. BPF leaders mobilized defeat of the proposed changes. A delegate wrote,

> This morning there was a heated debate over one of the resolutions . . . advocating feeding the starving and oppressed peoples of the world as a means of creating the mutual trust and fellowship for a just and durable peace. The chairman of the resolutions committee, Justin Wroe Nixon and Dan Poling and others of the same persuasion tried to emasculate the resolution and substitute a clause that would make it a virtual blessing of the war by the church. They tried to do it first by a trick of parliamentary procedure and then by an emotional appeal to the "mothers and fathers of 20,000 Baptist young men in the nation's armed forces." But due to the valiant efforts of Gene Bartlett, Shorty Collins, L. B. Moseley, and others the change was defeated on the floor of the convention.[15]

After a similar debate at the 1944 convention, an article was published complaining, as Carl Tiller recalls, "a resolution supporting our people engaged in war would probably undergo a process of emasculation at the hands of a strong group of pacifists who somehow always manage to get themselves elected to the committee of resolutions."[16]

---

[14]*Baptist C.O.*, no. 3 (November 1945): 1.
[15]LeRoy Day to Bette Mae Keith, personal communication.
[16]*PeaceWork*, May–June 1989, 3.

By the end of the Second World War, several thousand Baptists worldwide had a pacifist affiliation, including those who joined the Baptist Pacifist Fellowships in the United Kingdom and United States. Others joined the FOR but did not identify with the BPF. Given war propaganda of the time, hostility that COs confronted, and overwhelming support by the Christian churches for war in general and the Second World War in particular, it was not surprising that the figure was small. Perhaps what is surprising is that there were any Baptist pacifists at all.

Immediately after the war, the BPF concentrated on preventing a peacetime draft, raising funds for post-war relief, nurturing healing among the nations, and righting such wrongs as the wartime relocation of Japanese Americans. During the 1950s, attention shifted to the Korean conflict, avoidance of war with the Soviet Union, promoting the work of such organizations as the Church Peace Mission or FOR-USA, and encouragement by members of action such as writing members of Congress or participation in prayer vigils, walks for peace, and anti-war demonstrations. The BPF held meetings, sponsored resolutions, and set up exhibit tables at American Baptist assemblies. At breakfast gatherings, prominent pacifists addressed the group.

The BPF profile increased slowly—so slowly that several times pundits prematurely pronounced the BPF dead! It published a sporadic newsletter. It mailed to over six thousand American Baptist pastors an invitation to visit its exhibits or attend its breakfasts at the annual gathering of the American Baptist convention, along with information about various peace campaigns. Mailings included pamphlets by such prominent figures as Martin Niemoeller; petitions such as one to President Eisenhower asking him to call off nuclear weapons tests; or prayer requests, for example, to support the crew of the "Golden Rule," a trawler that sailed to a Pacific ocean nuclear test site. In 1956 and 1957, it conducted tours to Europe where emissaries of reconciliation led seminars and met with East European peace committees, the NATO Supreme Commander, and pacifists like Andre and Magda Trocme, Philippe Vernier, Kaspar Mayr, and his daughter Hildegard. While these were important initiatives, with a small membership and no staff, the BPF could not at the time sustain this level of activity. Still, the BPF won acceptance and exerted influence on the denomination. American Baptists elected several pacifists as presidents, including Edward Kunkle (1939–1940), Edwin Dahlberg (1946–1947), Carl Tiller (1965–1966), and

Culbert Rutenber (1968–1969). Long-time member Victor H. Gavel (d. 1993), of Bradenton, Florida, explained, "We were not an integral part of the convention, but we were tolerated. We managed to obtain a booth at our conventions in the exhibit halls—not always on the 'mid-way,' sometimes back in a corner—but we were there."[17]

Broadening the Mandate

The genius of the BPF was its focus on the spiritual basis of peacemaking. The BPF encouraged members to form groups for Bible study and prayer. It emphasized that, to follow Christ's gospel of peace, one must begin by purging sources of violence and war. At the same time, it resisted the temptation to spiritualize or privatize the biblical concept of peace. Baptist peacemakers named as evil the causes of war inherent within social structures such as threatened use of nuclear weapons, segregation, and poverty and began to organize around these issues.

One story illustrates the broadening mandate of Baptist peacemakers. In the 1930s, Clarence Jordan, an agriculture student at the University of Georgia, participated in reserve officer training. Unable to reconcile the Sermon on the Mount with the war machine, he abandoned thoughts of a military career and became a popular Southern Baptist preacher and Bible teacher at the Southern Baptist Theological Seminary in Louisville, Kentucky. The Second World War challenged Jordan's pacifism. During meetings of the Louisville chapter of the FOR, Jordan, his wife Florence, and Martin and Mable England, American Baptist missionaries on prolonged furlough due to the war in Asia, talked of trying to do something concrete about conditions among poor Southerners: inadequate housing, welfare, uncertain unemployment, and despair. In the fall of 1941, Jordan gave up the security of the seminary to work first with inner-city poor. In 1942, the two families left for Georgia to undertake a venture in discipleship. They bought a 440-acre rundown farm near Americus, Georgia. They renamed it Koinonia Farm. While the Englands

---

[17]Remarks to the fifth annual BPFNA summer conference, Ottawa, Ontario, 6 July 1990.

later returned to Asia, the Jordans worked to create an interracial community that held property in common (Acts 2:44-45, Eph 2:14–16).[18]

From the start, Koinonia Farm engendered hostility. For example, in 1948, the Jordans' congregation, Rehobeth Baptist Church, unhappy with the views of its Koinonia members on issues of peace and race, suggested that they resign voluntarily. The Jordans declined but were told that they were no longer welcome. One strategy used against Koinonia Farm was a boycott, which sought to prevent Koinonia from marketing its farm produce. There were also sporadic acts of hostility: machine-gunning of buildings, cancelation of insurance policies, beating of Koinonia workers, the visit of a 70-car Ku Klux Klan deputation. On one occasion, Jordan approached his brother, a successful banker, and asked him for assistance; his brother refused. Jordan confronted him with memory of having been baptized together. "You promised to follow Jesus; you just admire Him."

Among those who did respond to appeals for help were BPF members. Many traveled for varying periods of time to Georgia to work on the farm. Others assisted with gifts of encouragement, energy, and ideas. Jordan imbued Baptist peacemakers with the conviction. "It's not God is in heaven and all is well on earth, but God is here and all hell is breaking loose!" After years of controversy and non-violent struggle, Clarence Jordan died in 1969. Florence Jordan died in 1987. The ministry of Koinonia continues.

Prophetic voices—those of Clarence and Florence Jordan, Martin Luther King, Jr., Edwin Dahlberg and others—challenged the BPF to expand its scope. During the Second World War, most BPF members understood pacifism as not taking human life. Increasingly, BPF members acknowledged that this focus dealt only with negative peace. Baptists, and Christians generally, had a responsibility to work for positive peace. A joint meeting of the American and Southern Baptist commissions on Initiatives for Peace, which met in Chicago on 14 November 1958 under the chairmanship of Culbert Rutenber, expressed a growing consensus. Agreement was reached on motions that sought to encourage more exchange visits with people from abroad, foster a program of prayer for peace, develop a joint American and Southern Baptists effort on behalf

---

[18]Dallas Lee, *The Cotton Patch Evidence* (New York: Harper & Row, Publishers, 1971).

of Trick or Treat for UNICEF, and provide more literature to help Baptists to discern biblical and theological sanctions for Christian peacemaking. Delegates agreed that,

> the basic causes of war include hunger, population pressure, national rivalries, and racial tensions. It was further agreed that we must emphasize both our brotherhood in Christ and our kinship in creation, if humanity is not to fall over the brink of a suicidal race conflict. Concern for the survival of the human family must drive the Christian people to confront the issues which lead to war.[19]

With this as an agenda the BPF embarked on a period of growth.

Gradually, as members came to discern that there is no single way to peace, pressure grew to change the BPF's name. In 1960 the Baptist Pacifist Fellowship became the Baptist Peace Fellowship. Baptists who did not hold absolute pacifist convictions could now join—for example, those who may have supported war against Hitler but not in Vietnam. The switch allowed the BPF to widen the scope of its activity and to imbue older members with new focus.[20]

The importance of this shift became apparent during the 1960s, when issues of the draft and selective conscientious objection became concerns for many men during the Vietnam War. It was a period of heightened concern for peace and increased membership. In 1970, the BPF experimented by hiring an intern, James R. Lynch, a theological student at Bethany Theological Seminary in Chicago. He set up regional training seminars, encouraged the formation of local peace groups, improved the newsletter, and increased the effectiveness of the BPF. Lack of secure funding and other frustrations made it impossible for him to continue beyond a year. American Baptists, however, formed offices on international affairs and peace concerns.[21]

---

[19]"Minutes of the Meeting of American Baptist and Southern Baptist Commissions on Peace," BPFNA files.

[20]Interview with Olive Tiller, *PeaceWork*, May–June 1989, 3. In 1970–1971, the BPF took the name "Baptist Fellowship for Peace."

[21]Interview with James R. Lynch, 22 February 1989. Since 1987, Daniel L. Buttry has managed the peace program as part of the Board of National Ministries of the American Baptist Churches.

Another development gave evidence of a broad range of Baptist peace work. In 1964 Victor and Eileen Gavel endowed an award in honor of Edwin Dahlberg. They wanted "to give recognition to American Baptists who have worked constructively for peace with justice and freedom." Recipients have been Martin Luther King, Jr. (1964); L. Kijungluba Ao, for efforts to end violence in India stemming from Nagaland's rebellion against India (1965); W. Alvin Pitcher, for work in civil rights and economic development among blacks (1966); Kyle Hazelden, for leadership in opposing the Vietnam War and in race relations (1968); Leon Sullivan, for work in the development of economic opportunity for low income blacks (1968); Zelma George, for her work as director of one of the most successful job corps centres in the United States (1969); Frank M. Coffin, for work in international development assistance (1970); Shorty Collins, for a lifetime of campaigning against war and for peace (1971); Harold E. Stassen, for his role in formulating the United Nations Charter (1972); William Sloan Coffin, though not at the time related to an American Baptist Church, for his leadership in opposing the Vietnam War (1973); Mabel Martin, for her long term service as American Baptist representative to the United Nations (1975); Robert Hingson, for his role in eradicating epidemics through invention of the "peace gun" for inoculations (1977); Jimmy Carter, for his role in bringing about the Camp David accords (1979); Gustavo Parajon, for his work in Nicaragua with the Evangelical Committee for Aid and Development [CEPAD] (1981); Anna Dorothy Wylie, for her role in putting the nuclear weapons freeze on the ballot in Michigan and in the field of race relations (1983); George W. Hill, for helping launch a National Peace Academy (1985); George "Nick" Carter, for his service as national co-chairperson of the Coalition for a Nuclear Weapons Freeze (1987); Lucius Walker, director of the Interreligious Foundation for Community Organization, for his work with Pastors for Peace (1989); Carl and Olive Tiller, for their lifetime commitment to peacemaking (1991); and Margaret "Peg" Sherman for her work as the American Baptist Churches' representative to the United Nations coalition of non-government organizations.[22]

---

[22]*The Edwin T. Dahlberg Peace Award*, pamphlet, Peace Concerns Program, National Ministries, American Baptist Churches. For the most recent recipients, stories in *PeaceWork*, May–August 1987, 19; *PeaceWork*, July–October 1989, 21; *Baptist*

The Baptist Peace Fellowship flourished. By 1991, over thirty regional and conventional peace fellowships had come into being in Canada, Puerto Rico, and the United States. The growth of peacemaking initiatives among Southern Baptists was notable. A Southern Baptist Pacifist Fellowship existed during the Second World War but had not continued. In 1979, Southern Baptists launched a paper, *Baptist Peacemaker*, and many congregational peace groups. In 1983, when a journey of reconciliation to the Soviet Union brought together American and Southern Baptists, including Edwin T. Dahlberg, the stage was set for Baptists to break new ground.

Could Baptists make peace among themselves? Gathering 30–31 March 1984 at Deer Park Baptist Church in Louisville, Kentucky, Southern and American Baptists explored the possibility of cooperating in a single peace group. It was not an easy meeting. One of the participants, Rachel Gill, noted:

> There were fears. Would our cousins to the north like us? Would they think of us as just 'dumb old Southerners.' Would they grant us absolution for the sins of our separation? For our complicity in racism? . . . ABC people also had fears. They had a solid peace organization since the 1940s. Would these Southerners be out to get revenge? Would they just take over? Would they be willing to give financial support?[23]

Delegates determined to bring these two groups of Baptists together and to reach out to Baptists from other traditions and elsewhere in North America. Overcoming the doubts and fears, they identified an executive and gave birth to a wider Baptist Peace Fellowship of North America. Maintaining earlier emphases, the new body identified several goals: establishing peace groups at local, state, regional, and international levels; facilitating communication between these groups; and encouraging all

---

Peacemaker 11/2 (Summer 1991): 18 and 13/1 (Spring 1993): 17.

[23]Remarks to the fifth annual BPFNA summer conference, Ottawa, Ontario, 6 July 1990. Rachel Gill is a member of Oakhurst Baptist Church, Decatur, Georgia, and member of the BPFNA board. She has served as secretary since 1989. See also, Ken Sehested, "Baptist Peacemakers in North America: A Story, a Strategy, and a Theology," *Faith and Mission* 4 (1986): 13-26. Ken Sehested is a member of Prescott Memorial Baptist Church in Memphis, Tennessee, and Executive Director of the BPFNA since 1984.

Baptists to engage in active peacemaking. Within a year, it had taken on a staff, expanded and upgraded its newsletter, hosted a Parenting for Peace and Justice Conference, planned the first annual summer, weeklong conference, sponsored friendship visits to the Soviet Union and Central America, and, with support from the European Baptist Federation and Baptist World Alliance, begun to shape an international conference—all this for an organization that virtually had never had an income or an expense sheet before.

From 3–7 August 1988, a historic gathering in Sjovik, Sweden, brought together two hundred Baptists from over thirty countries. Under the theme "Seek peace, and pursue it" (Ps 34:14), participants explored three areas: the Anabaptist and Baptist heritage of peace; the Final Act of the Conference on Security and Cooperation in Europe, or Helsinki Accords; and practical strategies for implementing peace and justice ministries. The final communiqué envisioned future development of new initiatives among Baptists through growth in awareness of and involvement with other peacemakers, helping Baptists affirm peace as a crucial biblical concern, helping raise awareness of the Baptist peace heritage, and developing a network between groups and the creation of links with other Christian peace groups.[24] Planning for a second international Baptist peace conference in Nicaragua from 14-18 July 1992 began. This gathering brought together 220 Baptists from 35 countries and highlighted the Baptist peace witness throughout the world.

A few years ago, no one could have predicted such a flowering of Baptist peace activity. Heirs of the sixteenth-century Anabaptists, Baptists may assume a place among the historic peace churches. Having revived an emphasis characteristic at varying times and in varying strength, Baptist peacemakers attest that Christians must abandon themselves to the Kingdom Jesus announced, taught and lived.

Baptists and, indeed, all Christians need to recover the dreams of those who, through the Baptist Pacifist Fellowship, Fellowship of Reconciliation, and other religious peace groups, demonstrate that peace, justice, reconciliation, and love are at the heart of a living faith. During a workshop at the Seoul gathering of the Baptist World Alliance in August 1990, Setsuko Iijima, a Japanese Baptist leader, shared her dream

---

[24]*PeaceWork*, August–October 1988, 16. For proceedings of the conference, H. Wayne Pipkin, ed. *Seek Peace and Pursue It* (Memphis: BPFNA, 1989).

that the twentieth century, a century of war, will give way to a century of reconciliation. Let us see what becomes of her dream. That it might become reality, American Baptists would do well to recall a pledge formulated in 1978: "As American Baptists, we commit ourselves to seek peace and to pursue it, to emphasize peace education, to examine our lives so that we may be a better witness for peace and justice, and to work together with others pursuing these goals."

Conclusions

Throughout this century, North American Baptist peacemakers have given voice to their objections to war and to their conviction that the God of love wills peace. They have been courageous and prophetic. At times like a lightening rod, they have attracted the disdain of the majority of Baptist adherents.

Amidst a century of war, Baptist peacemakers have sought to apply the gospel of peace, reconciliation, and healing. This was the vision of Edwin T. Dahlberg. In 1965, he shared in a FOR-sponsored clergy visit to Vietnam. In talks given after the tour, he renewed his call for massive reconciliation. Once, he acknowledged that more was involved than ending the war in Vietnam. He called for development of a theology of peace to take the place of the theology of war. He appealed to the churches to come to grips with the power structures that keep the war system going—industry, government, and education—and to undertake a radical transformation, which, as he understood it, would entail a movement away from private religion and into places where the struggles for freedom must be won. Ultimately, he stressed, "we must go deep down into the soul of man if we are going to have a massive reconciliation." In another talk, he concluded, "Massive reconciliation may seem like an impossible task. But man has been given the intelligence, the imagination, and the power to effect it. Will he have the faith?"[25] The question remains a challenge to those who seek to bring healing among the nations.

---

[25]"Consideration of Massive Reconciliation," *Baptist Peace Fellowship Newsletter*, April 1970; "Massive Reconciliation," *Baptist Peace News*, August 1979.

Conclusions

"Are we facing a new moment in Baptist history?" With this question, Ken Sehested, executive director of the Baptist Peace Fellowship of North America (BPFNA) opened the first-ever international Baptist peace gathering in Sjovik, Sweden, in 1988. Speaking to an assembly of two hundred persons from nearly thirty countries, Sehested noted that one reason for the conference was to acknowledge the existence of a vital stream of Baptist peacemaking activity. "Baptists involved in justice and peace issues often feel like illegitimate children," Sehested noted. "Now we are discovering the presence of a worldwide community of Baptists who share our convictions, along with an almost-forgotten history of Baptist peacemakers."[1]

As indicated in the Introduction, this book is offered in part to Baptist peacemakers who need to unearth the tradition in which they move. It is a glorious tradition that reaches back to biblical times, to the remnant communities of the Hebrew prophets and the primitive New Testament communities who held all things in common, who ensured that there was not a needy person among them, and who, with great power, gave their testimony that Jesus had defeated the powers of this world (Acts 2, 4).

Although Baptists have not developed a consistent stance regarding issues of war, peace, non-resistance, or nonviolence, the tradition of Baptist peacemaking extends back to the Reformation era, when John Smyth, Thomas Helwys, and other early Baptists opposed war and began to work for positive peace. Some, informed by contacts with Anabaptists, Brethren, or members of the Society of Friends, or by their own reading of the Bible adopted the biblical conception of non-resistance, a concept that appeared in Baptist confessions of faith and writings by several Baptists. Amidst times of intermittent persecution and sporadic warfare, some Baptists verbalized love of enemies. Some declared their willingness to suffer or even die rather than to retaliate. Some refused to bear arms. Among the radical ideas put forward by followers of Smyth was

---

[1]The Reverend Kenneth L. Sehested, opening remarks, International Baptist Peace Conference, 3 August 1988.

the conviction that they should follow the unarmed and unweaponed, cross-bearing footsteps of Jesus. As a result, early Baptists ensured that peacemaking was securely part of the Baptist heritage even though the Baptist denomination did not become one of the historic peace churches.

Since the period of Baptist origins, and especially over the past two hundred years, peace thinking and action for peace have increasingly found a central place in Baptist life. War, oppression, radical non-conformity, evangelicalism, various streams of theological renewal, socialism, and other movements of social change have influenced Baptists in varying ways and to some extent. These have helped shape the strong Baptist peace movement of today.

Crucial in this development was reaction to the Napoleonic wars. In England and North America, Baptists exhibited a great deal of peace activity. After 1815, more and more Baptists spoke and wrote for peace. Many joined the Peace Society. Some were pacifists, believing all wars are contrary to the gospel of Christ or "mind of Christ." Others were pacificists, opposing offensive wars or working for peace through voluntary societies that sought the abolition of slavery, the end of *sati*, and other reforms.

Baptists campaigned for peace primarily through meetings, petitions, publications, and sermons. The peace ideal came to be intertwined with growing internationalism. Between 1870–1914, delegates (including Baptists) to over two hundred gatherings worldwide of one kind or another met to discuss peace. These sessions shaped twentieth-century international organizations.

The Crimean War and the United States Civil War were setbacks in the growing international movement for peace. Anti-war advocacy became more militant. At the time of the Anglo-Boer War, Baptists protested against the war and gave direction to efforts to prevent future wars. Early in this century, as the Baptist peace testimony became more intense and more visionary, pacifism found expression as principled opposition to all war. During each of the wars of this century, both the two World Wars and the myriad other wars, there have been significant numbers of conscientious objectors and many forms of witness against war.

A new stage in Baptist peace witness may be emerging. Peacemaking has become a powerful current in Baptist life. Will it become a mighty stream? It is possible. I believe it is both desirable *and* a gospel imperative. Even though this possibility seems to run counter to other threads of Baptist history and contrary currents at work among Baptists, peacemaking cuts across theological positions, approaches to social action or evangelism, and whatever else tends to divide Baptists. It is likely that, during the 1990s, more and more Baptists will join peace groups, receive training in techniques of non-violent resistance, and discover within themselves the faith, courage, and strength to face opposition, hostility, or, in some instances, martyrdom. Through initiatives such as summer North American conferences, friendship tours, and international gatherings, Baptist peacemakers are being knit into a strong international network. The movement has become more inclusive, drawing in more women, more lay people, and more people of color.

Historically, Baptist peacemakers have been practical idealists.[2] As a rule, they did not begin as utopian thinkers or revolutionary strategists. As believers, they responded to a gospel that sets on its head all old ideas of how we are to live with each other. In the face of laws that denied them liberty of conscience, they resolutely defended religious liberty. In the face of those who engaged in such forms of oppression as slavery or human rights violations, they defended the oppressed. Before those who engaged in violence, they adopted the way of the cross, suffered, and, in some instances, died for their convictions. Before those who waged war, they sought peace, justice, and reconciliation. Out of their own experience and out of their awareness of the needs of others, they sought to build a better world for themselves, the human community, and future generations. With humility and outstretched arms, they offered themselves in prayerful obedience to God and to the world. With patience and hope, they offered themselves as servants of Jesus, another practical revolutionary. This is the tradition that contemporary Baptist peacemakers must continue.

As indicated in the Introduction, this book has been written amidst dark days as war dashed hopes of a peace dividend following the apparent end of the Cold War. Now, more than two years after the end of intense military engagement in the Persian Gulf region, it is war as

---

[2]The phrase originates with M. K. Gandhi. See his "Freedom through Satyagraha," in K. Satchidananda Murty, ed., *Readings in Indian History, Politics and Philosophy* (London: George Allen and Unwin, 1967) 184, where Gandhi writes that he is not a visionary but a practical idealist.

usual. The guns are not silent in East Timor, in Mozambique, in the Western Sahara or elsewhere.

After the suffering, it is suffering as usual. The newly orphaned children are not silent in Kurdestan, in southern Iraq, in Bangladesh, in the famine stricken lands of the Sahel, or elsewhere.

After the business of arming the merchants of death, it is business as usual. The hawkers of F-15s, Tornado bombers, and cluster bombs freshly tested over Baghdad and Karbala are not silent in Birmingham, Great Britain; in Ottawa, Canada; in Washington D. C., or elsewhere.

A war that could have been avoided is ended and forgotten. Apart from dipping into one's pocket to give a few quid to help the newest waves of refugees, most people have consigned the Persian Gulf War to history and now disregard fundamental issues that led to the crisis in the first place, including over-consumption of oil, arms sales to the Middle East, and greed.

Each disaster that catches the attention of headline writers is troubling. All the domestic violence in the homes and on the streets of North America; all the mindless bloodletting in Ulster and the south African townships; all the suffering of the helpless, homeless, hopeless, and hugless among us—only some of which captures the attention of the media—all this is also troubling. No less troubling is the silence of Christians.

Perhaps we are overwhelmed by the challenge of following Christ in a war-weary, war-worried world. Perhaps we sense our helplessness in the face of such massive obstacles to world peace as global warming, erupting nationalism, nuclear proliferation, or population explosion, problems that seem to defy solution. Perhaps we have become indifferent to the perils of polluting the environment, rearming the nations, or living too comfortably. Whatever is the case, we face a collective crisis of the soul.

According to Mark, the gospel of Jesus Christ the Son of God began at a time when John the Baptist went among the people calling them to repent. Jesus was baptized and went through the Galilee repeating the call to repentance. Jesus proclaimed the gospel of God: "The time is fulfilled, and the kingdom of God has come near; repent, and believe in the good news" (Mark 1:15). During his earthly ministry, Jesus repeated this call to repentance. He assured women and men that God forgave them and summoned them to discipleship. He brought salvation, healing, and the possibility of a new creation to a world of brokenness and need. When Jesus reveals himself to us, his first call is still to repentance.

It is important to confess our sin, for our lives and the life of the world are broken by our sin. I write as a resident in one of the wealthier countries of the "North" but who has lived for several years and traveled widely among poorer countries of the "South." My roots are in the United States, a country prone to self-congratulation as the "West" emerges triumphant over the "East." I confess my complicity in war and oppression.

Collectively, I believe, we in the wealthy North and triumphant West need to declare our shame for what has been done over many decades by Christians and by our governments to plunge the poor nations of the world into an endless succession of traumatic crises. We need to declare our shame for failing to root out the causes of war and oppression, including our own affluent life-style.

We in the wealthy North and triumphant West confront a situation dissimilar in many respects to those faced by previous generations of peacemakers, including those discussed in this book. But in one respect, we face a common reality. It is impossible today as in the past to reconcile the gospel of Jesus Christ with the way the world is.

In quiet places and small circles, there are signs that Christians are stirring to confront the powers, principalities, and conditions that engender war. Let me cite three examples, two of which are quite personal. A few years ago, citizens of the Soviet Union lined up to see the movie *Repentance*, filmed in 1984 in Georgia, the Soviet Republic where Stalin was born. The film was about Stalin. Its release signaled the dawn of *glastnost* and *perestroika*.

The story centers on a grave digger who, in order to haunt the descendants of a Stalinist mayor named Varlan, digs up the corpse of his victims. Varlan's grandson ultimately commits suicide, which drives his father to repentance.

The film expresses the power of repentance, forgiveness, and eucharist. In one scene, we see several women in a muddy timber yard searching the ends of logs for the name of a loved one. (This was a way forced laborers communicated with relatives.) A woman finds her husband's name. Weeping, she caresses the rough wood as if it were truly her husband. Watching such scenes, many viewers of this remarkable film experience, no doubt, solidarity with her and with all victims of oppression.

In the final scene, an old lady asks a woman who makes cakes in the shape of a church, "Does this street go to the church?" "No," says the baker, "it is Varlan Street. A street named after Varlan can't lead to a church." "What good is a street that doesn't lead you to a church?" is the reply. The film ends as the old woman hobbles down an empty street looking for a church.

We are like the old woman, walking streets that do not lead to a church. What we need is a place where we, too, can repent our disobedience, both individual and collective, of the will of God. As indicated in my second and third examples, I see God moving people to repentance and amendment of life. This has been evident in my own experience.

Let me recall one situation. At the Ecole Polytechnique in Montreal, on 6 December 1989, a killer murdered fourteen young women, blaming feminists for the misfortunes of his life. This incident was part of a wider pattern of violence against women. Shortly after the Montreal killings, I made my confession for what I as a male may have contributed to the murders. I knelt alone in prayer at Almuth Lutkenhaus-Lackey's statue of the crucified woman.[3] A garden at Victoria University, Toronto, shelters the statue, which is startling and moving. As I meditated before the figure of a woman of sorrow and compassion, I recalled women in Jesus' life who wept at his grave and first proclaimed his resurrection. I encountered the grace of his presence. "Do not weep. Do not be afraid." Other words of Jesus gave me fresh hope: "Be of good cheer, I have overcome the world"

Another illustration grows out of circles seeking to respond to the Persian Gulf crisis. In December 1990, the BPFNA issued an appeal calling Christians to prayer and fasting.[4] Like many members of the BPFNA, my wife and I committed ourselves to daily prayer and weekly fasting for peace. We prayed and set aside a day each week for eight weeks. This was a time for repentance and renewal of our experience of the love of Jesus. Feeling helpless in the face of the enormity of the evil at work in the world, we found that the disciplines of prayer and fasting

---

[3]For other responses, Doris Jean Dyke, *Crucified Woman* (Toronto: United Church Publishing House, 1991).

[4]*Baptist Peacemaker* 11 (1991): 4.

helped us to focus on the love of Jesus as He prepared to be crucified, on the suffering of those who can not choose not to eat, on the wider community of believers with whom we shared the experience, and on the potential power of these spiritual disciplines for transforming initiatives. What if, for example during the Persian Gulf War, there had been a million of us fasting, say for forty days. We would not have done much else. If enough of us had been fasting and praying, perhaps we would have undermined the capacity of government to wage war in our name.

Repentance, prayer, and fasting enable one to experience forgiveness and healing. This is not, however, where matters end. The fast God requires is to loose the fetters of injustice, to untie the knots of the yoke, to snap every yoke and set free those who have been crushed, to share food with the hungry, and to take into my home the homeless poor (Is 58:6-7). In the Bible, the disciplines of prayer and fasting are linked with action. Repentance leads to reparation and amendment of life.

At the heart of repentance are the symbols of the cross and empty tomb. Martin Luther King, Jr. wrote, "The cross is the eternal expression of the length to which God will go in order to restore broken community. The resurrection is a symbol of God's triumph over all the forces that seek to destroy the beloved community." A time is coming, when this community will become reality. It will be a time

>—when swords will be hammered into ploughshares and nations shall not even study war (Isa 2:4);
>—when the proud shall be scattered, the mighty pulled down, lowly ones exalted and the hungry filled with good things (Luke 1:51-53);
>—when every tear shall be wiped away, neither shall there be mourning nor crying nor pain anymore . . . the river of life, sparkling like crystal, will flow from the throne of God and of the Lamb down the middle of a city street, with trees the leaves of which serve the healing of the nations (Rev 21:1-4, 22:2);
>—when death itself will be vanquished and creation set free from its bondage to decay (Rom 8: 19-24).

God will do this. We are the fragile instruments through whom God will work. Patience and unshakable faith will be required. Repentance will lead to amendment of life, prayer to action. There will be small beginnings. There will be setbacks. Crushed, like the wheat and grapes that become the bread and wine of communion, we will stretch out our hands and find one another for the long road ahead. Let us be prepared to work to end war and the things that make for war. Let us unite with others that, if the Lord tarries, the third millennium of the common era will be one in which the nations learn war no more. A little child will plant a tree, and it shall be for the healing of the nations.

Index

Abbot, Thomas, 124
AFSC, 262
Aked, Charles F., 67, 206
Allsop, 147
Ambrose, 19, 170
American Baptist Convention, 258, 263
American Baptist Churches, 258, 267, 268
American Peace Society, 47, 51, 53, 57
Amherstburg Association, 136, 139, 140
Anabaptist/Anabaptism, xix, 4, 7, 12, 13, 19, 20, 21, 121, 183-85, 269
Anglo-Boer War, 11, 46, 64-68, 73, 192, 206, 212, 241, 242, 272
Anthony, Susan B., 148
Anti-Slavery Society, 37, 41, 134
Ao, L. Kijungluba, 102, **164-66**, 267
Argentina, 252
Armenia, 144
Arminius, Jacob, 5
Associated Councils in the British and German Empires for Fostering Friendly Relations Between the Two Peoples, 79, 242
Augustine, 19, 96

Bainton, Roland, 89

Baker, Moses, 120, 129
Baptist Ministers' Pacifist Fellowship, 247
Baptist Missionary Society, 33, 41
Baptist Missionary Training School, 148
Baptist Pacifist Fellowship, xix, 1, **255-64**, 266
Baptist Peace Fellowship, xx, **252-53**, 266, 268
Baptist Peace Fellowship of North America, vii, xix, xx, **255-70**, 271, 276
Baptist Peacemaker, The, xx, 79, 268
Baptist Union, 33, 43, 61, 62, 79, 247, 253
Baptist Views of War and Peace, 252
"Baptist War," 120
Baptist World Alliance, 61, 70, 77, **82-84**, 85, 242, 269
Baptist Zenana Mission, 145
Barrow, David, 132
Beasley, Rene, 249
Belgian Congo, 71, 213
"beloved community," 16, 203, 233-37
Bennett, Reginald, 150
Bickley, Richard, 28
Bland, Marie Averill, 93
Boardman, George Dan, 57-59
Bolivia, 162-63, 168, 194
Bolivian Baptist Union, 163, 193

Boxer Rebellion, 190–93
Branton, Mary, 139
Brethren, Church of the Brethren, German Brethren, xiii, xix, 7, 13, 19, 20
Brethren of the Common Table, 218
Bristol Education Society, 33
British Baptist Pacifist Fellowship, **246-52**, 253, 254
British presence in Northern Ireland, 252
Broadus, John A., 188
Brock, Peter, 28
Brown, Louise Fargo, 26
Bryan, Andrew, 118
Bryan, Frank Colin, 247
Bunyan, John, 24, 25
Burchell, Thomas, 120, 121, 122, 124, 129
Burdette, Mary G., 149
Burgess, Walter H., 5
Burma, (Myanmar), xviii
Burmese-British War, 146
Burrows, Judge, 93
Busher, Leonard, 5

Calvin, John, 5
Calvinists, 5
Cameroon, xviii, 83, 160
Campbell, Alexander, 48
Canada, xviii, 30, 53, 134-39, 140, 141, 202, 257, 268, 274
Carey, Eustace, 126
Carey, William, 13, 126, 143, 146
Carr, Eseck, 30
Carter, George "Nick," 267

Carter, Jimmy, 267
Cary, Lott, 102, 155, **158-60**
Cary, Mary Ann Shadd, 137-39
Castro, Miguel Thomas, xxi
Ceadel, Martin, 12
CEPAD, xx, 267
Chad, xvii
Chartist principles, 39, 40, 63
Cheong, Michael, 253
Chessman, Daniel, 48
Children's House, 214, 219, 223, 224
Christadelphians, 244, 255
Christianity and the Social Crisis, 202, 203, 206
Christianizing the Social Order, 206
Christian Pacifist Forestry Land Units, 250
Church for the Fellowship of All Peoples, **174-76**, 178
Chute, Pearl, 101, 151, 152
civil rights movement, xvii, 228
Clark, Zella, 101, 152
Clarkson, John, 157
Clifford, John, viii, 17, **61-74**, 75, 76, 80, 242, 245
Cober, Kenneth L., 257, 258
Coffin, Frank M., 267
Coffin, William Sloan, 267
Cold War, 252, 273
Collins, Shorty, 171, 259, 262, 267
Congo, 144
congregationalist, 4, 35, 253
conscientious objectors, 181, **241-54**, 258-63, 266
Crawford, Isabel, viii, **148-50**

Crimean War, 11, 39, 40, 42, 45, 46, 272
Cross, James, 88
Crossroads Africa, xvii
Cuff, William, 73
Czech Brethren, 19, 183

Dabbs, Norman, 162, 193
Dahlberg, Edwin Theodore, 1, 201, 256, 259, 263, 265, 267, 268, 270
Davis, John William, 93, 94, 98
Dawn community, 137
Day, Dorothy, 224
Deavin, Derek, 251
Deer Park Baptist Church, 268
desegregation of schools and other public facilities, 228
development, underdevelopment, xvii
Diggers (also see Levellers), 103, 111-13
Dirks, Elizabeth, 185, 195
disarmament, 252
Dodge, David Low, 48
Dodson, Jualynne, xxi
Doke, Joseph James, 14, 70-71
Dominguez, Olivia Juarez, xx
Doras, Abraham, 137
Doty, Ava, xx
Douglas, Frederick, 138
DuBois, W. E. B., 138
Dunnico, Herbert, 245

Edwards, Thomas, 22, 23
Elements of Moral Science, The, 51, 54

El Salvador, xviii, xxi, 181, 184, 194, 195
England, Martin and Mable, 264
Erasmus, 19
Ethiopia, 2, 258
Evans, Benjamin, 36, 42, 45
Evans, Caleb, 33
Everard, William, 111
Eyes on the Prize, 179, 237

Fahkni, Mildred, 222
Falklands-Malvina Conflict, 252
Federal Council of Churches, 209, 255
Fell, Margaret, 20
Feller, Henrietta Oden, 53
Fellowship of Reconciliation, xviii, 81, 171, 172, 207, 214-15, 221, 242-45, 248, 249, 251, 253, 256, 257, 259, 261, 263, 264, 270
Fifth Monarchists, 6, 20, 26
First World War, 11, 70, 77, 80-82, 90-91, 221, 226, 241-43, 245, 246, 250, 251, 255, 256
Foley, Edwin, 245
For the Right, 200
Fosdick, Harry Emerson, 92, 256, 259, 261
Fox, George, 20, 43
Freedom Rides, 228
Freewill Baptists, 27, 31, 133,
Friends of Humanity Association, **132-34**
Fuller, Jackson, 102, 160
Fyfe, Robert Alexander, 135

Gaines, George, 56

Gandhi, 14, 70-71, 173, 215, 221-22, 224, 249
Gandhi Foundation, 223
Garrison, William Lloyd, 44, 134
Gater, Sarah, 109
Gavel, Eileen, 266, 267
Gavel, Victor H., 263, 264, 267
Gaunt, Elizabeth, 187, 195
General Baptists, 5, 22, 26, 27, 31, 186
George, David, 102, 155, **156-58**
George, David Lloyd, 70
George, Timothy, 6
George, Zelma, 267
German Baptists, 20, 77, 78, 79, 83, 133, 181
Gill, Rachel, 268
Gladden, Washington, 204
Godwin, Benjamin, 35, 36
Gomez, Maria, 181, **194-95**
Goodwill, 81-82
Graham, John William, 11
Grebel, Conrad, 19, 20
Gullison, Ben, 101, 152-54
Gullison, Mary Evlyn Erb, 152-54

Haden, William Henry, xix, 246, 247
Haley, Alex, 231
Halley's Comet, 177
Hall, Robert, 35, 36
Hargreaves, James, 36, 37, 38, 41
Harnack, Adolph von, 76

Hazelden, Kyle, 267
Hazzard, Dorothy, 24, 25
Hebrews, 181
Hell's Kitchen, 198, 199, 201
Helwys, Thomas, 5, 21, 103
Henson, Josiah, 137
Herald of Peace, 41
Hickman, William, 132
Hill, George W., 267
Hingson, Robert, 267
Hobhouse, Rosa Waugh, 217
Hobhouse, Stephen, 217
Hodgkin, Henry Theodore, 243
Holcombe, Henry, 49
Hosie, Laurence, 259
Howard, John, 37
Howe, Julia Ward, 56, 148
Hubberthorne, Richard, 20
Hughes, Charles Evans, 94
human rights, xvii
Humphrey, John and Thelma, 249
Hutchison, Anne, 29
Hutter, Jacob, 20
Hutterites, 7

IFOR, 215, 222, 253
Iijima, Setsuko, 269
Illingworth, Alfred, 36, 44
India, xviii, 150-54, 164, 165, 166, 168, 172, 173, 215, 221
international arms sales, 252
International Peace Research Institute, 39
Ireland, Northern Ireland, 2
Israel, 2

Jamaica, viii, 118
James, Howard Ingli, 182, 248-49
JeeJatchuch, Mandakini, 102, 155, **167**
Jehovah's Witnesses, 244
Johnson, Jennie, viii, 101, **139-41**
Johnson, Mammie, 102, 155, **159-60**
Jordan, Clarence and Florence, 182, 264, 265
Judson, Adoniram, 57, 146

Keeley, Kate, 172
Keith, George, 30
Kelly, Erasmus, 30
Kentucky Abolition Society, 133
Ketocton Association, 131
King, Alberta Williams, 227
Kingdom of God Is Within You, The, 212
King, Martin Luther, Jr., viii, xiii, 13, 14, 15, 16, 142, 170, 176, 181, 184, 204, 221, **227-39**, 256, 265, 277
King, Martin Luther, Sr., 227, 230
Kingsley Hall, 214, 217, 218, 219, 221, 222, 223, 224, 225
Klaassen, Walter, 11
Knibb, William, 13, 101, 120, **124-29**, 146
Kunkle, Edward, 259, 263

Labour Member of Parliament, 245
Lebanon, 2

Leland, John, 131
Lester, Henry Edward, 211
Lester, Kingsley, 213, 214
Lester, Muriel, viii, 172, 174, 181, **211-226**, 241, 249
Lester, Verona Doris, 212, 213, 218
"Letter from Birmingham Jail," 15, 234
Levellers, True Levellers (also see Diggers), 20, 25, 103, 111
liberty of conscience, religious liberty, 6, 26, 27
Liele, George, **117-20**, 129, 156
Lilburne, John, 25
Limma, Matthew, 102, **166-67**
London Baptist Association, 61
Lorkin, Peter, 252
love of enemy, 206
Ludhiana Medical College, 145
Luther, Martin, 229
Lutkenhaus-Lackey, Almuth, 276
Luwum, Janani, 184
Lynch, James R., 266

Macedonia, 71, 144
MacIntosh, Douglas Clyde, 17, **87-99**
Mack, Alexander, 20, 181
Madola, Diba, xxi
Majesty of Conscience, The, 246
Malcom, Howard, 52, 53
Mandela, Nelson, 2
Marshall, Abraham, 118
Marshall, Newton, 76
Martin, Mabel, 267

martyrdom, 4, 163, **183-195**, 273
martyr's theology, 184
Maurice, Frederick Dennison, 204
Maxson, John, 30
Mennonites, xix, 5, 7, 21, 259
Meyer, Frederick Brotherton, 14, 67, 68, 70, 71, 245
Military Service Act, 242, 243
Mitchell, William M., 135
Montgomery, Helen Barrett, 202
Montgomery, 16, 227, 232, 235-36
Moon, Charlotte Diggs, 188-91, 195
Moore, Joanna Patterson, 55
Munroe, Anne Catherine, 153, 154
Müntzer, Thomas, 19
Muste, Abraham Johannes, 174

Nahwooks, Reaves, xx
Nahwooksy, Clydia, xx
Napoleonic Wars, 34, 35, 241, 272
National Council of Evangelical Free Churches, 61
National Peace Academy, 267
National Service League, 241
Native Americans, viii, 105, 106, 107, 150
Native Indians, 103, 107
negative peace, 14, 115, 235
New Connexion Baptists, 33, 41, 120
New Lights, 31
New Model Army, 6, 25

Nicaragua, xix, xx, 267, 269
Niebuhr, H. Richard, 89
Niebuhr, Reinhold, 89
No Conscription Fellowship, 72, 81, 242, 244
non-resistance, 6, 21, 29, 31, 34, 60, 213, 273
nonviolence, 112, 236, 241, 257, 265
Norfolk Royal Commission, 241
Northern Baptist Convention, 202, 258, 259, 260

O'Neill, Arthur, 36, 39, 40, 41, 45, 46
Origen, 19, 38
Outler, Albert, 89
Overton, Richard, 25

pacifism, pacifist, 11-12, 29, 34, 60, 95, 96, 181, 245, 246, 248, 250, 251-253, 255-66, 272
pacificism, 12
Parajon, Gustavo, xx, 267
Parks, Rosa, 232, 233
Parsons, Sally, 55
Particular Baptists, 5, 31, 213
Partridge, Kate, 76
Paul, Nathaniel, 44
"peace gun," 267
peace societies, 30, **33-60**, 245, 272
Peggs, William, 145
Pemberton, Alice, 104
Persian Gulf, 2, 253, 254, 273, 274, 276, 277
Peru, 163

Peter, Jesse, 118
Phillippo, James M., 120
pietism, 20
Pilkington, George, 36-37, 40
Pitcher, W. Alvin, 267
Plymouth Brethren, 244
Po, Fernando, 160
Poole, Elizabeth, 25
positive peace, 14, 15, 143, 235
Poteat, E. McNeil, Jr., 259
Prayers of the Social Awakening, 198
Puerto Rico, xix, 268
puritan, puritanism, 4

Queen's Road Baptist Church, 182, 247, 249, 251
Quispe, Justino, 102, **162-64**
race, racism, xvii, 2, 60
Randall, Benjamin, 32
Rauschenbusch, Walter, viii, xiii, 171, 181, **197-209**, 233, 256, 257
Raven, Charles, 249
reconciliation, 2, 221-23, 270, 273
Reconciliation, 253
Regular Baptists, 31
Repentance, 275
Rice, Luther, 158
Richards, Timothy, 188
Richardson, Lewis Fry, 10
Richmond African Baptist Missionary Society, 159
Rippon, John, 119
Rivera-Pagan, Luis N., xxi
Robinson, Robert, 117
Rogerenes, 29, 54

Rogers, Alexander, 29
Rogers, John, 29
Romero, Oscar, 184
Royce, Josiah, 233
Rushbridge, Cyril, 251
Rushbrooke, James Henry, 17, 72, **75-85**, 242
Rushkin, John, 204
Rutenber, Culbert, 264, 265

Saddle Mountain, Indian Territory, OK, 149
Salazar, Francisco, 163, 193
Sale, Elizabeth, 145
Sale, John, 145
Sandy Creek, NC, 31
Sati, 144, 272
Sattler, Michael, 19
Schachter, Zalman, 177
Schleitheim Confession, 7, 19
Schmidt, Nathaniel, 200
Schwimmer, Rosika, 93
Scott, Catharine, 29
Scudder, Ida, 152
Second World War, 97, 181, 223, 246, 248, 249, 252, 263, 264, 265, 268
Sehested, Ken, xxii, 271
separatist, separatism, 4, 104
Serempore, India, 188
Sermon on the Mount, The, 1, 59, 207
Seventh Day Baptists, 5, 30, 31, 133, 186
Shadd, Harriet, 137
Sharpe, Dores Robinson, 198, 207, 256-57
Sharpe, Granville, 130

Sharpe, Samuel, viii, 123
Sheppard, Dick, 249
Sherman, Margaret "Peg," 267
Shreve, Elizabeth Shadd, 101, 137, 138, 161
Siegmund-Schultze, Friedrich Wilhelm, 80, 243
Sierra Leone, 159
Silver Bluff, 118
Simons, Menno, 20
Sjovik, Sweden, xx, 269, 271
Slade, Tom, 251
Smith, Everett, 151
Smyth, John, 4, 12, 21, 103, 271
socialist, socialism, 57, 63, 64
Society of Friends, Quakers, xiii, xix, 4, 7, 13, 19, 26, 29, 30, 35, 54, 188, 243-44, 259
Society for the Promotion of Permanent and Universal Peace, 34
Soper, Donald, 249
South Africa, xix, 72, 102
Southern Christian Leadership Conference, 227, 228, 234-35
Soviet Union, 83, 263, 268, 275
Spurgeon, Charles Hadden, 35, 42, 45, 62
Sri Lanka, xix
Stassen, Glen, xx
Stassen, Harold E., 267
Stearns, Shubal, 31,
Stiles, Ezra, 30
Stock, John, 42, 45
Stokes, William, 36, 38, 39, 40, 41, 45, 46

Stride Toward Freedom, The Montgomery Story, 234
Sturge, Joseph, 128, 129
Sullivan, Leon, 267

Tagore, Rabindranath, 173, 215
Tarrant, Carter, 132
Taylor, Alan John P., 12
Taylor, John, 23
Territorial and Reserve Forces Act, 241
Tertullian, 19, 38, 183
Theology for the Social Gospel, A, 207
Thorndike, Sybil, 224
Thurman, Howard, **169-80**, 230, 258
Tiller, Carl, 262, 263, 267
Tiller, Olive, 267
Tillich, Paul, 229
Tolstoy, Leo, 204, 212, 213
"trail of blood", 4, 183
Traske, Dorothy, 181, 185-86
Traske, John, 186
Tule, John, 161
Tule, Mary, 102, 155, **161**
Turkey, Turkish atrocities, 71

Union of Soviet Socialist Republics, 2, 83
United States, xix, 92, 188, 190, 191, 193, 228, 230, 231, 233, 255, 256, 257, 263, 267, 272

Vietnam War, 228, 266, 267, 270
Voting Rights Act, 228

Waldensians, 19
Walker, Lucius, 267
Ward, William, 145
Wayland, Francis, 51-52
Wells, H. G., 224
Welsh nationalism, 252
White, George, 69
Whitfield, George, 31
Why Forbid Us?, 219, 220
Wieman, Henry Nelson, 229
Wilberforce, William, 130
Williams, Leighton, 200
Williams, Roger, xiii, 29, 103, **104-109**, 114, 115, 117, 259
Williamson, George, xxi
Winks, Joseph Foulks, 36, 41
Winstanley, Gerrard, 103, **109-13**, 114, 115

Women's American Baptist Baptist Foreign Mission Society, 202
World Alliance for Promoting International Friendship through the Churches, 80, 81, 242
World Federation of Brotherhoods, 61
World Priorities Institute, 39
Wyclif, 4, 19
Wylie, Anna Dorothy, 267

YMCA, 90, 201, 262
YWCA, 262

Zurich, Switzerland, 19
Zwingli, 19

GOLDEN GATE SEMINARY LIBRARY